Fantasy Fiction

Also available in this series:

Fantasy Fiction:
An Introduction

LUCIE ARMITT

continuum
NEW YORK • LONDON

2005

The Continuum International Publishing Group Inc
15 East 26 Street, New York, NY 10010

The Continuum International Publishing Group Ltd
The Tower Building, 11 York Road, London SE1 7NX

www.continuumbooks.com

Printed in the United States of America

Library of Congress Cataloging-in-Publication Data

Armitt, Lucie, 1962–
  Fantasy fiction : an introduction / Lucie Armitt.
     p. cm.
  Includes bibliographical references and index.
  ISBN 0-8264-1685-3 (pbk. : alk. paper)—ISBN 0-8264-1686-1 (hardcover :
alk. paper)
  1. Fantasy fiction, English—History and criticism.   2. Fantasy fiction,
American—History and criticism.   I. Title.
  PR830.F3A76 2005
  823'.0876609—dc22

                                                                    2005000580

Contents

Dedication

For Bethany and Rowan —
fantastic, both

'Only the impossible is worth the effort,'
Jeanette Winterson, *The PowerBook*

Acknowledgments

I would like to thank the following, all of whom have helped in the preparation and completion of this book: the Brynmor Jones Library at the University of Hull, for permitting me access to their holdings on Edith Wharton; Janet Cowen, for kindly allowing me to read an advance copy of her essay 'Old Sir Thomas Malory's Enchanting Book: *A Connecticut Yankee Reads Le Morte d'Arthur*'; the University of Wales, Bangor, for granting me a semester's study leave during the early months of this book's preparation; many of my colleagues and students, who have helped in a variety of ways from discussing and so furthering my understanding of issues, periods, and texts, through to the loan of books. Among those I would particularly acknowledge the help of the following: Tony Brown, Andrew Hiscock, Margaret Locherbie-Cameron, Catrin Haf Williams, Chiara Luis. Linda Jones has, as always, been a stalwart of calm and assured assistance. I am especially grateful to my two nieces, Jennifer and Rosemary Sibley, for their insights into the Harry Potter books. Above all, I wish to thank Scott Brewster for sharing with me his encyclopaedic knowledge, his facility for the mot juste, and simply for always being there. Finally, by way of apology to my two wonderful children, Bethany and Rowan, I dedicate this book; there will now be so much more space and time, I promise . . .

Chapter One

What Is Fantasy Writing?

'When we decide that something is unreal, the real it isn't
need not itself be very real . . .'[1]

Introduction

'Fantasy' is a word commonly disparaged by literary and nonliterary
voices alike. Summed up in the dismissive phrase 'castles in the air,'
fantasy takes on a kind of vertical trajectory that must be flattened,
smoothed out, replaced with a more acceptable 'horizontal' outlook. So we are encouraged, in life, to keep our feet on the ground
and our ambitions firmly anchored while fantasy writing guiltily
reaches for 'blue sky.' What *is* fantasy writing? Utopia, allegory,
fable, myth, science fiction, the ghost story, space opera, travelogue,
the Gothic, cyberpunk, magic realism; the list is not exhaustive, but
it covers most of the modes of fiction discussed in this book as 'fantasy.' Where fantasising is 'airy-fairy,' then, realism is 'grounded' (the
recent colloquial meaning of this phrase underlying the positive
implications of the distinction). It is, from this point, an easy slippage to glide from 'realistic' to (literary) realism. Literary realism is
certainly the type of fictional writing adopted most readily by the
canon, seen as most fitting for serious or weighty subject matter.
Certainly, it is difficult to imagine a work of fantasy attaining the
gravitas of Tolstoy's *War and Peace* (1863–69). Then again, the same
might be said for most other works of literary realism, and Milton's
epic, *Paradise Lost* (1667), is far closer to fantasy than it is to real
life, with Maureen Duffy going so far as to call it 'our longest and
greatest romance work of science fiction.'[2]

What is it about literary realism that endows it with this innate privilege over fantasy? In essence, the advantage seems to reside in the perceived proximity between realism and 'the real.' The very term 'mimesis' (describing 'the imitative representation of nature or human behaviour'[3]) implies a documentary relationship between the world and its fictions, in the process endowing fiction with a false sense of truth. And yet, as specialists of literary realism remind us, there is no more a genuinely direct connection between realism and the real than there is between fantasy fiction and the real; fiction is fiction is fiction. As Lilian R. Furst puts it,

> The realists' insistence on equating truth with illusion [fiction] means that they could achieve their aims only on the level of pretense, by prevailing upon their readers to accept the validity of their contentions and to believe without reservation in the reality of the fictive worlds they created. They were remarkably successful in doing so because they were able largely to conceal the literariness of their practices. In a sense, therefore, the realist novel can be seen as a prodigious cover-up.[4]

The first proviso we must therefore accommodate in tracing out the question 'What is fantasy writing?' is one apparently bending back upon itself: all fiction is fantasy, insofar as narrative scenarios comprise an interiorised image (one having existence only in the author's head) projected outwards onto a blank page. Through the intervention of a reader, one who brings his or her own reading fantasies to that book, we have a dynamic meeting point giving shape to the unique pleasures inherent in every readerly encounter.

Fantasy, then, is the basis upon which all reading and writing is founded. In his 1908 essay 'Creative Writers and Day-Dreaming,' Sigmund Freud identifies this process in the following terms:

> Might we not say that every child at play behaves like a creative writer, in that he creates a world of his own, or, rather, rearranges the things of his world in a new way which pleases him? . . . [T]he creative writer does the same as the child at play. He creates a world of phantasy which he takes very seriously . . . while separating it sharply from reality.[5]

So far so good, but our aim in this book is to establish a specific type of writing that exists as fantasy in a more rigorously defined sense. In identifying this aspect of fantasy writing, we need to be clear that Freud's word 'phantasy' is not synonymous with the word 'fantasy' as it is employed here. 'Phantasy' is a psychoanalytic term referring to that storehouse of fears, desires, and daydreams that inspire all fictions equally and that has its ultimate source in the unconscious.[6]

I have noted that 'phantasy' is not the same as 'fantasy'; nevertheless, those same fears and longings upon which our unconscious is founded frequently find their most resonant surface manifestations in fantasy literature. Fantasy enjoys—along with the unconscious—a greater freedom from that overdetermination to order, organise, and package the chaotic set of experiences we call 'real life' than classical literary realism can. There is, however, a third element of interest in Freud's words, which is the natural relationship he identifies between children and phantasying. For those of us who work in the field of literary fantasy, we are all too aware of the tendency to dismiss fantasy writing as childish: children read fantasy; adults read realism. Nor would we wish to deny that some of the most influential fantasy narratives *were* written for children: Lewis Carroll's Alice books (1865 and 1871), Kenneth Grahame's *The Wind in the Willows* (1908), J. R. R. Tolkien's *The Hobbit* (1937), C. S. Lewis's *Chronicles of Narnia* (1950–56), and most recently, of course, J. K. Rowling's Harry Potter books (1997–present). Nevertheless, this is not the same as identifying all fantasy as innately childlike.

What literary fantasy and psychoanalysis have in common is their shared need to construct narratives to explain the utterly inexplicable: what drives us, what terrifies us and why, and what our greatest desires might be. In examining, as we will in this book, texts such as Tolkien's The Lord of the Rings, Swift's *Gulliver's Travels*, Orwell's *Animal Farm*, or Shelley's *Frankenstein* (among others), we know we are not reading children's literature. Nevertheless, it is perhaps *as* children that the kind of questions these narratives raise ('What do we most fear?' 'What is the most exotic place we can imagine?' 'Who are we?' 'What will become of us if . . . ?') loom largest, and when we are most receptive to them. As we mature, the questions remain, but our philosophising on them becomes more complex and our response to their irresolution more intense. What we also realise is that while, as children, we pose these questions as individuals, as adults we know them to have a collective social and cultural significance. Similarly, although as children we believed there might be a precise geographical location where such dream worlds reside ('Second to the right and then straight on till morning'[7]), on reaching adulthood we need to discern locations of a more philosophical kind. It is here that we return to our differentiation between vertical and horizontal axes. The desire to fly is a common childhood fantasy, one that narratives such as *Peter Pan* exploit to good effect. But the challenge facing fantasy writing for adults is to take that vertical trajectory and give it a more grounded dimension while still enabling it to take flight. One of the means by which it does so is in its use of the horizon itself.

Beyond the Horizon

In his fine essay on utopia, Louis Marin examines the horizon as a symbol of simultaneous limit and infinity: 'The conquest through the discovery of mountain landscape at the end of the eighteenth century, of higher and higher viewpoints, moved the horizon further and further back, until it vanished . . .'[8] Though capable of being pinpointed with mathematical precision, absolute in its refusal to allow access beyond it, the horizon can never be reached, for it continually recedes as we approach. For Marin, this is the essence of utopia: a vista onto unknowable promise. It is in this same complex relationship between geometric precision and an utter sense of the impossible that the essence of fantasy fiction in general is born: a hyperbolic, endlessly expansive desire for the uncontainable, trapped within the constraints of a literary genre in which narrative closure is ruthlessly effected.

Though not all utopias are fantasy narratives as such (More's, as we shall see in Chapter 5, is not, and critics such as Louis James happily embrace Defoe's *Robinson Crusoe* [1719] as a utopia, though it is difficult to accommodate under the generic term 'fantasy'), it is easy to see how those early encounters with 'scientific investigation[s] of the habitat and lifestyles of alien peoples'[9] paved the way for later subgenres such as science/speculative fiction. As James himself observes, one of the many intertextual influences *Crusoe* can be seen to have had on subsequent adventure narratives includes the making of cult sci-fi films such as *Robinson Crusoe on Mars* (1964).[10] When, as is so often the case, fantasy utopias do amalgamate fictive futurism with a utopian rereading of ancient mythological sources such as Eden or classical Greek legends, they become enabled to carve out spaces no longer beholden to time, allowing for a thorough deconstruction of the basic structural principles of realism.

Many of the points Marin makes about sea travel are equally valid for space travel, so much of the terminology of space navigation being of maritime origin. Hence the notion of a journey into the unknown, interrupted by forces unforeseen, epitomises the plot of H. G. Wells's *The First Men in the Moon* (1901). Whilst by no means a 'no place' (not least because the moon is a specific location familiar to us all—if only from a distance), the difference between the moon and the Earth, combined with a perceived difficulty in the ability to return to Earth, results in Earth being considered utopian by contrast in the minds of the central protagonists:

> 'Daylight!' cried I. 'Daybreak, sunset, clouds, and windy skies! Shall we ever see these things again?'
>
> As I spoke, a little picture of our world seemed to rise before me, bright and little and clear, like the background of some old Italian picture. 'The Sky that changes, and the sea that changes, and the hills and the green trees and the towns and cities shining in the sun. Think of a wet roof at sunset . . . Think of the windows of a westward house!'[11]

It is perhaps primarily when horizon meets ocean or space, rather than land, that utopianism fulfils its most alluring potential, for like water running through our hands, no matter how hard we try to shape it, horizons trace the point at which sea strives to become air but fails to be either. In Samuel Taylor Coleridge's Romantic Gothic ballad 'The Rime of the Ancient Mariner' (1797–98), the shooting of the albatross propels the mariner and his crew into an obsessive relationship with that imaginary line of navigation:

All in a hot and copper sky,
The bloody Sun, at noon,
Right up above the mast did stand,
No bigger than the Moon.

Day after day, day after day,
We stuck, nor breath nor motion;
As idle as a painted ship
Upon a painted ocean.

Water, water, every where,
And all the boards did shrink;
Water, water, every where,
Nor any drop to drink.
(lines 111–22)

While the horizon is literally absent for Coleridge's reader (no mention being made of it in these lines), its presence, paradoxically, is insisted upon through the immense but still ocean framed by the horizon in the same manner in which the 'painted ship' and 'painted ocean' are framed by (again, literally absent) wood. Marin identifies a more characteristic pattern emerging in literature from this period:

> The limitless horizon is one of the main characteristics of the Romantic landscape, and seems to be related to the attempt to display transcendence: at this extremity it seems possible to glimpse the other side of the sky, a 'beyond-space' which can be encountered through the poetic and rhetorical figure of twilight—through which a bridge is established between the visible and the invisible. Then beyond the horizon, in the imagination, appear Utopias.[12]

Arguably, faced with the uncanny aspects of Coleridge's poem, it is the view across the 'horizon' into the delights of marriage that proffers (no place!) the possibility of bliss. The encounter takes place on the very brink of this new world: the ceremony over, 'The Bridegroom's doors are opened wide . . . The guests are met, [and] feast is set' (lines 5 and 7). Hence the wedding guest can see the party but is prevented from joining in. Stuck upon the boundaries of that vision of promise, by the end of the poem he turns away without partaking, and 'went like one that hath been stunned . . . A sadder and a wiser man' (lines 622 and 624).

Nor is this vision of the horizon only applicable to spatial interpretation; it also has relevance to our understanding of time. As Susan Stewart puts it, a typical and contradictory pattern describes our shared relationship with time whereby, on the one hand, we 'see events as discrete, having discernible beginnings and endings,' while on the other we see 'time itself as infinite, beyond any knowledgeable origin or end.'[13] Similarly, left to its own devices there is an inherent structural paradox in fantasy writing. While it projects us beyond the horizon on the level of content, creating what J. R. R. Tolkien calls the 'Secondary World inside which the green sun will be credible,'[14] it harnesses us within clearly defined constraints on the level of narrative structure. Multiple 'Secondary' worlds may proliferate, but the boundaries established around those worlds must remain constant in order for the narrative to succeed. This static identification enabled Vladimir Propp, in 1928, to execute an entire project dependent upon identifying a finite list of what he calls key narrative 'functions' within the fairy tale. Basing his work on a scientific breakdown of 450 fairy tales, he discovered he could identify a set of 150 such functions spanning the entire corpus. Paring down these functions, he claimed they cohere into one single common function pairing, prohibition versus violation or, as he refers to it elsewhere, the 'principle of freedom' set against 'little use of this freedom.'[15] Herein lies the difference between modes of genre fantasy such as fairy tale, science fiction, fable, and allegory and more disruptive, open-ended narratives of the literary fantastic such as magic realism and certain types of supernatural/ghost narrative. Where genre fantasy imposes absolute closure, the fantastic opens up onto Marin's 'fraying edge.'

This sense of fraying can be usefully developed in relation to Tzvetan Todorov's pivotal understanding of the literary fantastic, a mode of writing distinct from genre fantasy in two main ways. First, where genre fantasy deals in enclosed worlds, the literary fantastic deals in disruptive impulses. Second, where genre fantasy implies complicity on the part of readers, the literary fantastic actively seeks out reader hesitancy as a means of building in competing readings of the text, typically revolving around two choices, the psychological or the supernatural. As Marin expounds his theory of the limit, he brings in a more complex sense of the finite. Taking the Latin term *limes* ('a path or a passage, a way between two fields'), he continues by noting what happens to this sense of a limit, once two distinct edges track each other without meeting: 'The limit [becomes] at the same time a way and a gap . . .'[16] In maintaining plural readings, possible choices track each other—perhaps on occasions veering towards one or another—but while hesitancy remains, so does this fraying edge of semantic possibility.

How, then, can texts as diverse as the biblical Book of Genesis, Tennyson's poem 'The Lady of Shalott,' Orwell's novel *Animal Farm*, J. M. Barrie's play *Peter Pan*, and Bunyan's allegory *The Pilgrim's Progress* all shelter under the same literary umbrella, fantasy? The answer lies in the fact that they share two primary characteristics. First, as already implied, they deal in the unknowableness of life. A reader of Doris Lessing's realist first novel, *The Grass is Singing* (1950), may find she can relive at least an element of that literary experience by reading up on or even visiting present-day Zimbabwe, but none of us can holiday in the Garden of Eden. A child who delights in Anna Sewell's *Black Beauty* (1877) may try to recapture that pleasure through learning to ride, but no reader of *Animal Farm* can teach beasts to speak, any more than they can make pigs fly. To reiterate: fantasy sets up worlds that genuinely exist *beyond* the horizon, as opposed to those parts of our own world that are located beyond that line of sight but to which we might travel, given sufficient means.

Epic Space

Second, a fantasy narrative threatens infinity in the manner described by Stewart in *On Longing*: it conveys 'a world not necessarily known through the senses, or lived experience.'[17] One supreme instance of this lies in the potency of legends and myths, the primary instance of which—at least in the Anglo-American tradition—are those relating to the tales of King Arthur. Indeed, there is a sense in which Arthur himself *is* a fantasy narrative: lacking any clear anchor point in historical reality, writers and readers return endlessly to

Arthurian legend as if driven by the impossible need for closure. A paradox is clearly at work here. Though there are those like Graham Phillips and Martin Keatman, who have embarked on a quest to find the historical figure behind the legend (in their case, painstakingly tracing it back to Owain Ddantgwyn 'the Bear,' a sixth-century Prince of Gwynedd in North Wales), legend it remains.[18] In this dynamic, we see a replication of longing and miniaturism, for by taming Arthur in text after text, we 'cut him down to size' and at the same time render him larger than life. Explication also miniaturises Arthur. Phillips and Keatman draw attention to the fact that 'their' Arthur came from the Votadini, a tribe sympathetic to the Romans at a time when the Britons as a whole were divided. As such, they suggest he

> may well have adopted a name which personified both [Briton and Roman] sympathies in order to avoid any implication of favouring one faction more than the other. If his tribal title was the Bear, he may not only have used the Brythonic word *Arth*, but also the Latin word for bear, *Ursus*. His original title may therefore have been *Arthursus*, later shortened to *Arthur* . . . [19]

Here, however, pinning King Arthur down to one individual identity comes immediately into conflict with the endowment of a battle name. For if Arthur is a battle name, it further contributes to his larger-than-life hyperbolic status, in the same way that pseudonyms such as the Black Panther or the Yorkshire Ripper mythologise serial killers. It is perhaps through this concertina-like desire to aggrandise and reduce, accompanied by the inability to reconcile both, that Arthur becomes the stuff of dreams, shifting out of focus however hard we peer. Hence, satisfactorily indistinct, Arthur can become his own text, across which we inscribe projections of heroism, cultural struggle, leadership, and romance. For (and here is the crux of the 'beyond the horizon' aspect of fantasy) despite impressive studies such as Phillips and Keatman's, the quest for Arthur must remain open, fantasy ending at the moment of realisation.

How, then, do we reconcile this view of Arthur with the fantasy formula already offered, in which each world functions as a discrete entity in order for the formula to work effectively? To some extent, though individual texts may satisfy the closure dynamic, once seen as a drive to read (or write) the next (hence more definitive) Arthurian narrative, sequences of texts accumulate in a manner that complicates the fantasy model. In these terms, the enforced closure of the formula exists in tension with the expansive elements of all our fantasies (positive and negative). According to J. R. R. Tolkien, the most appropriate metaphor to use to describe the diachronic composition of Arthurian legend is that of the soup cauldron simmering on the hob: the essence remains the same, but the precise flavour and ingredients change.[20] As history mingles with myth and faerie, the result is a composite, the original an impossible quest. From here it is easy to see how Arthurian fantasy changes shape to accommodate its readers and, in addition, the societies they represent: 'King Arthur has always been many things to many people . . . from [him] being an extra-terrestrial to his being the king of Atlantis . . . and in the 1980s, King Arthur was again sensationalised in the wake of the "Dungeons and Dragons" craze.'[21]

This lack of historical specificity is a particular feature of epic fantasy in general. Tolkien's Lord of the Rings trilogy, as its recent adaptation for cinema reveals, has a similar aptitude for capturing the shifting preoccupations of successive generations of readers—Tolkien was named 'Author of the Century' in the year 2000 by a readers' poll in the UK. Peter Jackson's recent films have fuelled the popular appeal of the series to even more exaggerated heights. As Michael Coren observes, the initial short trailer for *The Lord of the Rings: The Fellowship of the Ring* (New Line Cinema, 2001) was 'downloaded more than 1.7 million times. That was twice the number of downloads for the trailer for *Star Wars: Episode I: The Phantom Menace*, which had previously held the record . . .'[22] One of the reasons *Lord of the Rings* allows for such reinterpretations is that its vast cartographic canvas (another version of elongation) opens across epic space in the same way that *Star Wars* opens across outer space, or Arthur opens across time. Like the Arthurian tales, it is specific enough in its vision of heroism, comradeship, and corruption to mirror the world we know, while being general enough for us to flesh out the detail with the vision of monstrosity most pertinent at the time.

In mirroring our own world, we return briefly to realism and the role played by reflection in that form. As Furst observes, 'In attributing to both mirror and eye the capacity for faithful representation, the realists wanted to have it both ways, by ascribing transparency to the reflection and so inscribing it with truthfulness.'[23] In fantasy writing, mirrors draw attention to themselves, and in so doing, they become simultaneously more compelling and their glassy surfaces more effectively breached. In fact, what they take on is a kind of architectural function, offering an aperture into a second fictive world that makes the cinema screen one of its most effective canvases. In turning, now, to consider the development of fantasy writing across the ages, the mirror's reflections become contemplative, tracing a path from classical antiquity to the twenty-first century, while evoking possibilities of a perfect future.

Notes

1. Irving Goffman, *Frame Analysis*, 560–561. Cited in Susan Stewart, *On Longing: Narratives of the Miniature, the Gigantic the Souvenir, the Collection* (Durham: Duke University Press, 1993), 25.

2. Maureen Duffy, *The Erotic World of Faery* (London: Hodder and Stoughton, 1972), 175.

3. *Collins English Dictionary, Third Edition* (Glasgow: HarperCollins, 1991).

4. Lilian R. Furst, *All Is True: The Claims and Strategies of Realist Fiction* (Durham: Duke University Press, 1995), 9–10.

5. Sigmund Freud, 'Creative Writers and Day-Dreaming' in the *Penguin Freud Library, Vol. 14, Art and Literature*, Albert Dickson, ed. (Harmondsworth: Penguin, 1990), 129–141 (p. 131–132).

6. For a fuller discussion of the interrelationship between 'phantasy' and 'fantasy,' see Lucie Armitt, *Theorising the Fantastic* (London: Arnold, 1996), 39–42.

7. 'Peter Pan, Or the Boy Who Would Not Grown Up,' Act I, in *The Plays of J. M. Barrie in One Volume* (London: Hodder and Stoughton, 1928), 29.

8. Louis Marin, 'The Frontiers of Utopia,' in *Utopias and the Millennium*, Krishan Kumar and Stephen Bann, eds. (London: Reaktion Books, 1993), 7–16 (p. 7).

9. Louis James, 'From Robinson to Robina, and Beyond: *Robinson Crusoe* as a Utopian Concept,' in *Utopias and the Millennium*, Krishan Kumar and Stephen Bann, eds. (London: Reaktion Books, 1993), 33–45 (p. 34).

10. *Robinson Crusoe on Mars* (dir. Byron Haskin), Paramount, 1964. See James, 'From Robinson to Robina,' 45.

11. H. G. Wells, *The First Men in the Moon* (1901; London: Everyman, 1993), 100.

12. Marin, 'The Frontiers of Utopia,' 7–8.

13. Stewart, *On Longing*, 117.

14. J. R. R. Tolkien, 'On Fairy-Stories,' in *Tree and Leaf* (London: HarperCollins, 2001), 1–81 (p. 49).

15. Vladimir Propp, *Morphology of the Folktale*, Laurence Scott, trans. (Austin: University of Texas Press, 1968), 64, 111.

16. Marin, 'The Frontiers of Utopia,' 9.

17. Stewart, *On Longing*, 38, 44.

18. Graham Phillips and Martin Keatman, *King Arthur: The True Story* (London: Century, 1992).

19. Phillips and Keatman, *King Arthur*, 128.

20. 'Speaking of the history of stories . . . we may say that the Pot of Soup, the Cauldron of Story, has always been boiling. . . . It seems fairly plain that Arthur . . . boiled for a long time, together with many other older figures and devices, of mythology and Faeries, and even some other stray bones of history . . .' J. R. R. Tolkien, 'On Fairy-Stories,' 27–29 passim.

21. Phillips and Keatman, *King Arthur*, 3.

22. Michael Coren, *J. R. R. Tolkien: The Man Who Created The Lord of the Rings* (Basingstoke: Boxtree, 2001), 4.

23. Furst, *All Is True*, 9.

Chapter Two

Fantasy as Timeline

Introduction

With the exception of Sir Thomas More's *Utopia* (1516) and
Jonathan Swift's *Gulliver's Travels* (1726), all of the fantasy narratives discussed in any detail in this book are written after 1800.
However, this is not to suggest that fantasy is, in any way, predominantly a post-1800 narrative phenomenon—quite the reverse. In
fact, it is with the introduction of narrative fiction in novel form
around this time that fantasy first starts to become surmounted by
the newly emergent narrative realism. This chapter therefore briefly
examines some of the key pre-1800 concepts that have shaped and
conditioned post-1800 fantasy, concluding with one of the key
debates provoked—around 1800—by an element of critical hostil-
ity towards the new realism: the relationship between fancy and
imagination as discussed by Samuel Taylor Coleridge in his
'Biographia Literaria.'

The Origins of Modern Fantasy

Whether it be the gods of ancient Greece or the Yahweh of the Old
Testament, writings of the gods typically employ narrative modes
we would now call 'fantasy':

> . . . Mercury prepared to obey his exalted Father's com-
> mand. First he laced on his feet those golden sandals with
> wings to carry him high at the speed of the winds' swift
> blast over ocean and over land alike. Then he took his wand;
> the wand with which he calls the pale souls forth from the

Nether World and sends others down to grim Tartarus, gives
sleep, and takes sleep away, and unseals eyes at death. So
shepherding the winds before him with his wand, he swam
through the murk of the clouds.[1]

The relationship between the real and the unreal during the classical period was far more fluid than our own rather prosaic determination to assert reality at all costs. We may well attach much of the
strength of fantasy in the writings of the ancients to the fact that
mythology was, during that time, wrestling with ideas that may have
appeared monstrous in scale. As Kathryn Hume puts it, these myths
'assert values that cannot be validated scientifically, and the stories
they tell are most decidedly not verifiable—creation, activities of
the gods, the deeds of semi-divine beings and culture heroes.' By
extension, this has an effect upon character construction: 'Displaced
from the mythic level, we find tales of men, many of whom still deal
with marvelous adversaries since such enemies are necessary to
define the heroes as heroes.'[2]

Intriguingly, however, the encounter with fabulous monsters can
also work to render the central character heroic in a more modern
sense: not by setting him apart from the rest of humanity, but by
strengthening the common ground between him and the reader. It
is, in fact, this aspect of heroism, rather than the cosmological significance of the gods, that tends to be conveyed in more recent writings. Hence, in John Bunyan's comparatively recent allegory, *The
Pilgrim's Progress* (1684), one of the ways in which Christian main-
tains his status as Everyman is through the figurative implication
that each of us must be prepared to face our share of periods in the
Slough of Despond and encounters with whatever constitutes, for
us, our personal Apollyon, in order that we might reach the resolution and consolations of our Celestial City. To evoke an obvious
comparison, Christian's pattern is identical to Frodo's in *The Lord of
the Rings*.

While Bunyan happily employs the traditional fantasy device of
the dream narrative for his Christian allegory, it is interesting that,
though the Old Testament section of the Bible is full of wonderful
fables and dreams, the New Testament insists on realism, almost to
the exclusion of any other mode of writing.[3] This overemphasis on

realism remains a strong facet of contemporary Christianity—particularly in its more evangelical guises. So the Harry Potter series continues to receive a lot of adverse criticism from Christians anxious about its apparent promotion of magic to an avid generation of child readers. (As an aside, I once knew a Christian couple who refused to allow their children to believe in Santa Claus, fearing that when they discovered Santa Claus to be 'made-up' they would believe Jesus was 'made-up,' too.) Hume reads this phenomenon more historically, blaming much of the current prejudice against fantasy writing on early Christian works that, she claims, 'unconcernedly perpetuated mimetic assumptions,' partly as a reaction against the fantasy favoured in the pagan myths of Greece and Rome.[4]

And yet, of course, without the significant presence of equally appreciative Christian fantasists there would be no *Pilgrim's Progress*, no *Chronicles of Narnia*, and no Lord of the Rings trilogy either. The view of J. R. R. Tolkien, a 'devout and orthodox Catholic,'[5] is clear and in direct contravention to those who deem fantasy to somehow imperil the Christian faith: in its determination to reach beyond the limits of the real, fantasy takes us closer to the act of divine creation than mimesis can possibly allow, hence becoming a form of devotion in its own right. To put it in Tolkien's own words, fantasy empowers a storyteller to divorce 'green from grass, blue from heaven, and red from blood,' cloak him- or herself in 'an enchanter's power,' and in remixing and creating anew, 'put a deadly green upon a man's face and produce a horror . . . cause woods to spring with silver leaves . . . and put hot fire into the belly of the cold worm . . . [I]n such "fantasy" . . . new form is made; Faërie begins; man becomes a sub-creator.'[6]

Early Modern Fantasy

It is presumably this ability of fantasy to create the world anew that makes it, during the early modern period, such a valuable technique for certain key canonical writers. William Shakespeare's *The Tempest* (1623), for example, parallels the discoveries 'really' taking place in the New World at the time by placing a new island paradise centre stage. In the process, the central protagonist, Prospero, flaunts his power to effect freedom and slavery in one fell swoop, freeing the airy spirit Ariel from the 'foul witch Sycorax,' who had trapped him physically within a cloven pine, but only at the expense of enslaving him anew, rendering Ariel the conduit for many of his 'charms' (Act I, Scene 2, ll.257–99). Though classified by Shakespearean scholars as a 'pastoral drama,' *The Tempest*, in its wholesale use of magic and faerie—not to mention its masque elements drawing on the gods of classical antiquity—is clearly a work of fantasy as we understand the term. And like the later fairy stories, Shakespeare bases his play on other, more popular, ancient oral literatures, 'saga, ballad . . . and folktale.'[7] Unlike *A Midsummer Night's Dream* (1600) or the contemporaneous *Twelfth Night* (1623), however, both of which also employ faerie as part of their dramatic foundation, there is a developed sense of the sinister in *The Tempest*, conjuring occult forms to undermine the paradisiacal, creating a sense of haunted space. Faerie is, as Maureen Duffy reminds us, available 'in manifestations of light and dark, beautiful and ugly, enchanting and terrifying. The Fairy Queen is balanced by the witch; the Fairy King [Prospero?] by the devil . . .'[8]

On a far grander scale, then, we see similar developments in the warring factions between good and evil filtered through a framework of fantasy in John Milton's *Paradise Lost* (1667). As Margaret Kean puts it, through the employment of fantasy Milton is enabled to convey 'the world in its creational perfection' whereby, as part of that process, 'the poem discovers a new space where, freed from the limitations of mortal existence . . . an ideal fiction can be developed.'[9] Immediately, we see the connections with Tolkien's vision of the 'sub-creator,' also embodied wholesale in Shakespeare's demonic Prospero. As Duffy observes, part of the ambivalence in evidence in literary and aesthetic representations of faeries involves their taking on a religious guise as 'rebel angels who didn't fall all the way when they were turned out of heaven'[10]: the comparison with Milton's Satan and his fall from Paradise is self-evident.

When we come to consider some of the similarities in the use of imagery between *The Tempest* and *Paradise Lost*, one of the first traits that springs to mind is the 'vertical' factor with which we opened Chapter One. Ariel is, as his name suggests, of the air, and to some extent, he is a product of those elemental surroundings—

by which I mean that much of *The Tempest* (as its very name suggests) concerns the potency of wind-borne things. Thus it is difficult to separate Ariel from the 'music of the spheres,' described in Act III, Scene 2, as 'Sounds and sweet airs' (l.134) that haunt and torment Caliban. Similarly, in *Paradise Lost, Book IV*, we are made as aware of the 'gentle gales / Fanning their odiferous wings' (ll.156–157) around Eden as we are of the equally wind-borne Satan, who 'flew, and on the tree of life / The middle tree and highest there that grew, / Sat like a cormorant . . .' (ll.194–196).

As Duffy tells us, the presence of winged creatures in faerie guise is a new phenomenon during this period. Puck, Ariel's equivalent in the earlier Shakespearean fantasy, *A Midsummer Night's Dream*, is devoid of wings, and in the opening dialogue between Puck and a Fairy in Act II, Scene 1, of that play, Puck asks, 'Whither wander you?' (l.1), receiving the reply 'I do wander everywhere . . . And I serve the Fairy Queen, / To dew her orbs upon the green / . . . I must go seek some dew-drops here, / And hang a pearl in every cowslip's ear' (ll.6–15 passim). In other words, these are land-based forms, whereas the later Ariel is defined by or in flight. Duffy reads this shift entirely performatively, citing the influence of the flamboyant architect and stage designer Inigo Jones upon early modern staging techniques and subsequent play texts. Under Jones's influence, the stage could, for the first time, become visually transformed into 'Rocky wastes, moving waves, clouds descending with personages . . . ,'[11] the dramatic possibilities of which Shakespeare was quick to grasp. Once fairies were winged, moreover, the ease with which religious imagery could become attached to them, and hence the combined power of pagan and Christian mythology, helped to render their new physical form irresistible.

'Tree' Versus 'Leaf': Reading the Present Through the Past

From the early modern period, Duffy moves her encyclopaedic study forward again, taking in the eighteenth century and such mock epic poems as Pope's 'The Rape of the Lock' (1712–14) with its own winged forms in the shape of 'airy elves' (l.31) and 'Sylphs [who] aloft repair, / And sport and flutter in the field of air' (ll.65–66) before rejoining the core territory of this book in the form of *Gulliver's Travels* and on to the emerging Gothic novel. There is, however, no one easily defined sense of the progression of fantasy through the ages, because of the commingling of cultural and historical influences that rise and fall at any one point. For instance, Tolkien's sense of the development that became nineteenth- and twentieth-century fantasy differs in many ways from that of more contemporary critics. Where commentators such as Bruno Bettelheim or Jack Zipes[12] come to fantasy/faerie in the form of fairy tales, through European sources such as the German Märchen (later collected by Jacob and Wilhelm Grimm as *Kinder- und Hausmärchen* [1812–15]), or Charles Perrault's earlier French collection, *Contes du Ma Mère L'Oye* (*Tales of Mother Goose*) (1697), Tolkien traces a lineage through Old Norse legends, Anglo-Saxon tales, and on through Arthurian myth. From this genealogy, Tolkien dwells on three aspects of lineage: '*independent evolution* (or rather *invention*) . . . *inheritance* from a common ancestry; and *diffusion* at various times from one or more centres.' As he acknowledges, however, 'All three things . . . have evidently played their part in producing the intricate web of Story. It is now beyond all skill but that of the elves to unravel it.'[13]

Tolkien was, in his 'dayjob,' the Rawlinson and Bosworth Chair in Anglo-Saxon at Oxford University, his actual field of study being Old and Middle English.[14] It is therefore by no means surprising that, with the exception of contemporary popular Arthurian novels, it is primarily through his work that the ongoing relevance of the medieval period to the field of twentieth- and (via Jackson's cinematic versions) twenty-first century fantasy is maintained. In the Lord of the Rings trilogy, Middle Earth seems to coincide with the Middle Ages, an era of horsebacked conflict and tribal warfare. This also accords with the dates set towards the end of *Volume III, The Return of the King* (1955) where the battle to secure the Shire once more is titled 'the Battle of Bywater, 1419, the last battle fought in the Shire, and the only battle since the Greenfields, 1147 . . .'[15] As we will see in Chapter 3, even medieval dream vision continues to have currency in his work. But there is more to this than the employment of medieval themes within fiction. Even the title of his critical book *Tree and Leaf* retains connections with what Angus

Fletcher refers to as 'the medieval allegory of virtue and vice,' which takes its shape from the tree:

> Thus the parable of the two trees is used during the twelfth century to the point of threadbareness, the reason being that the highly articulated structure of the growth of nature could lodge complicated systems of abstraction and their upward development could be interpreted step by step— or rather, branch by branch.[16]

In Tolkien's *Tree and Leaf* (or at least the part of it encapsulated by the essay 'On Fairy-Stories'), we could argue that the 'tree' constitutes the etymological genealogy of fantasy, while the 'leaf' constitutes its surface manifestation as narrative. Tolkien foliates the tree in the following manner:

> We read that *Beowulf* 'is only a version of *Dat Erdmänneken*'; that '*The Black Bull of Norroway* is *Beauty and the Beast*,' or 'is the same story as *Eros and Psyche*' . . . Statements of that kind [i.e. tree] express . . . some element of truth; but they are not true in a fairy-story sense . . . It is precisely the colouring, the atmosphere, the unclassifiable individual details [i.e. leaf] of a story . . . that really count.[17]

In the context of more modern narratives Fletcher substitutes the word *leaf* with *ornamentation*, but with the proviso that, in this sense, ornamentation need not be aesthetically pleasing: 'The horrid scales and joints of the metamorphosed Gregor Samsa are . . . no less ornaments than the invented trappings of Swift's Flying Island . . . or the heraldic costuming of knights in *The Faerie Queene*.'[18] In other words, to ornament is to 'flesh out,' with all the beauty, gore, filth, or corpulence the average body can muster.

Phantasm Versus *Fantasia*

We know that a different relationship existed between literary representation, reality, and fantasy during the medieval period, largely due to the extensive faith held in the supernatural (both divine and demonic) at the time. As Mark Philpott observes, 'In the Middle Ages the dead were universally present with the living,' to the extent that there was even legislation covering the walking of ghosts.[19] However, rather than revealing an atavistic fascination, via Augustine the Middle Ages conceived an understanding of haunting that meshes with far more recent debates about psychology than we find in, for example, many nineteenth-century narratives.

> For [Augustine] memory was vital to cognition, and fantasies were vital to the working of memory . . . Among the terms Augustine used for such images were 'phantasia' and 'phantasma' . . . Fantasies were mental images of objects perceived, products of sensory motion and counter-motion, and themselves motions of the mind . . . Phantasms, 'like images of images,' were the result of memory working on itself; they were the vital link between memory and the creative usage of the imagination . . . [20]

It is the word *phantasm* that enables the slippage between meanings here, for it can refer to either a phantom, an 'illusory perception,' or 'objective reality as distorted by perception.'[21] As we move through these three distinct nuances, we perceive that the sense of empirical reality lessens to accommodate a matching increase in creative cognitive function. As fantasia and phantasm progress, therefore, we return to a similar pattern to that identified with Louis Marin's 'fraying edge' in Chapter 1, namely 'a path or a passage, a way between two fields,' which may result in the two veering towards or away from each other without actually meeting.[22] Hence, in Philpott's quotation, *phantasia* and *phantasma* are treated as synonyms, though in fact *fantasia* is a term we more commonly associate with music.

Not so during the period of Romanticism, however, in which Samuel Taylor Coleridge returned to the term *phantasia* (deriving from the Greek) and compared it to another apparent synonym, the Latin term *imaginatio*. Just as I am arguing for a distinction between *phantasm* and *phantasia*, Coleridge saw *phantasia* and *imaginatio* as 'two distinct and widely different faculties.' Once we examine the nature of his distinction carefully, however, we realise it is not one of etymology but of perceived quality: 'Milton had a highly imaginative, Cowley a very fanciful mind.'[23] The distinction, then, lies in these two writers' respective relationships with the literary canon and, by inference, *imaginatio* takes precedence over *phantasia*. As we trace these two lines, we see that, whereas in the Middle Ages fantasy's etymological ancestry was derived from high philosophy, by the start of the 1800s it had been brought down to earth. Though Cowley is no more a writer of fantasy than Milton (in fact, rather less so), the linguistic affinity between *phantasia* and *fantasy* is as clear as the negative implications the latter carries.

In *Tree and Leaf*, Tolkien tries to reverse this negativity, combining within *phantasia* two further aspects, 'the Sub-creative Art in itself and a quality of strangeness and wonder in the Expression . . . a quality essential to fairy-story.' It is here that Tolkien's use of the terms *Primary* and *Secondary Worlds* comes to the fore, which he employs in association with a kind of vertical trajectory: 'That the images are of things not in the primary world . . . is a virtue not a vice. Fantasy (in this sense) is, I think, not a lower but a higher form of Art, indeed the most nearly pure form, and so (when achieved) the most potent.'[24] The terms *phantasia* and *fantasy* are not always direct or even indirectly synonymous, of course. D. H. Lawrence writes his *Fantasia of the Unconscious* (1922) without making a single recourse to fantasy, but in his case the inheritance comes through Freud and equates with that understanding of phantasy we outlined in Chapter 1, namely 'a psychoanalytic term referring to that storehouse of fears, desires, and daydreams that inspire all fictions equally and that has its ultimate source in the unconscious.' In other instances, however, *fantasia* and *fantasy* have greater synergy.

Take, for example, Walt Disney's animation film *Fantasia* (1940), a film playing directly on the slippage between the musical nuances of the term and *fantasy* in the sense that we are tracing it in this book. Disney's animation is constructed around eight individual movements, many of which have a natural affinity with fantasy, such as Tchaikovsky's *The Nutcracker* suite, Paul Dukas's *The Sorcerer's Apprentice*, and Ponchielli's 'Dance of the Hours.' Even, however, in the case of pieces that might have a more natural affinity with classical realism (such as Beethoven's *Pastoral* Symphony), Disney places a clear fantasy interpretation upon them. So Beethoven's composition is interpreted through a landscape of Arcadia, complete with satyrs, unicorns, centaurs, winged horses, and a range of gods from Zeus to Hephaestus. *Whimsy*, then, becomes *fancy*, before effecting a slippage directly into fantasy. In fact, Disney's *Fantasia*—with its window onto fairy and folklore, magic and superstition, animal allegory, classical mythology, the Gothic, the ghost narrative, and epic fantasy—offers perhaps the closest parallel, within the boundaries of one single work, to the range of fantasy covered in this book. But irrespective of the manner in which fantasy—and its derivations—has shifted in perception, literary status, or terminology over the centuries, it cannot and does not exist at all until read. With that in mind, let us turn to the role of reading in fantasy.

Notes

1. Virgil, *The Aeneid*, W. F. Jackson Knight, trans. (Harmondsworth: Penguin, 1958), 104.

2. Kathryn Hume, *Fantasy and Mimesis: Responses to Reality in Western Literature* (New York: Methuen, 1984), 33.

3. The obvious exception to this rule, of course, is the Book of Revelation, in which fantasy is given free rein, it being a vision of an apocalyptic future.

4. Hume, *Fantasy and Mimesis*, 6.

5. Flieger, *A Question of Time*, 96.

6. J. R. R. Tolkien, 'On Fairy-Stories,' in *Tree and Leaf* (London: HarperCollins, 2001), 1–81 (pp. 22–23).

7. Frank Kermode, 'Introduction' to William Shakespeare, *The Tempest* (The Arden Shakespeare, London: Methuen, 1964), xi–xciii (p. lxiii).

8. Maureen Duffy, *The Erotic World of Faery* (London: Hodder and Stoughton, 1972), 89.

9. Margaret Kean, 'Dreaming of Eve: Edenic Fantasies in John Milton's *Paradise Lost*,' in *Writing and Fantasy*, Ceri Sullivan and Barbara White, eds. (London: Longman, 1999), 77–94 (p. 77).

10. Duffy, *Erotic World of Faery*, 185.

11. Duffy, *Erotic World of Faery*, 174.

12. See Bruno Bettelheim, *The Uses of Enchantment: The Meaning and Importance of Fairy Tales* (Harmondsworth: Penguin, 1991) and Jack Zipes, *Fairy Tales and the Art of Subversion: The Classical Genre for Children and the Process of Civilization* (New York: Routledge, 1983).

13. Tolkien, 'On Fairy-Stories,' 20–21.

14. According to Tom Shippey, 'Anglo-Saxon' was a term Tolkien disliked, preferring 'Old English.' *J. R. R. Tolkien: Author of the Century* (London: HarperCollins, 2001), xii.

15. J. R. R. Tolkien, *The Lord of the Rings, Volume III: The Return of the King* (1955; London: HarperCollins, 1999), 357. Further quotations from this novel will be referenced within the main body of the text, accompanied by the abbreviation *RK*.

16. Adolf Katzellenbogen, *Allegories of the Virtues and Vices in Medieval Art* (London, 1939), cited in Angus Fletcher, *Allegory: The Theory of a Symbolic Mode* (Ithaca: Cornell University Press, 1964), 133–134.

17. Tolkien, 'On Fairy-Stories,' 18–19.

18. Fletcher, *Allegory*, 143–144.

19. Mark Philpott, 'Haunting the Middle Ages,' in Sullivan and White, *Writing and Fantasy*, 48–61 (p. 48).

20. Philpott, 'Haunting the Middle Ages,' 53.

21. *Collins English Dictionary, Third Edition*, 1991.

22. Louis Marin, 'The Frontiers of Utopia,' in *Utopias and the Millennium*, Krishan Kumar and Stephen Bann, eds. (London: Reaktion Books, 1993), 7–16 (p. 9).

23. Samuel Taylor Coleridge, 'Biographia Literaria, Chapter 4,' in *The Portable Coleridge*, I. A. Richards, ed. (Harmondsworth: Penguin, 1978), 465–481 (pp. 476, 477).

24. Tolkien, 'On Fairy-Stories,' 47, 48.

Chapter Three

How to Read Fantasy; or, Dreams and Their Fictional Readers

Introduction

The reader is, in many ways, often sidelined in fantasy criticism. Genre determines readership, we are told, and readers who like science fiction will like science fiction *because* it is science fiction. In my opinion, a reader fulfilling this criterion doesn't like books at all. We are, in fact, far less likely to be consoled by formula in literary texts than we are repeated encounters with predictability in life: we expect literature—of any kind—to be creative, whereas we expect (indeed prefer) significant chunks of our lives to be reliably forecast. So, when an intelligent reader is surprised, or even perplexed, by the refusal of a work of fantasy to take the predictable route, she is far more likely to respond with interest than with disappointment. Fantasy narratives are literary texts before and beyond being fantasy narratives.

To talk of reading in this way, however, is to consider it purely within a synchronous frame. What about when we consider readership across the spectrum of history? Do we always read fantasy narratives in the same way, irrespective of whether we read them in 1500 or 1900? Clearly, the answer is no, and as Tolkien reminds us, we have to place reading, as well as writing, within a historical frame:

> . . . when we have done all that research—collection and comparison of the tales of many lands—can do; when we have explained many of the elements commonly found

embedded in fairy-stories (such as step-mothers, enchanted
bears and bulls, cannibal witches, taboos on names, and the
like) as relics of ancient customs once practised in daily life,
or of beliefs once held as beliefs and not as 'fancies'—there
remains still a point too often forgotten: that is, the effect
produced now by these old things in the stories as they are.[1]

A twenty-first-century reader well versed in narrative realism
and coming to *The Pilgrim's Progress* (1684) for the first time, may
well feel alienated by or at least to some extent impatient with the
allegorical style of Bunyan's book, despite being more at ease, perhaps, with the equally allegorical content of Orwell's *Animal Farm*
(1945). Similar accommodation is likely to be required by most
contemporary readers of a Victorian ghost story, for—in general
terms—the supernatural holds far fewer terrors for us than it did for
the majority of nineteenth-century readers. Nevertheless, in both of
these examples the necessary shifts in readerly focus are relatively
easily achieved, and without a significant loss of understanding of
these texts' significance either to us now or at the time when they
were first written. However, when the distance between the date of
writing and the date of reading is greater, lack of awareness of such
disparities may result.

Take, for instance, the inclusion of the monster Grendel in the
Anglo-Saxon text *Beowulf*. While we will certainly read Grendel as
a creature of fable, and may therefore endow him with primarily
allegorical or metaphorical significance dependent upon the particular antagonists we mythologise in our own society (Al Qaeda, glob-
alisation, child poverty, AIDS), Kathryn Hume reminds us that the
audience sitting and listening to the *Beowulf* poet may well have
believed Grendel to have actual existence and thus would mentally
replace fable with realism.[2] Such differences in perception are not,
of course, particular to fantasy: they operate in all modes of literary
writing. What we will now consider is a key structural aspect that *is*
more particular to fantasy than other modes, namely the changing
nature of the representation and interpretation of dream structures
in literary texts over time and how this may affect their reading(s).

In his book *The Dynamics of Literary Response*, Norman N.
Holland quickly recognises the particular advantage fantasy narra-

tives have over other literary forms when considering the reading process: 'Often, when literary works ask us to enter an environment explicitly labelled as fantastic, we are being asked to merge orally into that new world . . . take it in and be taken into it.'[3] In other words, where realism holds up a mirror to the world and, in the process, doubles the distance between what we can see and what we can touch, fantasy swallows us whole. The only experience we have that is similar to this, beyond reading, is when we enter into the night world of dream. There, too, we are plunged 'bodily' into danger, desire, confusion, and chaos; there, too, we struggle to piece together meaning out of what does not immediately reflect the known; and from there, too, we re-emerge unscathed, conscious that what we have experienced is different from the world, but informs that world and is in turn informed by it. It is for this reason that we here focus, in detail, on some of the differing ways in which dreams are used to structure the relationship between reader and fantasy text, beginning with the work of Sigmund Freud.

Reading Dreams

Sigmund Freud's essay 'Creative Writers and Day-Dreaming,' already alluded to in Chapter 1, sets the norm for the structure of a fantasy text. Typically, two or more chronotopes are established within the narrative frame, the protagonist retreating from the world of outer realism into another world, one taking on a dream-like representation. Lewis Carroll's *Alice in Wonderland* (1865)[4] is, in that sense, the archetypal narrative model for such fictions. Alice begins this story in the world of narrative realism, sitting by her sister on a riverbank; however, within half a sentence she is immersed into another world—one not of dream, but of fiction: 'once or twice she had peeped into the book her sister was reading, but it had no pictures or conversations in it, "and what is the use of a book," thought Alice, "without pictures or conversations?"'[5] This is, then, a fantasy framed in terms of reading and writing. Only once she has dipped her toe into the world of reading and drawn it hurriedly out again does Alice take the plunge and immerse herself fully into creative writing/dreaming:

> So she was considering, in her own mind (as well as she
> could, for the hot day made her feel very sleepy and stu-
> pid), whether the pleasure of making a daisy-chain would
> be worth the trouble of getting up and picking the daisies,
> when suddenly a white rabbit with pink eyes ran close by
> her. (*AW*, 25)

We remember that, in Freud's essay, the parameters between
worlds are very clearly defined ('In spite of all the emotion with
which he cathects his world of play, the child distinguishes it quite
well from reality').[6] In Carroll's text, however, though the parameters of the world inside Alice's sister's book and the relationship
they bear to the world beyond that are clearly distinguished, the
precise point of slippage from fantasy to reality is not. In fact,
despite my suggestion that it is the second sentence of Carroll's text
(quoted above) that demarcates the shift from one world into the
next, arguably it is the third:

> There was nothing so very remarkable in that; nor did Alice
> think it so very much out of the way to hear the Rabbit say
> to itself, 'Oh dear! Oh dear! I shall be too late' (when she
> thought about it afterwards, it occurred to her that she
> ought to have wondered at this, but at the time it all
> seemed quite natural) . . . (*AW*, 25–26)

Having rejected a role for herself as reader within the text, Alice
here unwittingly elides her own response with that of the 'real'
reader. The second sentence, which I suggest marks the shift
between worlds, only takes on application as fantasy retrospectively
—just as 'it all seemed quite natural' to Alice 'at the time.' Hence,
even though it would be perfectly proper for a work of narrative
realism to incorporate the second sentence—though obviously not
the third—into its frame, the moving rabbit traces the horizon
between worlds.

Yet here we find a further complication to Freud's model, in a
question the reader of *Alice in Wonderland* must consider: namely,
'How many Alices are there in the text, one or two?' Or, to put it
another way, 'Is the Alice who is "in" Wonderland the same as the
Alice who dreams of Wonderland?' The answer, surely, is no: Alice

dreams/writes herself into Wonderland, while remaining, 'in reality,' dreaming/reading on the riverbank beside her sister. Alice is, then, in literary terms two characters, not one. As dreamer she is a character of realism; only as an outward projection of the self within dream does she become a character of fantasy. Moreover, the Alice who is within Wonderland—despite her refusal to adopt the role of reader at the start, repeatedly intervenes to impose a kind of readerly role upon herself:

> 'It was much pleasanter at home,' thought poor Alice, 'when one wasn't always growing larger and smaller, and being ordered about by mice and rabbits . . . I do wonder what *can* have happened to me! When I used to read fairy tales, I fancied that kind of thing never happened, and now here I am in the middle of one! There ought to be a book written about me, that there ought!' (*AW*, 58–59)

Through such self-interrogation, Alice becomes dreamer and interpreter in one.

A similar dynamic is noticeable in *The Two Towers*, the second volume of Tolkien's Lord of the Rings trilogy. A number of metafictional references to tales and their telling are made at the start of the book and, towards the end, Sam refers to Frodo and himself as characters within the tales of others in a manner very similar to that Alice employs:

> . . . we shouldn't be here at all, if we'd known more about it before we started. But I suppose it's often that way. The brave things in the old tales and songs, Mr. Frodo: adventures, as I used to call them. I used to think that they were things the wonderful folk of the stories went out and looked for . . . But that's not the way of it with the tales that really mattered, or the ones that stay in the mind. Folk seem to have just landed in them, usually—their paths were laid that way, as you put it . . . and not all to a good end, mind you; at least not to what folk inside a story and not outside it call a good end . . . But those aren't always the best tales to hear, though they may be the best tales to get landed in! I wonder what sort of a tale we've fallen into?[7]

What Sam is outlining, here, is not just his place as a character within a narrative, but also his existence as a reader beyond it ('those aren't always the best tales'). If Middle Earth is a land of dreams, and Sam and Frodo's quest a journey into Tolkien's unconscious (which a Freudian reader might well argue), then we need to consider to what extent this dream structure is affected by Tolkien's knowledge of an earlier literary dream model, that of the medieval dream vision. In doing so, we will also consider how this structure affects our reading of more recent fantasy narratives.

Medieval Dream Vision

Kathryn L. Lynch, in her book on the subject, traces medieval dream vision poetry back to an eighth-century religious text recounted by the venerable Bede, which details the story of the vision of a good and prosperous man, Drycthelm. Having died in the night, Drycthelm returns to life at daylight ready to tell his tale. Here we have another variant on Carroll's Wonderland, for this dreamer, having operated as reader to his own text through the secondary elaboration he retains on waking, goes on to act as writer of his own dream. Lynch continues:

> . . . the Dreamer's experience can easily be analysed into three parts—his existence before the vision, the vision itself, and his life afterward. In this way, the vision is like any rite of passage, in which . . . the initiate travels through three different stages: separation, when he is detached from his stable cultural group . . . limen or margin [the vision experience itself,] . . . and aggregation, when he returns to normal life with a newly defined role . . . [8]

Under the terms of this framework, the 'newly defined role' for Drycthelm is one of reader/writer as well as experienced dreamer. By definition the solitary nature of his position also turns the dream into a form of quest: here one after truth. The perceived isolation of the dreamer, however, offers a further parallel with the dynamics of reading. For we also immerse ourselves into the 'dreamworld' of the text in order to reach a level of understanding we believe experience alone cannot give us. Indeed, preoccupied as we are with the minutiae of existence beyond the text, the readerly retreat from reality into the text is where we are, perhaps, best enabled to wake up to a more transcendent understanding. And yet, even when medieval dream vision is used in this way, it is important not to confuse 'clarity' for ease of understanding on the part of the reader. Interpretation is as much a problem here as in more recent works, for as John of Salisbury (ca. 1120–1180) argued, they contain 'images of events wrapped as it were in a cloak of disguise, and it is with this disguise that the art of interpreting dreams deals.'[9]

For us, it is almost impossible to separate the phrase 'the interpretation of dreams' from the work of Sigmund Freud, but medieval scholars would turn to the Bible for dream models and, in particular, to the Old Testament's Book of Daniel or the story of Joseph and his brothers in the Book of Genesis, Chapters 37–50. In both of these books, as much as in the texts under consideration in this one, the issue of how a dream is read proves crucial. In the Book of Daniel, for instance, the relationship between dreaming and the reading of texts is made literal. Having gained fame for interpreting the dreams of King Nebuchadnezzar, Daniel is called before his successor to interpret a mysterious text supernaturally inscribed upon the wall by the 'fingers of a man's hand.' Prior to Daniel being called upon, however, we learn that 'the wise men, the astrologers, have been brought in before [the King], that they should read this writing, and make known unto [him] the interpretation thereof: but they could not shew the interpretation of the thing . . .'[10] In other words, the interpreter of dreams is a kind of super-reader (a role, of course, that Freud also outlined for himself in 'reading' his analysands' words and actions, writing their stories, and then reading/interpreting them in entirely self-fulfilling terms). Sure enough, Daniel proves himself up to the job, deciphering the text as follows:

'. . . ME-NĒ, ME-NĒ, TE-KĒL, U-PHAR-SIN.'
   This is the interpretation of the thing: ME-NĒ: God hath numbered thy kingdom, and finished it.
   TE-KĒL: Thou art weighed in the balances, and art found wanting.
   PE-RĒS: Thy kingdom is divided, and given to the Mēdes and Persians.'[11]

Here, not only is the ability to interpret seen as a direct connection with the divine, but the passage also draws attention to the advantages that can be afforded through deliberate misinterpretation. One need not be a biblical scholar to notice the discrepancy between the message inscribed and Daniel's reading of it. Not only is his version an abbreviation (*me-nē* appears twice in the original and only once in Daniel's reading), it also employs lexical substitution (*pe-rēs* for *upharsin*). Scholars generally accept the gist of the interpretation to be a humorous critique 'of the kings of the Neo-Babylonian Empire,' but are divided on the precise meaning of the wordplay.[12] What matters for our purposes is the larger critical consensus of biblical commentators on Daniel's actions, namely 'that an interpretation . . . need not correspond exactly to the actual language of what is interpreted,' and secondly that the importance of Daniel's reading lies in his prioritisation of making 'the mysterious words immediately relevant to the situation of the king,' rather than offering a fully accurate transliteration of them. Thus, sanction is given to employ discursive power where the effect may be more expedient than the truth. Norman W. Porteous goes further, applauding Daniel for his willingness to deal with 'traditional materials . . . freely and imaginatively . . . to convey their truth in the most impressive way possible.'[13] In fact, what strikes me as most trustworthy about Daniel is that he puts very little effort into concealing his discrepancy (something less easily said for 'super-readers' such as Freud!).

As far as twenty-first-century readers are concerned, medievalists are split about whether or not Freudian readings can be retrospectively applied to the structure of medieval dream vision. Lynch has reservations, making the point that our own era is so dominated by Freudian readings of dream theory that recourse to Freud risks rendering medieval dream visionaries 'mere forerunners' and 'differences such as those between the "supernatural" in a medieval world view and the "unconscious" in a modern one . . . simply differences of "terminology."'[14] Nevertheless, one element remaining common to the approaches of Lynch, Freud, and the Carroll of the Alice texts is the shared metaphor of travel or quest employed by all three writers. Psychoanalysis traces a journey into subjectivity, and Alice, as we have seen, leaves the inert world of realism and exchanges it for one in which she rarely stays still. Even at the Mad Tea Party, where she is seated, each diner moves around from place to place, Alice never having the chance to drink tea before moving on to the next setting. Lynch, citing Winthrop Wetherbee, identifies in medieval dream vision a similar kind of mobile patterning, but in this case it has a metaphorical rather than literal application. So Wetherbee talks of the dream as a form of 'intellectual pilgrimage' enabling the dreamer to transcend the limitations of realism and 'attain a vision of truth' that often carries with it a form of divine message.[15] According to medievalists, such journeys can also be charted in more secular terms: 'At the most simplistic level . . . a diagram of many high medieval philosophical poems resembles in broad outline the medieval diagram of brain function . . . charting a journey through imagination, reason, and memory, involving will and intentionality . . .'[16] A further similarity exists within the apparently diverging philosophical bases for the two models. Where medieval dream vision takes its inspiration from belief in God, psychoanalytic readings of dream structures take their inspiration from belief in the unconscious. As faith systems, the two have much in common, despite appearances to the contrary. God is unseen, unknowable, and His/Her existence impossible to prove; all three things can equally be said of the unconscious. If we consider the parallels between literary fantasy and dream motivation further, we might argue that, just as God and the unconscious present us with the possibility that there is another, unseen side to life—a storehouse of fears and possibilities, an unknown world beyond the senses—then literary fantasy offers a shape for those fears and possibilities that cannot be captured in any other way.

Immediately, then, we are aware of the differing ways in which dreams can be read and, if we take the dream world as existing in parallel to the structures of competing worlds in fantasy narratives, we can see the value in exploring readerly connections between them. Though medieval dream vision is commonly read as divinely inspired, Constance B. Hieatt develops this further, arguing that this is not the sole perspective from which we should interpret it:

> All of this medieval opinion appears to fall into one of three patterns: first, that dreams are divinely (or diabolically)

caused, and therefore may show the future or impart knowledge in a supernatural way; second, that dreams have purely physical or psychological causes; or, third, that some dreams have supernatural causes, while others have purely physical causes.[17]

In fact, this commonsense approach also defines Hieatt's understanding of the role 'reality' plays in the literary representation of dream vision in general: '[Dream vision poetry] makes a good deal of poetic "sense," and its connection with the everyday sort of common sense is that it makes sense as a dream.' At the same time, the existence of that dream is situated within what one might call a larger 'reality context':

> [In such poetry] waking up, for example, serves as a way to terminate a sequence with which the poet has gone as far as he wishes. Of course, the frequency with which the dreamer wakes up and goes back to sleep not only serves to extricate the poet from his material, so he can go on to something else without the need of tying up loose ends, but also is a constant reminder to his audience that this is a dream.[18]

It is here that we identify perhaps the key structural distinction between medieval and contemporary dream structures in relation to the literary reader. As we have seen, Alice's Wonderland dream begins when she falls asleep. In this sense, the relationship between dreamworld and realist frame is mimetic, tracing the shape we expect such a relationship to take. J. R. R. Tolkien, however, is highly critical of this type of fantasy text, accusing it of employing what he calls 'the machinery of Dream' to produce 'a good picture in a disfiguring frame.'[19] More satisfactory, one assumes, would be the use of dream typically adopted in the medieval text, whereby the protagonist *awakens* into dream, thus allowing for the 'chance to open the veiled eye of the flesh to clearer vision of the absolute.'[20] This type of dream takes on an almost theological quality entirely appropriate to Tolkien's larger Christian vision. It is a freeing from the restricted vision of earthly life in order to become endowed with an enhanced vision (indeed, to become a visionary). Hence, as Verlyn Flieger observes, in the Lord of the Rings trilogy, 'Tolkien's dream narrative manages to suggest dream without identifying it, as if Carroll had left Alice down the rabbit hole.'[21] It is only once we have established this distinction that the ending of Tolkien's own Lord of the Rings trilogy makes any sense.

Towards the end of *Volume III, The Return of the King*, Gandalf leaves Frodo, Sam, Merry, and Pippin on the East Road close to the borders of the Shire. Merry turns to the others and observes, 'Well here we are, just the four of us that started out together . . . We have left all the rest behind, one after another. It seems almost like a dream that has slowly faded.' Frodo responds, 'Not to me . . . To me it feels more like falling asleep again.'[22] To a contemporary reader, Merry's remark makes a great deal more structural sense than Frodo's. The epic journey that spans the trilogy becomes, in Merry's terms, a dream, the border between sleeping and waking seemingly locating itself on the borders of the Shire. In this sense, the journey into Middle Earth works in a structurally identical manner to the journey into Wonderland, and like Alice, these four travellers immerse themselves fully into it and fully return again. For Frodo, the key dreamer of Tolkien's trilogy, this is clearly not the relationship he holds to dream by this stage. His journey into dream has functioned as a moment of enhanced enlightenment, resulting in him being more fully alive when 'dreaming' than when 'awake'; but also, and as with Drycthelm, for Frodo dream and death (or the threat of death) are never far apart.

The fear of death or danger is, in fact, the key characteristic of Frodo's dreaming. The first instance of sleep overtaking him occurs in *Volume I, The Fellowship of the Ring*, as the travellers walk through the Old Forest prior to Pippin and Merry being attacked by the willow tree: 'Sleepiness seemed to be creeping out of the ground and up their legs, and falling softly out of the air upon their heads and eyes.'[23] The next dream sequence is perhaps the key one of the trilogy and takes place inside Tom Bombadil's house. Three of the four characters have nightmares here, in part inspired by their adventures in the wood; but while Pippin dreams he is back inside the willow, 'listening to that horrible dry creaking voice laughing at him again,' and Merry dreams he is being drowned, 'water streaming down gently, and then spreading, spreading irresistibly all around the house . . . rising slowly but surely' (*FR*, 168), it is Frodo's nightmare (described as 'a dream without light' [*FR*, 167]) that is the most important. This is the only moment in *Volume I, The Fellowship of the Ring* at which Frodo has the type of dream structurally analogous with medieval dream vision, in that it provides him with a future vision of things that he, and we as readers, have not yet encountered, but will in *Volume II, The Two Towers*:

> Then he saw the young moon rising; under its thin light there loomed before him a black wall of rock, pierced by a dark arch like a great gate . . . On its top stood the figure of a man . . . Suddenly a shadow, like the shape of great wings, passed across the moon. The figure lifted his arms and a light flashed from the staff that he wielded. A mighty eagle swept down and bore him away . . . There was a noise like a strong wind blowing, and on it was borne the sound of hoofs, galloping, galloping from the East. 'Black Riders!' thought Frodo as he wakened, with the sound of the hoofs still echoing in his mind. (*FR*, 167)

Despite the fact that this appears as a nightmare vision of darkness, it turns out to be a forecast of a vision of salvation. The location corresponds with the description Merry offers of Isengard, Saruman's lair, in *Volume II, The Two Towers*, namely 'a sort of ring of rocks . . . with a flat space inside and an island or pillar or rock in the middle, called Orthanc' (*TT*, 95). What Frodo foresees, it turns out, is the freeing of Gandalf from Isengard by the eagle, Gwaihir the Windlord, following Gandalf's battle to the death with the Balrog. At the point of dreaming, of course, Gandalf has no need of salvation, the battle not yet having happened; it is therefore unclear to both Frodo and the reader why he would be foreseen at the top of Isengard. Furthermore, the visual similarity between Gandalf and Saruman makes it possible for the reader to misinterpret this nightmare as an encounter between Saruman and one of his great winged Nazgûl (also encountered for the first time in *Volume II, The Two Towers*). In fact, when Gandalf does recount the tale of his freedom to Gimli, Legolas, and Aragorn, his reappearance leads them initially to mistake him for Saruman. Notice, also, that Gandalf does not recount this narrative directly to Frodo. Had he done so, we might have read it as a vision of the future anterior. In fact, because this dream is the only moment at which Frodo is exposed to this tale firsthand (because Tolkien subdivides each volume of the trilogy into two books, when the reader hears Gandalf's explanation Frodo is 'elsewhere'), it becomes a dream of prophecy in the medieval sense.

Further contributing to the deliberate use of misrecognition/misreading, though the dream censor operates to ensure that Frodo interprets the sound of hooves as belonging to the Black Riders, once we place this dream in the future narrative context we realise they 'actually' belong to their allies, the riders of Rohan, who will join forces with Aragorn's group and Gandalf to fight Saruman and the Orcs at the battle of Helm's Deep. Frodo's mistaking of the Riders of Rohan for the Black Riders demonstrates the difficulty the dreamer has in interpreting his own dream, a difficulty we, as readers, share at this point in the text. This scene also seems to problematise the wider relationship existing between twentieth-century fantasy and the medieval dream vision, for in the medieval originals the isolation of the dreamer from the world of everyday reality is typically compensated for by his relationship to dream characteristically having 'an unfamiliar clarity and freshness.'[24] At this stage, such clarity apparently eludes Frodo, a point perhaps accounting for the necessary distinction between Frodo's passive fear of this dream in *Volume I, The Fellowship of the Ring*, as opposed to his positive reclamation of the realm of dream at the end of *Volume III, The Return of the King*, where his perception has become so heightened by experience that a return to 'normality' would constitute a negative falling into sleep.

In addition, immediate clarity of vision seems to be something Tolkien mistrusts. This is nowhere more overtly demonstrated than in the dangers inherent in the One Ring itself. As Frodo gives in to temptation, fearing the coming onslaught of the Black Riders on Weathertop hill, he dons the Ring and immediately discovers that 'though everything else remained as before, dim and dark, the shapes became terribly clear . . . In their white faces burned keen and merciless eyes . . . Their eyes fell on him and pierced him, as they rushed towards him' (*FR*, 258). Though the consistent effect of the Ring in Tolkien's trilogy is to awaken the bearer into a world of heightened perception, where in medieval dream vision this carries divine qualities, in the Lord of the Rings its associations are demonic. Hence, in enhancing Frodo's own vision it does so simply to propel him into a world of nightmare and, by reciprocation, the Black Riders' 'vision' is rendered more acute. Just prior to this passage, Strider/Aragorn tells the group that the Black Riders 'do not see the world of light as we do, but our shapes cast shadows in their minds, which only the noon sun destroys; and in the dark they perceive many signs and forms that are hidden from us: then they are most to be feared' (*FR*, 250). According to Tolkien, then, it seems that a gradual awakening into insight is preferable to immediate revelation. This emphasis on an initial cloaking of vision, which gradually lifts as the dreamer focuses more clearly on the veiled message is, of course, a further metaphor for reading texts of all kinds. It also takes us on to another key scene in *Volume I, The Fellowship of the Ring*, concerning the Mirror of Galadriel in the elven kingdom of Lórien, a realm that is described as 'present and yet remote, a living vision of that which has already been left far behind by the flowing streams of Time' (*FR*, 490).

The World in/of the Mirror

Galadriel's Mirror, which is associated with and named by the Lady of Lórien, is formed by filling a shallow silver basin with water. As each character peers in turn into its surface, the Lady explains, 'Many things I can command the Mirror to reveal . . . and to some I can show what they desire to see. But the Mirror will also show things unbidden, and those are often stranger and more profitable than things which we wish to behold' (*FR*, 475). In other words, the mirror maps out the world of dream, aspects of which we frame through our conscious minds (remnants of the preoccupations of the day), others of which lie beyond our control. It is interesting that some critics interpret Lórien as a state of mind rather than a place or region and, as a result, Flieger draws attention to the fact that, where dreams abound in the rest of *Volume I, The Fellowship of the Ring*,

> [i]t is notable that none of the Fellowship is described as having dreams in Lórien . . . Rather, it would seem that the experience of being there is itself the dream. Treebeard

translates Lothlórien as 'Dreamflower' and comments to Merry and Pippin that its inhabitants are 'falling behind the world' . . . From the early stages of Tolkien's mythology, *Lórien* was the name of the God of Dreams . . . I suggest, then, that Lórien itself is in a very real sense a dream sent or dreamed by the God of Dreams and that the Company in Lórien is, in one sense at least, inside that dream.'[25]

If we accept Flieger's reading, it is clear that the mirror is, within the parameters of this 'dreamworld,' a metonymy for the place Lórien holds within the cartography of the text as a whole: namely a *reflection* upon the world of dream. In that sense, it also parallels Sam's allusions (discussed earlier) to being in a story within the story in which he is himself read. As Flieger also observes, not all dreams attract the same degree of narrative attention—or internal interpretation—as others. However, when connected sequentially, she identifies within them a kind of 'trail' set for the reader to follow:[26] part quest and part map, the dreams almost work as a palimpsest to the main narrative, shadowing but also commenting on what happens on the surface. Hence the mirror is also, in part, a clue about how to read texts: it cautions patience and careful attention, employing the worthy character Sam as our model readerly representative. As Sam first approaches the mirror, he finds the water 'hard and dark,' reflecting only stars: 'Then he gave a low gasp, for the stars went out. As if a dark veil had been withdrawn, the Mirror grew grey, and then clear' (*FR*, 475). Like any reader, he comes to this 'text' cold, finding initially only a 'hard and dark' barrier to knowledge. Gradually, that barrier becomes permeable, 'melts' away into gauze, and like the veil, can operate as the means by which revelation as much as concealment takes place.

Vision, then, is the key sense for medieval dream theory. It is, as Hieatt observes, 'what the poet *sees* rather than . . . what he hears or thinks' that counts.[27] With that idea in mind, let us take another text, equally influenced by medieval thinking yet also written comparatively recently, and examine how typical such visual structures are in relation to dream. Alfred, Lord Tennyson's poem 'The Lady of Shalott' (1842), brings us into contact with another 'Lady' and another mirror. Like the Lady of Lórien, Tennyson's Lady is trapped outside time, here set apart on an island, contained by 'Four grey walls, and four grey towers' (part I, stanza 2, line 6). Framed by two glass surfaces, facing an enchanted mirror, her back to the window whose vista is reflected in the mirror, the Lady is also an artist who 'weaves by night and day / A magic web with colours gay' (part 2, stanza 1, lines 1–2), based on the images of the world she perceives in the mirror's surface. Like Sam's, her relationship with that world in the mirror is, at first, only dimly perceived, Tennyson initially describing the resultant images as 'shadows' (part 2, stanza 1, line 3). Gradually, nevertheless, the Lady's readerly frustration gathers force in her eventual exclamation: '"I am half sick of shadows," said / The Lady of Shalott' (part 2, stanza 4, line 8).

This dimness heralds, it transpires, the shattered revelation, as desire enters the frame and dullness gives way to an abundance of light. As Sir Lancelot passes across her line of vision, the sun's rays blazing against his armour become magnified by their reproduction in the windowpane and are described as having 'flashed into the crystal mirror' (part 3, stanza 4, line 7). Here shadows not only give way to clarity; dimness becomes bedazzlement. To what extent, however, can this be described as a dream vision? No mention of sleep is made in the poem, but there is, as we have seen, mention made of enchantment and, as she leaves the island, the Lady is compared directly to a 'bold seer in a trance, / Seeing all his own mischance— / with a glassy countenance' (part 4, stanza 2, lines 2–4). In essence, what the poem allows for is 'the same detachment from reality that we find in our own dreams.'[28]

The perspective on dreams offered by Gestalt therapy, however, might also help to interpret a poem such as 'The Lady of Shalott.' Gestalt therapy is 'a phenomenological-existential therapy . . . in which . . . [e]xplanations and interpretations are considered less reliable than what is directly perceived and felt.' So, as Frederick S. Perls observes, 'all the things in a dream, be they people, objects, or parts of the landscape, [become] part of the dreamer.'[29] Elsewhere I have argued that what may at first appear to be freedom from imprisonment for this Lady is, in actuality, the exchange of an actively creative role as artist for the reductively stereotypical one of passive objet d'art.[30] So the wood of the vessel in which she lies down frames her like a portrait and the Lady's ultimate fate is to become passively consumed by the masculine gaze: 'Lancelot mused a little space; / He said, 'She has a lovely face; / God in his mercy lend her grace, / The Lady of Shalott' (part 4, stanza 6, lines 6–9).

Lancelot's naming of the Lady in the final line of the poem therefore adds a third tier of embedded enclosure to it, for it is not just the central character who bears the name 'The Lady of Shalott,' but also the poem itself and, via Lancelot's own words, her image as self-portrait. Through her role as artist, weaving into art all the sights she sees passing across her glass canvas, Camelot, Lancelot (for he is originally the object of *her* gaze), the web, and the loom, all function as outward projections of her and take on definition only in relation to she who names them. This makes the presence of the mirror particularly apt. If, under Gestalt therapy, 'A man who dreams of himself in a desert can be told to "be the desert," and can then be asked "What does the desert feel?"'[31] then we can use this approach to question the fixity of subject/object relations in Tennyson's poem. In these terms, Lancelot remains merely an outward projection of the Lady's ego, her departure from the tower offering her a means of *taking on* the role of Lancelot, in the process looking at herself as if in a mirror. This would explain the strangely inseparable quality of Tennyson's Lady and her environs. She is the spider at the centre of the web she is spinning; therefore it is impossible for her to leave it 'in reality' and it still remain intact.

Thus the mirror in Tennyson's text not only frames a sense of ego projection, but also takes on what is perhaps the most familiar function of mirrors for readers of fantasy narratives, namely the means by which characters are enabled to move between worlds. Carroll again offers an archetypal example of such writing, this time in *Alice Through the Looking Glass*. Holding up to the mirror a recalcitrant kitten, Alice threatens: 'if you're not good directly . . . I'll put you through into Looking-glass House.' Her vision then continues by detailing the world beyond the mirror:

> First, there's the room you can see through the glass—that's just the same as our drawing-room, only the things go the other way . . . Well then, the books are something like our books, only the words go the wrong way: I know that, because I've held up one of our books to the glass, and then they hold up one in the other room.[32]

However, where in 'The Lady of Shalott' everything becomes subsumed by the Lady/creator at the centre of the mirror, here Alice's reflection in the glass becomes divorced from her sense of self. So she shifts, in the phrase 'I've held up . . . then they hold up,' from first to third person and, in the process, is also rendered plural. Nevertheless, and like Tennyson's Lady, we never lose the sense of Alice being her own creator within the dreamworld, as she immediately adopts the rhetoric of storytelling in the art of constructing the dream: 'Let's pretend there's a way of getting through into it . . . Let's pretend the glass has got all soft like gauze, so that we can get through. Why, it's turning into a sort of mist now, I declare!' (LG, 181 and 184). As Lilian R. Furst observes, 'let's pretend' is a phrase heralding the type of play that requires 'no props' at all,[33] a fact that appears to negate the necessity for a mirror, were it not for the fact that its presence is a metaphor for the veil beyond which sleep lies. As in Tennyson's poem, then, the relationship to sleep is merely indirect here. Earlier in the passage, we read that Alice is 'half talking to herself and half asleep' (LG, 176), but this is prior to her rallying, on discovering the kitten making merry with a ball of wool (the nature of the aforementioned recalcitrance). Nevertheless, we once again carry with us a presiding impression of the boundaries between dream and waking worlds breaking down, with the mirror itself establishing a kind of dreamtext to be interpreted (or read) by the character who peers into its surface in just the same manner as one interprets/reads the dream.

To conclude, then, in dream narrative we find a metaphorical model for the reading of fantasy texts in general. It is primarily during sleep that we are made aware of the existence of a world beyond our own, which drives and motivates us in the same way that fantasy inspires our imaginations. And yet, just as we fuel our dreams from the material of everyday while taking from them material inspired by that other, unknown nocturnal world, so fantasy texts are a complex combination of the familiar and the unfamiliar. In Chapter 4, we look in detail at a selection of the most familiar fantasy narratives and, in doing so, demonstrate how central fantasy is to our current cultural preoccupations, beginning, as we leave here, with the Alice texts.

Notes

1. J. R. R. Tolkien, 'On Fairy-Stories,' in *Tree and Leaf* (London: HarperCollins, 2001), 1–81 (p. 31).

2. Kathryn Hume, *Fantasy and Mimesis: Responses to Reality in Western Literature* (New York: Methuen, 1984), 87.

3. Norman N. Holland, *The Dynamics of Literary Response* (New York: W.W. Norton, 1975), 35.

4. Lewis Carroll, 'Alice in Wonderland,' in *The Annotated Alice*, Martin Gardner, ed. (Harmondsworth: Penguin, 1970), 17–164.

5. Carroll, 'Alice in Wonderland,' 25. Further quotations from this story will be referenced within the main body of the text, accompanied by the abbreviation *AW*.

6. Sigmund Freud, 'Creative Writers and Day-Dreaming' in the *Penguin Freud Library, Vol. 14, Art and Literature*, Albert Dickson, ed. (Harmondsworth: Penguin, 1990), 129–141 (p. 132).

7. J. R. R. Tolkien, *The Lord of the Rings, Volume II: The Two Towers* (London: HarperCollins, 1999), 399–400. Further quotations from this novel will be referenced within the main body of the text, accompanied by the abbreviation *TT*.

8. Kathryn L. Lynch, *The High Medieval Dream Vision: Poetry, Philosophy, and Literary Form* (Stanford, CA: Stanford University Press, 1988), 47. Note, also, that Lynch's choice of the term *limen* or *margin* evokes Marin's use of the term *limes* in his essay 'The Frontiers of Utopia,' in *Utopias and the Millennium*, Krishan Kumar and Stephen Bann, eds. (London: Reaktion Books, 1993), 7–16.

9. Joseph B. Pike, ed. and trans., *Frivolities of Courtiers and Footprints of Philosophers . . . Selections from the Seventh and Eighth Books of the Policraticus of John of Salisbury* (Minneapolis, 1938), pp. 76–77. Cited in Constance B. Hieatt, *The Realism of Dream Visions* (The Hague: Mouton & Co., 1967), 28.

10. Book of Daniel 5:5.

11. Daniel 5:25–8.

12. Depending on whether one deems there to be three words or five here (five coming from *mina* multiplied by two + *tekel* + *upharsin*—through division between *upharsin* and *peres* also becoming multiplied by two), either three or five kings are being brought into disrepute. Norman W. Porteous suggests that we can add a slur, indicating the kings be of little worth by drawing attention to the ease with which *menē* and *tekel* can be (mis)heard as the monetary values *mina* and *shekel* respectively, with *peres* ('divided') implying a half-*mina*. In these terms, each successive king is shown to be of lesser 'value' in the eyes of God. *Daniel: A Commentary* (London: SCM Press, 1965), 82–83.

13. Porteous, *Daniel*, 83.

14. Lynch, *High Medieval Dream Vision*, 3.

15. Winthrop Wetherbee, *Platonism and Poetry in the Twelfth Century: The Literary Influence of the School of Chartres* (Princeton, NJ: Princeton University Press, 1972), 8. Cited in Lynch, *High Medieval Dream Vision*, 42–43.

16. Lynch, *High Medieval Dream Vision*, 45.

17. Hieatt, *Realism of Dream Visions*, 23.

18. Hieatt, *Realism of Dream Visions*, 97.

19. J. R. R. Tolkien, 'On Fairy-Stories,' 13–14.

20. Hume, *Fantasy and Mimesis*, 128.

21. Verlyn Flieger, *A Question of Time: J. R. R. Tolkien's Road to Faërie* (Kent, OH: The Kent State University Press, 1997), 80.

22. J. R. R. Tolkien, *The Lord of the Rings, Volume III: The Return of the King* (London: HarperCollins, 1999), 333. Further quotations from this novel will be referenced within the main body of the text, accompanied by the abbreviation *RK*.

23. J. R. R. Tolkien, *The Lord of the Rings, Volume I: The Fellowship of the Ring* (London: HarperCollins, 1999), 153. Further quotations from this novel will be referenced within the main body of the text, accompanied by the abbreviation *FR*.

24. Angus Fletcher, *Allegory: The Theory of a Symbolic Mode* (Ithaca: Cornell University Press, 1964), 348.

25. Flieger, *A Question of Time*, 192, original emphasis.

26. Flieger, *A Question of Time*, 167.

27. Heiatt, *Realism of Dream Visions*, 18.

28. Fletcher, *Allegory*, 349.

29. This definition of Gestalt therapy is taken from Gary Yontef, 'Gestalt Therapy: An Introduction' (1993), http://www.gestalt.org/yontef.htm. Frederick S. Perl's observation is from *Gestalt Therapy Verbatim* (New York: Bantam, 1971). Cited in Hume, *Fantasy and Mimesis*, 183.

30. For a fuller discussion of 'The Lady of Shalott' as artist/art object, see Lucie Armitt, *Contemporary Women's Fiction and the Fantastic* (London: Macmillan, 2000), 8–9.

31. Hume, *Fantasy and Mimesis*, 183

32. Lewis Carroll, 'Through the Looking-Glass and What Alice Found There,' in *The Annotated Alice*, Martin Gardner, ed. (Harmondsworth: Penguin, 1970), 165–345 (pp. 180–81). Further quotations from this story will be referenced within the main body of the text, accompanied by the abbreviation *LG*.

33. Lilian R. Furst, *All Is True: The Claims and Strategies of Realist Fiction* (Durham, NC: Duke University Press, 1995), 28–29. In her challenge to the duplicity inherent in literary realism, Furst reminds us that adult behaviour encourages scepticism about pretence, seeing within it all the dubiousness of falsehood. Nevertheless, literary realism absolutely relies on the embracing of 'let's pretend,' the book itself being our only prop.

Chapter Four

The Best and Best Known

Gulliver's Travels (1726)

Frankenstein (1818)

Edward Lear (1812–88)

The Alice books (1865 and 1871)

The Time Machine (1895)

The First Men in the Moon (1901)

Animal Farm (1945)

The Lord of the Rings trilogy (1954–55)

The Harry Potter series (1997–2003)[1]

Introduction

Here we have a chance to consider, in detail, a selection of some of the key fantasy narratives written in the last 300 years, and where else could one begin but with J. R. R. Tolkien? Tolkien's oeuvre has, surely, never enjoyed a higher profile in fantasy writing or literary culture more generally than it has now. To the great astonishment (and no little pique) of a substantial section of the literary establishment, Tolkien has been consistently voted Author of the (Twentieth) Century by a variety of polls.[2] Peter Jackson's recent films of the Lord of the Rings trilogy have augmented this recognition still further, bringing to Tolkien's writing a new, younger audience and re-energising the reading and study of quality fantasy writing more generally. In the process, Jackson's films have demonstrated that good old-fashioned epic fantasy still has a message to communicate to our increasingly secular, cynical age. It is therefore only fitting that Tolkien should be given pre-eminence in this chapter on 'The Best and Best Known,' as well as featuring as the key exemplar of fantasy writing in this book as a whole.

Jonathan Swift's *Gulliver's Travels* and Mary Shelley's *Frankenstein* also merit inclusion in this chapter as examples of texts that have, over three and two centuries respectively, successfully transcended the serious/popular divide and continue to speak in a myriad of ways to academic and nonacademic readers alike. Fantasy has, as Rosemary Jackson made clear in 1981,[3] a significantly subversive function to fulfil, and both Swift and Shelley have their subversive side: Swift is as famous for his political treatises on the state of Ireland as he is for his fiction, and Mary Shelley's controversial elopement with the married poet Percy Bysshe Shelley led to her eventual exclusion from polite society. In some fantasy narratives, such as Orwell's *Animal Farm*, the purely political is at the forefront of the narrative message, but it is more common, as in the case of Swift and Shelley, for raw politics to combine with other issues of social or cultural significance, as can also be seen in the writings of H. G. Wells. Wells is certainly one of the most respected science/speculative fiction writers of all, and like Shelley, he enjoyed the company of a wide and eminent circle of literary influence. The author of both realist and fantasy fictions, Wells also employed his scientific knowledge in nonfictional essays on the social and political effects of scientific invention, including the consequences of technological warfare. Of his *sf* works, *The Time Machine* is arguably the best known and most widely read, with *The First Men in the Moon* also being worthy of inclusion here for its characteristic attention to the detail of alien life.

Fantasy, like all modes of writing, moves in and out of popularity with literary critics according to the trends. When I first started publishing on fantasy writing at the start of the 1990s, the feminist movement had given fantasy writing a 'currency boost' among critics. Now, ten to fifteen years later, we have hit a similar—and arguably a higher—peak. Tolkien's resurgence has done much to pave the way for that peak, but by happy coincidence, 'the Tolkien phenomenon' has met its match through the birth of an unanticipated rival, the likes of which we have perhaps never seen before: I refer, of course, to the Harry Potter craze (for what other term could sum up such an ebullient fanbase?). With J. K. Rowling gripping child and adult readers alike and Tolkien returning from comparative inattention to do similarly all over again, there has never been a better time to read, write, or write *on* fantasy. No current discussion of 'best of . . .' could therefore fail to include a section on Harry Potter and this chapter proves no exception to the rule. Nevertheless, lest we forget, there would be no Harry Potter without the tradition that has preceded it and, with that proviso in mind, we open with an examination of the work of two of the all-time greats of children's fantasy writing, Lewis Carroll and Edward Lear.

Carroll and Lear are, when taken together, the primary founders and practitioners of that subgenre of fantasy known today as nonsense literature. In considering their contribution to literary fantasy more generally, we begin with the relationship fantasy holds to play (more specifically child's play) before going on to consider the relationship nonsense holds to 'the real.' The interface between nonsense and other fantasy subgenres such as utopia and the travelogue will also be explored as a precursor to examining the role of geography and cartography in fantasy in general. Where, in realism, space and time are usually fixed, in fantasy both become freed up for interrogation. This allows for the founding of territories such as Tolkien's Middle Earth, a land by now so familiar to us its contours almost take on a palpable texture of their own. Freeing up the fixtures of time and space, however, also enables a freeing up of perspective—in the most literal, visual sense. So, in comparing Lord of the Rings with Jonathan Swift's *Gulliver's Travels*, we come to consider how juxtapositions of competing scale (the miniature versus the giant, the myopic versus the hypermetropic) frame our readings of the world around us, 'reality' being shown to be interpretive rather than absolute.

Such distortions in perspective are perhaps most compelling when metamorphoses in the human frame move us inexorably away from the human towards the inhuman, adapting to a grotesque or even monstrous form. In the second part of this chapter we compare the differing species of Tolkien's Lord of the Rings trilogy with the fantasy monsters of *Frankenstein, The Time Machine, The First Men in the Moon*, and Harry Potter. In doing so, we consider what these monsters tell us about the societies that give rise to them and how their existence in fictive form can offer comment on certain historical or sociocultural debates topical at the time of publication. The ultimate question fantasy narratives raise, perhaps, is whether in inventing these monstrous alteregos we are drawn into more empathetic relations with the foreigner or stranger in our midst, or whether their effect is simply to reinforce a desire to purge.

Next, and as an extension of the other/stranger/foreigner debate, the chapter concludes with a consideration of the role played by gender in fantasy fiction. Beginning with a detailed discussion of the function desire has in fantasy narratives, we come to a more specific focus on the feminine. Ultimately, this takes us to the mother, that site of origin shared by all and, in metaphorical terms, one of the chief features of fantasy writing (hence the 'mother ship' of science fiction or the 'motherland' of utopia). Consequently, where the chapter opens with a consideration of children and the role adopted by play in fantasy writing, it concludes with parenthood and the wider family structures, including the manner in which fantasy narratives aid the adolescent in his/her journey into the 'real' adult world. Turning full circle, then, let us take our first teetering steps into the unknown.

Play and Nonsense: Lewis Carroll and Edward Lear

Lewis Carroll's *Alice's Adventures in Wonderland* (1865) and *Through the Looking Glass* (1871) are, in many ways, archetypal fantasy texts. Structurally, both offer a clear-cut immersion into the world of the unreal and an equally clear-cut retreat from it. In addition, the world into which the reader is immersed in each case is structured using certain archetypal fantasy 'features' (dreamscapes, talking animals, mythical creatures, a magic mirror) combined with the characters and lexicon of nonsense literature. This is possibly most evident in the Mock Turtle and his song in *Wonderland*: 'Will you walk a little faster?' said a whiting to a snail, / There's a porpoise close behind us, and he's treading on my tail'[4] or, in *Looking-Glass*, in the 'Jabberwocky' poem, the first stanza of which Carroll initially published in a private periodical titled *Misch-Masch*, under the heading 'Stanza of Anglo-Saxon Poetry': ''Twas brillig, and the slithy toves / Did gyre and gimble in the wabe.'[5] Both texts also function as travelogues, the central protagonist journeying through a strange and alienating landscape, encountering strange and alienating forms as she goes (the connection with forerunners such as *Gulliver's Travels* is obvious). As Jean-Jacques Lecercle puts it,

> The reader of *Alice's Adventures in Wonderland* is in the position of an explorer: the landscape is strikingly new, new plants swim into his ken, and a new species is encountered at every turn, each more exotic than the one before . . . As we read the text, we experience the same sense of wonder that Charles Darwin felt when exploring the Patagonian wonderland. There are indeed pages in *The Voyage of the 'Beagle'* that read like Carroll . . . [6]

Not only does this endow texts with a sense of natural history, it also endows them with a narrative cartography. This is made particularly clear in *Looking-Glass*, where we gradually come to realise that all of Alice's movements have been plotted out on a chessboard, and that in order to complete her journey she must win the game. Games are, of course, the key structural feature of both Alice books and have a particularly close relationship to fantasy writing in general. Like much fantasy literature, they are also, as Susan Stewart observes, central to our understanding of other social boundary formations, for without understanding the 'rules' of the social game, we will be as alienated from our environs as Alice is from hers.

Nevertheless, there remains a distinction to be drawn between our understanding of how games operate in reality and how they operate in fantasy writing. The game of chess, for instance, holds an allegorical relationship to a traditional battlefield, the pawns representing the front line, forming a mass in comparison with more individualised pieces such as the knights or the bishops, and being far more expendable in strategic terms. The nature of the relationship between the game and reality is therefore based upon a mimetic code. In the Alice books, on the other hand, the play mechanisms within the texts, though based on chess and cards, gesture inwards rather outwards. To put it another way:

> With Carroll's games of cards, chess, and croquet, the
> metonymic of the game is maintained, and, at the same
> time, is traversed by a substitution of elements that are
> incongruous with both game and plot . . . We should
> remember that the croquet game in *Alice in Wonderland* is
> being played by a pack of cards; one game is imposed over
> another.[7]

Though apparently central to the action, however, 'play' is more superficial to the Alice books than we might presume. Certainly, toys feature centrally in them, the White Rabbit's house becoming miniaturised to doll-size as Alice grows, and Tweedledum and Tweedledee fighting over a spoilt rattle; nevertheless, unlike more supine forms of children's writing such as A. A. Milne's *Winnie-the-Pooh* (1926) or *The House at Pooh Corner* (1928), Carroll's toys are not encountered primarily as toys, but as antagonists whom Alice must outwit in order to stay safe. There is a strange uncanniness to these narratives, enhanced by John Tenniel's original illustrations, which certainly captures the Gothicism of Alice's characterisation.[8] With the enhanced knowledge of the dubious moral subtext to the creation of the Alice books and, in particular, the manner in which Charles Dodgson (the man behind the Lewis Carroll pseudonym) used his skill in photography to prey upon young girls, they provoke a sense of disquiet in any adult reader that we now find almost impossible to separate from a post-Freudian reading of them. In these terms, the depiction of the cantankerous pigeon in Chapter 5 of *Wonderland*, fearing for the safety of her eggs when faced by the unnaturally serpentine elongation of Alice's neck, is easily interpreted as the aggressive mother, fiercely defending her children from the phallic threat posed by the rude intervention of an adult male outsider into her household.

J. R. R. Tolkien is keen to stress that the common tendency to relegate fantasy to the nursery, or to perceive it as a form of writing out of which one grows, is a false one. Instead, he makes a neat comparison about the manner in which the willing suspension of disbelief is shared between adults and children beyond the world of books:

> A child may well believe a report that there are ogres in the
> next county; many grown-up persons find it easy to believe

of another country; and as for another planet, very few adults seem able to imagine it as peopled, if at all, by anything but monsters of iniquity.[9]

As noted earlier, fantasy narratives work via boundary negotiations. In formal terms, the first boundary violation they commit is that relating to narrative realism. The distinction between literary fantasy and literary realism is less that literary realism mimics 'the real' while fantasy does not—for, in fact, fantasy does this too—than the fact that realism sticks more closely to the *restrictions* placed upon us by 'the real' than fantasy does. For instance, where, in literary realism, a character cannot move from 1853 in Chapter 16 to 1953 in Chapter 17, in science fiction she/he can. Other boundary negotiations derive from these initial deviations. Hence, while one may encounter galloping horses in both realism and fantasy, in the latter they might also be able to fly or talk. And whilst, in realism, characters can only be drawn from human or, more rarely, animal species, in fantasy a host of imagined species can occur, from centaurs to cyborgs and on to Cyclops. Later in this chapter, we will come to consider the relationship between negotiating parameters and anatomical metamorphoses. For now let us consider another kind of mutation: that which occurs when *sense* gives way to *nonsense*.

Nonsense literature is a type of writing typically associated not only with children, but also with childishness. Its two major practitioners, Lewis Carroll and Edward Lear, both attracted the adoration of children because of their interest in nonsense, just as both perceived it as only part of a larger arena of play in which—and unlike in Freud's example—the distinction between real life, writing/daydreaming, and fantasy was often unclear ('Nonsense is the breath of my nostrils,' wrote Lear[10]). Easily dismissed by the literary snob, nonsense writing often engages with great semantic complexity and uses play (particularly wordplay) once again to explore boundary negotiations:

A nonsense text, on the one hand, plays with the bounds of common sense in order to remain within view of them, even if it has crossed to the other side of the frontier; but it does not seek to limit the text's meaning to one single interpretation—on the contrary, its dissolution of sense

> multiplies meaning. This is because a nonsense text requires
> to be read on two levels at once—two incompatible levels:
> not 'x means A,' but 'x is both A and, incoherently, B.'[11]

The precise nature of the relationship between fantasy and non-sense literature is, to some extent, summed up in relation to this dis-course of boundaries. Both interrogate our relationship with reality by offering a way of reaching out to impossibility. Lear began his career as an illustrator of natural history books on flora and fauna, only later employing these skills to develop his passion for nonsense writing and art. That this dual aspect of his life reflects the interface between limits and their transgressions is made clear through Vivien Noakes's observation that 'All his life [Lear] sought wide horizons —both the real width of the landscape he explored in his travel and his drawings, and the symbolic width of tolerance expressed in the landscape of his nonsense . . .' (*EL*, xx–xxi). As Jean-Jacques Lecercle points out, one might well argue it is the hyperbole inher-ent in Carolus Linnaeus's attribution of Latin names to plants dur-ing the eighteenth century[12] that inspired, in Lear's playful hands, his own genre of nonsense botany, two examples of which are given in Figures 4.1 and 4.2.

However, that nonsense was seen as a reward for diligently pur-suing common sense might also be assumed from Lear's presenta-tion of two nonsense sketches (lunar landscapes) to Mrs. Stuart Wortley, in thanks for her purchase of a more 'serious' painting. Lear was the son of a stockbroker, although, as he was the penultimate of twenty-one children, his family was not as wealthy as one may suppose. A sickly child, by the age of seven he suffered from what he called 'the Morbids' (*EL*, xx), and during his teens, his parental family unit having broken down, he and his eldest sister, Ann, set up house together. Immediately, he put his mind to earning a living through illustration, a set of circumstances that would always ground his nonsense work in an apparently paradoxical sense of 'real' need. This does, I think, place a different emphasis on Lear's development of nonsense to Carroll's, whose own relationship to nonsense is conventionally perceived as escapism from the dry and, to him, rather intimidating world of Oxford academia.

This is not to suggest there is no orthodox aspect at the root of Lear's writing. John Lehmann perceives in it 'a kind of transposed

Figure 4.1   *Tigerlillia Terribilis* from Vivien Noakes, ed., *Edward Lear: The Collected Verse and Other Nonsense* (Harmondsworth: Penguin, 2001).

Romantic poetry, written with remarkable skill, with a sense of rhythmic architecture and word music that recalls the masters, especially his beloved Tennyson . . .'[13] But what of Lear's nonsense work in relation to the broad sweep of fantasy writing in particular? For Lecercle, there are clear connections between Lear's work and the traditions of folklore, nursery tales, and Arcadia, or what he calls

Figure 4.2 *Pollybirdia Singularis* from Vivien Noakes, ed., *Edward Lear: The Collected Verse and Other Nonsense* (Harmondsworth: Penguin, 2001).

'the counting rhymes of shepherds.'[14] Vivien Noakes traces it back predominantly through oral literatures and song. In the process, we recognise further parallels with Carroll, as well as with epic fantasy writers such as Tolkien, for Noakes identifies elements of nonsense, not just in the classical Roman period, but also in the Anglo-Saxon musical tradition, that of the medieval minstrels, and on to the tradition of the Shakespearean fool (*EL*, xxiv).

In terms of fantasy genres, Lear's nonsense spans a broad spectrum from animal fable to utopian travelogue and on to science/

space fiction. In relation to two science-fiction sketches, sent to Mrs. Stuart Wortley in a letter dated February 26, 1882 (now given the title 'The Moon Journey'), Lear describes them as being 'of singular —I may say bingular value,—as they were done in the Moon, to which I lately went one night, returning next morning on a Moonbeam' (*EL*, 435). However, be it lunar or terrestrial, travel and the foreign are Lear's major preoccupations—both in his writing and in his life. To give an earthly example, his short story 'The Story of the Four Little Children Who Went Round the World' (1867) is considered by Lecercle to be a parody of Defoe's *Robinson Crusoe* (1719). In other words, there is certainly a kind of utopian drive to the writing of nonsense, a belief that lexis can be manipulated to such an extent that it can take us to a point of 'elsewhere.' And yet, while that is its aim, much like other aspects of utopia it is ultimately unrealisable; for as we struggle to navigate ourselves, as readers, to that 'elsewhere point,' we continually find ourselves left behind—there is something we are missing, some secret door into a garden that, rather like Alice, we keep discovering we cannot get through. If only we could find it, we tell ourselves, the text and its meanings would fall into place. In some ways, of course, this heightens, rather than lessens, the utopian dimension:

> There is a strong flavour of archaism to nonsense texts— they all look back to a lovely June afternoon, to an Oxford still immune from the nastier consequences of modernity . . . At the same time . . . they look forward, even if unconsciously, to a more advanced state of knowledge and understanding . . . and the result is that they are in tune with the modernity of today's reader—they have not aged as most . . . texts have.[15]

The 'cherished' quality of a poem such as Lear's 'The Owl and the Pussy-Cat' (1870) makes it almost impossible to consider from a completely fresh perspective. When we do so, however, we notice how clearly it is rooted—despite apparent evidence to the contrary —in a clear and logical framework of causality. Two ill-matched lovers undertake a sea voyage into unknown territory in order to start a life free from public censure. Lear's characteristic 'realism' about economics is reflected in the fact that they take 'plenty of money' with them, so much that they can afford to treat a five-pound note as a wallet, and it is with this money that they purchase the ring that will allow them to marry (and so attain respectability). The poem itself achieves the conventional closure of all romance narratives, the couple 'danc[ing] by the light of the moon' in the final line, and it is also worth noting that, with very little exception, all the items referred to in the poem have utter familiarity to recommend them: a guitar, a 'Piggy-wig,' a turkey, mince, quince, sand, and the moon. Only, in fact, their ultimate destination ('the land where the Bong-tree grows') and the piece of cutlery with which they consume the wedding breakfast ('a runcible spoon') are alien to us. In fact, this is one of the most conventional and homely of Lear's texts—which may explain its enduring appeal to children everywhere.

What both texts once again share is what we are finding to be the recurrent application of Marin's fascination for the importance of that ever-receding horizon, be it geographical or topographical, semantic or philosophical, or, as in many of Lear's examples, elemental. By further considering the role of the horizon, Lecercle turns back to classical antiquity, drawing on the *De Natura Rerum* for illustration:

> Lucretius wonders what would happen if, having reached the end of the world, [he] threw [his] javelin beyond [it] . . . Either [his] javelin would cross into something else, or it would rebound against something. There is always something beyond the limit, if only the limit itself . . . [N]onsensical words either rebound into grammaticality or else cross into a type of a-grammaticality that turns out to be no chaos.[16]

Lecercle's project is a linguistic one and, via nonsense writing, he demonstrates how our relationship to syntax and lexis shapes our awareness of the 'real world.' Hence, in his discussion of nonsense monsters, what matters to Lecercle are the coinages that accompany them (the bread-and-butter fly, the mock turtle, etc.), for to him this is the basis upon which much language development is based: 'When I analyse "hamburger" into "ham" and "burger," I am analysing the same string *a second time*, since the correct analysis, "Hamburg" and "-er" logically precedes the incorrect one.'[17] Yet, in analysing our relationship to the world in terms of our relationship to language, what Lecercle also draws attention to is the fact that what I have called utopianism does not necessarily equate with escapism. The drive towards utopia involves an agonistic wrestling with meaning, 'not a cooperative undertaking for mutually rewarding ends.'[18]

This returns us to 'The Owl and the Pussy-Cat' or, at least, the sequel text to it: 'The Later History of the Owl and the Pussy-Cat' (1884). This is not the title given to a poem (although purportedly Lear had plans to write one), but to a letter written by Lear to a child, Violet, whose younger sister had sent him a collar for the 'pussy-cat' of the original poem. Lear's response to Violet is cruel: 'It was very good of [your sister] to think of this, but she evidently has not known, what it is very painful for me to elude [sic] to, that the Owl has long been a widower . . .' As he goes into the further details of the cat's death, the effect is increasingly callous, describing a 'party of persons, who threatened the Pussy-Cat most violently with a pair of Tongs & a Pepperbox,' the cat fleeing to the safety of a tree to escape them, only to fall to her death (*EL*, 450–51). Though clearly playful on one level, one wonders if either Violet or her younger sister would have found the letter as entertaining as did Lear. Its tone, throughout, is one of gentle chastisement, inferring that Violet's sister is guilty of insensitivity or, at best, having committed a social faux pas. What shocks, here, is not the undermining of a previously consolationist poem, but the targeted nature of the correspondence. Just as Lear tells the children that the cat, immediately before falling to its death, had ingested a sealed paper, suggesting it having had a toxic effect, so the ingesting of this particular 'poison-pen letter' will require the older sister to relay this information to the younger, having the additional result of the hurt being apparently inflicted by Violet rather than Lear. The nature of the conclusion he offers to the letter is equally cruel: 'Please to read this letter to your sister . . . as slowly & opprobriously as you can in order to save her feelings from a too sudden shock' (*EL*, 451). This is the worst of Lear's offences, being deliberately deceitful. 'Opprobrium' being the conveyance of scornful reproach, it emphasises the tone of mock hurt with which Lear begins his letter while, far from sparing the child's feelings, the slow pacing will emphasise the pain caused, humiliating as well as chiding her. If this is 'play,' it is of the kind employed by another type of 'pussy-cat'—that which taunts and tortures a mouse.

Cartographies and Geographies of Fantasy: *Animal Farm* and *Gulliver's Travels*

Irrespective of which fantasy text one is discussing, borders and parameters remain its key themes, and spatial and topographical concerns its key motifs. Maps form an integral aspect of reputable editions of narratives from Jonathan Swift's *Gulliver's Travels* (1726) to J. R. R. Tolkien's The Lord of the Rings (1954–55) and, though Tolkien's son Christopher is credited with drawing the maps of Middle Earth, J. R. R. Tolkien is reputed to have been fastidious in his production of the cartography for the book(s) and compulsive in his checking of the publisher's 'redrawing of the maps' for publication.[19] Even in his Prologue to the trilogy, such geographical specificity is introduced: 'The Shire was divided into four quarters, the Farthings . . . North, South, East, and West; and these again into a number of folklands . . . Outside the Farthings were the East and West Marches: the Buckland . . . and the Westmarch added to the Shire in S.[hire] R.[eckoning] 1462.'[20] In fact, it is in relation to the reading of maps that Frodo first identifies the spirit of quest within his own character: '[T]he old paths seemed too well-trodden. He looked at maps, and wondered what lay beyond their edges: maps made in the Shire showed mostly white spaces beyond its borders . . . Often he was seen walking and talking with the strange wayfarers that began at this time to appear in the Shire' (*FR*, 57).

In this context, let us yet again return to Louis Marin:

> The utopian representation always takes the figure, the form of a map . . . But at the very moment that I look at the map—when I follow with my finger the route of a road, a contour-line, when I cross here and not there a frontier, when I jump from one bank of a river to the other—at this very moment a figure is extracted from the ground and the map, the figure of a projected journey, even if it is an imaginary one, a dreamed one.[21]

Even leaving aside, for a moment, the final clause of the quotation, Marin's impetus here moves from the space of the 'real' straight into the world of fantasy. We look and, in the act of looking, 'perceive' ourselves projected into any number of possible fantasy voyages: myself, 'jump[ing] from one bank of a river to the other,' conquering Striding Edge in the English Lake District, driving through Death Valley pursued by a speeding truck, navigating the Mississippi at the helm of a nineteenth-century paddle steamer. But of course, even without this wish-fulfilment fantasy, all maps, and paradoxically, by dint of their existence as metonymies *of* the real, necessarily remain at a stage of removal *from* the 'real.' They are miniatures, souvenirs—'fantasy narratives' in that sense, too. When reading a map, one does not 'follow with my finger the route of a road,' one follows with one's finger a coloured line on a page that stands in for the road one follows, not with one's fingers at all (unless as a circus stunt), but with one's feet; and follow with their feet these characters do.

In George Orwell's *Animal Farm* (1945), for instance, the first act the animals perform, having banished the human farmers from their territory, is to 'gallop in a body right round the boundaries of the farm, *as though* to make quite sure that no human being was hiding anywhere upon it . . .'[22] The phrase 'as though' implies that the search for human intruders is purely motivational: the 'real' act carries more of a ritual significance, that ritual being based on charting territory. In a novel such as *Gulliver's Travels* (1726), the relationship to territory is less ritualistic and more idealistic. Lemuel Gulliver's arrival in Lilliput is a result of shipwreck. As he finally manages to drag himself ashore, he collapses on the ground with exhaustion and, on waking, discovers himself tethered along the full length of his body by the tiny inhabitants of that empire. On regaining his feet, his first 'aerial' view of Lilliput is couched primarily in terms more typical of the model village: 'The Country round appeared like a continued Garden, and the enclosed Fields, which were generally Forty Foot square, resembled so many Beds of flowers. These Fields were intermingled with Woods of half a Stang, and the tallest Trees, as I could judge, appeared to be seven Foot high.'[23] What we find, in both these textual examples, is that fantasy landscapes take on shape in relation to those through whose eyes they are projected. It is also the case that they reflect on the parameters between the text and a larger reality.

In *Animal Farm*, territory is largely static and very small in scale. All the action takes place on Manor Farm, the only broader development of that canvas being in relation to its two neighbours, these being described primarily in terms of how they impinge on border territory. So Foxwood Farm, on one side, is described—as its name might imply—as 'a large, neglected, old-fashioned farm, much overgrown by woodland, with all its pastures worn out and its hedges in a disgraceful condition' (*AF*, 34). The other neighbour, similarly aptly named Pinchfield Farm, is 'smaller and better kept,' its owner being 'a tough, shrewd man, perpetually involved in lawsuits and with a name for driving hard bargains' (*AF*, 35). In *Gulliver's Travels*, the scale is larger, though while the main protagonist moves between landscapes, frontiers remain very clearly defined. Though Gulliver travels, as the title informs us, little mobility is in evidence in terms of exchanges out of Lilliput, Brobdingnag, or the Land of the Houyhnhnms. Each territory exists as a kind of set piece or vista, going on as before, after Gulliver has left. What happens to territory, then, when its cartography shapes the nature of the fantasy explored within it to such an extent that one cannot imagine its existence apart from the quest? This is the type of backdrop one encounters in epic fantasy, no better example of which exists than J. R. R. Tolkien's The Lord of the Rings trilogy (1954–55).

J. R. R. Tolkien, The Lord of the Rings

Cartography is, by definition, an attempt to tame the world around us, to transform it into a product of our own making and, in being able to write and read it, cut it down to our size. As such, it enacts a type of miniaturising effect that traces a surprisingly paradoxical route. On the one hand, as Susan Stewart observes, it operates through 'metaphors of containment' whilst simultaneously 'threaten[ing] infinity.'[24] In other words, we are back to the dual effect of the sublime, as discussed in Chapter 1: staring from the summit of Snowdon, then looking at the point at which you are standing as represented on the Ordnance Survey map, one is almost as struck by the impossibility of transcribing physical geography into the codes of mapmaking and map reading as by the view itself.

In literature it is difficult to retain that awesome sense of hyperbolic contrast in scale and form, the actual size of the fictive map on the page holding a one-to-one correspondence to the size of the text, and the graphic artistry of fictional map illustrating bearing a far closer relationship to the graphology of the printed page than OS codes do to rock forms and scarps. The distinction between the two fictive forms lies more in quantity (number of pages of text to each illustration) than in kind. And yet, a text such as the Lord of the Rings attempts to return that sense of awe to literary narrative because, as Middle Earth only exists in our readerly imagination, while map easily equates to page, reading enables the true panorama of Middle Earth to explode *off* the page. However, this, too, is an effect of limited duration. Despite its vastness and its epic quality, the scale of the Lord of the Rings will always be bound, as fast as Gulliver in Lilliput, by its generic limitations.

Thus, while Tolkien can have a character travel the length and breadth of Middle Earth and take a lifetime to do so, that character will never be able to leave it, as the 'white spaces' Frodo locates at the edges of the Shire maps are actually made most clearly manifest in the borders tracing the edges of every page: there is nothing beyond Middle Earth, because Middle Earth is nowhere—it only exists in the act of reading. In fact, this may be one of the reasons for the immense success of Peter Jackson's three recent films: once projected in visual terms onto a screen, the monumental scale of Isengard becomes manifest, along with the flight from the Black Riders through the woods and across the foothills as the travellers race for the Ford of Rivendell. Furthermore, once we have purchased the video or DVD versions, we can re-create them repeatedly in time and space: map them directly onto our minds.

A further paradox attaches to this sense of vastness, in that characters are, in traditional quest myths, magnified in stature by the foes and monsters they encounter en route. Yet this never quite happens to Tolkien's hobbits, whose existence as 'Halflings' always gives them a sense of perpetual childlikeness, even in the thick of battle. Gandalf, sweeping Pippin up onto the back of Shadowfax as they gallop across the plain at the end of *Volume II, The Two Towers,* does so in the manner of a loving but chiding father, who sweeps his naughty little boy into his arms or sits him on the back of his bicycle as they ride home for tea. Even as Frodo nears the Mount of Doom and the culmination of his quest, his physical stature, rather than becoming aggrandised by the role, actually diminishes in line with the significance of the task set: Sam ultimately has to carry him as if bearing 'a hobbit-child pig-a-back' (*RK,* 259).

This sense of littleness is, from that perspective, something to which we can all relate. Not only do we recall our own childhood adventures, setting out on treks and expeditions armed with anything from buckets and spades to bicycles and binoculars, but we also recall that we, like Pippin, associated childhood adventures with food. One needs to read relatively little of Tolkien's trilogy before one recognises that food is one of its characters' central preoccupations. On occasion this takes on a kind of sacramental quality, such as when Frodo, Sam, and Gollum shelter in a hollow from the mountain winds of Cirith Ungol towards the end of *Volume II, The Two Towers.* As they do, they sit down to 'what they expected would be their last meal before they went down into the Nameless Land, maybe the last meal they would ever eat together.'[25] Evocations of the Last Supper are obvious here and, along with them, the implication that Gollum will play Judas to his 'master.' And, as if Tolkien is determined to ensure we do not miss such an allusion, what they eat is a version of the communion supper: 'wafers of the waybread' given to them by the Elves and a 'sparing' amount to drink, imbibing 'only enough to moisten their dry mouths' (*TT,* 399). In Pippin's case, however, it is simply that endless preoccupation with eating that most of us can only fully indulge as children. So, while others muse on the tragedy of Lothlórien, his memories of the Elven Kingdom are dominated by a yearning for their 'bread, surpassing the savour of a fair white loaf to one who is starving; and fruits sweet as wildberries and richer than the tended fruits of gardens' (*FR,* 109). Even after the flight to Minas Tirith at the start of *Volume III, The Return of the King,* no sooner have they reached their destination and Gandalf has left him with the warning that 'tomorrow will be certain to bring worse than today,' than Pippin muses, 'Nine o'clock we'd call it in the Shire . . . Just the time for a nice breakfast by the open window in the spring sunshine. And how I should like breakfast! Do these people ever have it, or is it over? And when do they have dinner, and where?'[26]

Metaphorically, diminution also draws attention to the insignificance of the individual: the means by which we are all dwarfed—throughout our lives—by challenges and circumstances we struggle to master, and then move beyond. In that sense, each of the hobbits is a kind of twentieth-century equivalent to John Bunyan's Christian, though in some ways it is as much Sam as the more obvious Frodo who most resembles Bunyan's traveller, both in his unswerving loyalty and dedication and in the simplicity of his needs and desires:

> As Sam stood there, even though the Ring was not on him but hanging by its chain about his neck, he felt himself enlarged, as if he were robed in a huge distorted shadow of himself . . . Wild fantasies arose in his mind; and he saw Samwise the Strong, Hero of the Age, striding with a flaming sword across the darkened land . . . He had only to put on the Ring and claim it for his own, and all this could be.
>
> In that hour of trial it was the love of his master that helped most to hold him firm; but also deep down in him lived still unconquered his plain hobbit-sense: he knew in the core of his heart that he was not large enough to bear such a burden . . .
>
> . . . He had not gone far before he had shrunk again to a very small and frightened hobbit. (*RK*, 206–207)

Nor is this to minimise the 'adult' significance of the trilogy. Epic, by its very nature, dwarfs us because its panorama is similarly rendered small-scale. Tolkien takes the world and, though continuing to stress its vastness, gives it a topography that can be paced, climbed, even delved, on foot. In part, the longevity of hobbit life contributes to this, for it gives a sense of childhood lasting proportionally longer, and maturity (as the community sees it) taking longer to be attained. Hence, though we discover, just before he sets out on his quest as ring bearer, that Frodo's 'forties were running out, and his fiftieth birthday was drawing near' (*FR*, 56), we cannot help but retain a sense of Frodo as being in his early to mid-twenties. Only as the hobbits near the borders of the Shire on the return leg of their journey does Gandalf finally judge: 'You are grown up now . . . and I have no longer any fear at all for any of you' (*RK*, 332).

In effect, what Tolkien gives us in the Lord of the Rings is a narrative requiring us, as readers, to negotiate profound shifts in perspective—more so than any realist narrative could manage and still retain coherence. Once the travellers leave the cosy familiarity of the Shire, we are almost immediately struck by the vast emptiness of the landscapes through which they travel. This is particularly consistently sustained in *Volume II, The Two Towers*, landscape and its forbidding qualities being enhanced by the realisation that we, as readers, will travel the entire scope of this volume and neither reach our outward destiny nor return home. It is here where we hear the tale of Gandalf's battle with the Balrog, a narrative the parameters of which encompass dizzying contrasts in scale and which, immersed in a form of readerly homesickness as we are, affects us with a true sense of the sublime:

> 'Long time I fell . . . and he fell with me. His fire was about me. I was burned. Then we plunged into deep water and all was dark. Cold it was as the tide of death: almost it froze my heart.'
>
> 'Deep is the abyss that is spanned by Durin's Bridge, and none has measured it,' said Gimli.
>
> 'Yet it has a bottom, beyond light and knowledge . . . Thither I came at last, to the uttermost foundations of stone. He was with me still. His fire was quenched, but now he was a thing of slime . . . We fought under the living earth, where time is not counted. Ever he clutched me, and ever I hewed him, till at last he fled into dark tunnels . . . Far, far below the deepest delvings of the Dwarves, the world is gnawed by nameless things . . . In that despair my enemy was my only hope, and I pursued him . . . Thus he brought me back at last to the secret ways of Khazad-dûm . . . Ever up now we went, until we came to the endless Stair . . . From the lowest dungeon to the highest peak it climbed . . . until it issued at last in Durin's Tower carved in the living rock of Zirakzigil, the pinnacle of the Silvertine.' (*TT*, 122)

It is in response to such topographical extremes that we, like the characters, feel most in need of a means by which that landscape may be tamed and controlled, and perhaps it is fitting for it to be Gandalf who turns for this to Legolas the Elf, because of Legolas's gift of excellent first sight. The Elf's ability to see accurately and at great distance enables the travellers to 'read' and hence 'map' the landscape and, in the process, clearly differentiate between natural and unnatural elements. Nor is it accidental that this happens in conjunction with a narrative model for the sublime, for the picturesque is often set up as a kind of antidote to it. As Angus Fletcher puts it:

> Picturesque might best be defined as inverse, or microscopic, sublimity: where the sublime aims at great size and grandeur, the picturesque aims at littleness and a sort of modesty; where the sublime is austere, the picturesque is intricate; where the sublime produces 'terror,' or rather, awed anxiety, the picturesque produces an almost excessive feeling of comfort . . . [27]

For us, too, Legolas's ability to see microscopic movement becomes a source of reassurance. And yet, such feelings are never uncontaminated by violence in Lord of the Rings—nor, according to Fletcher, is the picturesque: 'The picturesque challenges the spectator . . . by a direct attack on the senses, such that . . . it is likely to mix pleasant scenes with troubling, disturbing scenes of a morbid nature.'[28] However, as we saw in Chapter 3, immediate clarity of perspective is not always valued by Tolkien. So, as Gandalf turns towards Helm's Deep and asks Legolas what he can see ahead, the Elf's first perceptions are only dim:

> There are shapes moving . . . but what they are I cannot tell. It is not mist or cloud that defeats my eyes: there is a veiling shadow that some power lays upon the land, and it marches slowly down stream. It is as if the twilight under endless trees were flowing downwards from the hills. (*TT*, 155)

This is immediately interpreted not as a limitation in Legolas's perception but as a sense of 'visible' uncanniness, which here takes on the shape of a cloak that simultaneously outlines and conceals. This should perhaps be compared with the role of ocular perception in realism for, as Stewart puts it:

Often the eye of realism in literature or film, moving from one object in a room or a landscape to another, brings each object to the attention of the reader/audience, creating a notion of a surrounding, an appropriate context, in which a character first appears. The realistic eye is centered, focused, in the literal and metaphorical sense, and an illusion of opacity and sharpness is created. The realistic eye is narrative—one event follows another, is contingent upon the event that has passed before it and causes the event that follows it. It is an eye that moves primarily in time, an eye with a past and a future.[29]

Stewart's words evoke another passage involving Legolas and Gandalf, here one in which Legolas first spots a stranger approaching through the trees, but lacks clear perception of who it is. Hence, though we are in no doubt about his appearance, his identity remains unclear. Assuming Gandalf to be lost to death, the travellers unquestioningly assume this person can only be Saruman:

'Yet here we are—and nicely caught in the net,' said Legolas. 'Look!'
'Look at what?' said Gimli.
'There in the trees.'
'Where? I have not elf-eyes.'
'Hush! Speak more softly! Look! . . . Cannot you see him, passing from tree to tree?'
'I see, I see now!' hissed Gimli. 'Look, Aragorn! . . .'
Aragorn looked and beheld a bent figure . . . It was not far away . . .
Gimli gazed with wide eyes for a while, as step by step the figure drew nearer . . . (*TT*, 109–110)

Notice how, as Stewart might put it, each character's eyes bring, in turn, this 'object' to the reader's attention as well as theirs. This chain of vision is indeed 'narrative,' in the sense that we are conscious of almost every individual step this stranger takes and the effect of that sequence of movement upon the watchers as they are urged, by Aragorn, to 'Watch and wait!' (*TT*, 110)

What we are almost given, in the specifically framing function of vision in this part of the trilogy, is a sense of apertures opening up and reclosing—or at least becoming temporarily obscured—like shutters. This, in itself, maps on to a larger narrative patterning in the Lord of the Rings, where Tolkien employs a variety of closure mechanisms for effect. Each new stretch of territory into which the group travels operates as an opening into adventure: a space of possibility, an entry into the unknown. But this is often conjoined with a series of mini-closures, often very abrupt ones. So characters tend to part unexpectedly (the end of *Volume I, The Fellowship of the Ring*, being a perfect example of this) and the final thrusting of the Ring into the fire—when it eventually comes—actually happens precipitately. In each of these two cases, narrative climaxes are eschewed in favour of a sense of readerly disillusion. We tend to be left wondering whether we have been looking for the wrong aim, enabling Tolkien to raise more profound questions about resolution. Here we come to his treatment of irresolution through melancholia, a theme that Verlyn Flieger identifies as the key theme in Tolkien's writing and that must impinge on loss in relation to quest.

Melancholia is, as Sigmund Freud observes, a condition related to mourning. However, where mourning constitutes a temporary 'reaction to the loss of a loved one . . . one's country, liberty,' gradually resolved over time, melancholia 'is in some way related to an object-loss which is withdrawn from consciousness . . .' with the effect that 'we [may not] see what it is that is absorbing [the melancholic] so entirely.'[30] Many have argued Tolkien's relationship to melancholia to be both personal and cultural. Having lost his parents while still a child (his father at the age of four and his mother at the age of twelve) and having served in the First World War and been a survivor of the infamous Battle of the Somme (occurring at the same time as Freud published his essay 'Mourning and Melancolia' in 1917), like many young men of his generation Tolkien is generally believed to have been emotionally scarred for life. Under the circumstances, Maureen Duffy adopts a rather casual stance on the war and its connection with Tolkien's work:

> For intellectuals there was reassurance in the Hobbits of Tolkien with their underground homes like wartime dugouts . . . Perhaps it was the wish 'there must be more to it than this,' struggling with the discoveries of cosmology and

physics, that led to the taking up of one faintly numinous writer after another . . . [31]

Flieger is more sympathetic, but at the same time refuses to read the trilogy as an allegory about war, harshly criticising any reader who might be tempted to reduce the Lord of the Rings books, first published in the mid-1950s, to a symbolically encoded World War II narrative, 'with Gandalf and his forces as the Allies, Sauron and company as the Axis powers, and the Ruling Ring, the super-weapon, as—what else?—the atom bomb.'[32] Instead, she focuses on Tolkien's determination to employ his work as a means of part escaping and part revisioning that horror, drawing attention to the fact that he began work on the construction of his own mythology while serving in the trenches—not to mention, of course, the fact that his academic specialty in Anglo-Saxon and medieval literature placed him as a man 'out of time.'

Irrespective of any biographically based assumptions we may be tempted to impose upon the Lord of the Rings, there is certainly a clear element of melancholia threaded through it. The realm of Lórien, as a whole, is based on a melancholic ethos, the realm being shown to have come adrift from time. Associated with the fair folk (the word *Elf* derives from the Anglo-Saxon term *ælf*, meaning "fairy spirit"[33]), Lórien is a land of great beauty. However, as the travellers cross it they become aware of a darker side to the terrain: 'The air was cool and soft, as if it were early spring, yet they felt about them the deep and thoughtful quiet of winter' (*FR*, 470). As their queen, the Lady Galadriel, reveals to Frodo, his quest directly impinges on their fate: '[I]f you fail, then we are laid bare to the enemy. Yet if you succeed, then our power is diminished, and Lothlórien will fade, and the tides of Time will sweep it away' (*FR*, 479). Furthermore, of course, the group of travellers enter the Elven king-dom in a state of mourning, Gandalf having just, as they believe, plummeted to his death from the Bridge of Khazad-dûm.

In fact, not just those awaiting the freedom to die in Lórien, but the quest as a whole takes on the structure of melancholia, a point explaining Frodo's own relationship to death at the end. After his return to the Shire in *Volume III, The Return of the King*, the wound he sustained on Weathertop Hill continues to wear him down until he takes Sam with him on one final journey. As they reach the tree behind which Frodo hid from the Black Rider when they first set out from the Shire in *Volume I, The Fellowship of the Ring*, they hear the Elven folk approaching in song. Recalling that the Elves must now dwindle away, the Ring having been destroyed, Frodo goes with them, accompanied, like a funeral cortege, by Sam, Pippin, and Merry. As they travel back through the Shire, it is as if death already clothes them: 'Though they rode . . . all the evening and all the night, none saw them pass, save . . . here and there some wanderer in the dark who saw a swift shimmer under the trees, or a light and shadow flowing through the grass . . .' (*RK*, 376). Attending the several occasions, throughout the journey across Middle Earth, when the narrator alludes to characters leaving and never again returning, there is a kind of less specific companionate wistfulness. So, again on the road to Lothlórien, as Gimli the Dwarf insists on paying homage to Durin's Stone and the beauty of its surrounding vale, Pippin turns to face Sam—who is not directly part of the scene— and unexpectedly asks him, 'What did you see?' Neither we nor Pippin ever find out, for the narrator tells us that Sam 'was too deep in thought to answer' (*FR*, 438). In terms of character construction, of course, this is a far more 'realistic' sense of character than we tend to find in most works of literature, where nothing is ever given narrative presence unless it impinges directly on plot structure. Here, Sam's unexplained wistfulness contributes to a general sense of melancholic contemplation, coupled with the lack of resolution such melancholia brings.

As such isolated contemplative moments imply, for all its usage of a variety of species and monsters, Tolkien's the Lord of the Rings is primarily a trilogy concerning the future of humanity. As Flieger observes, 'Tolkien made it clear that he intended Hobbits to be a subvariety of humankind, not a different species altogether,'[34] and as a fleeting observation shared by Gimli and Legolas in *Volume III, The Return of the King* shows, the fate of Middle Earth lies also with 'us':

> 'It is ever so with the things that Men begin: there is a frost in Spring, or a blight in Summer, and they fail of their promise.'

'Yet seldom do they fail of their seed,' said Legolas. 'And that will lie in the dust and rot to spring up again in times and places unlooked-for. The deeds of Men will outlast us, Gimli.'

'And yet come to naught in the end but might-have-beens, I guess,' said the Dwarf.

'To that the Elves know not the answer,' said Legolas. (*RK*, 170)

One of the problems twenty-first century readers bring to Tolkien's trilogy is the belief that it is structured in terms of an old-fashioned, light-and-dark, good-and-evil binary divide that is too easily mapped on to conventional Christian orthodoxy. And yet, and as the previous discussion of melancholia aims to show, one of the most intriguing aspects of the whole trilogy concerns those elements eschewing resolution of a number of kinds. In *Volume I, The Fellowship of the Ring*, this is predominantly conveyed through a form of character ambivalence that renders our response to individuals (including those with whom we are encouraged to both identify and empathise) problematic.

It is the Ring that is seen to instil this ambivalence in the characters, even before the novel proper starts, with the Prologue concerning Bilbo's successful challenge of Gollum for it. In these terms, Bilbo Baggins, from whom Frodo inherits the quest, attracts a kind of Gothic darkness, not dissimilar to that of Oscar Wilde's Dorian Gray: '[I]t seemed unfair that anyone should possess (apparently) perpetual youth as well as (reputedly) inexhaustible wealth. "It will have to be paid for," they said. "It isn't natural, and trouble will come of it"' (*FR*, 27).[35] Jackson's film captures Bilbo's ambivalence brilliantly. As Bilbo attempts to snatch the Ring from Frodo, his eyes undergo a hideous mutation in which the iris becomes white and the cornea darkens. In this simple but unsettling and unexpected reversal Jackson provides us with easily the most shocking visual image of the film, rendering an almost abject response of disgust in the spectator. Tolkien's original depicts this less through an objective metamorphosis in Bilbo than in a sudden and distressing shift in visual perception on the part of Frodo: ' . . . [H]e was no longer looking at Bilbo; a shadow seemed to have fallen between them, and through it he found himself eyeing a little wrinkled creature with a hungry face and bony groping hands. He felt a desire to strike him' (*FR*, 304).

Though Frodo looks at Bilbo, what he sees is Gollum and, in that instance of skewed vision, he encounters a metaphor for the means by which lineage can be displaced by illegitimacy on more than just the level of character. The Lord of the Rings luxuriates in having, in generic terms, an epic lineage that Tolkien can and does trace back to *Beowulf* via medieval allegory. Paradoxically, it is this lineage that endows the text with much of its contemporary socio-ethical relevance, for the struggle between good and evil is timeless: 'Debates ever recurring, battles repetitiously taking on the same form, reversals and discoveries always couched in the same heraldic diction . . .'[36] Nevertheless, the Lord of the Rings also aims at being more than this—it is a trilogy of novels in the twentieth-century sense and, as such, Tolkien attempts to endow each of them with a genuinely complex sense of 'character' (the very thing allegorical writing lacks). In doing so, the lineage of high fantasy is allowed to mutate through close contact with that 'bastard' usurper, the novelistic 'good read,' and to revel, as a result, in a degree of 'realism' that is all the more unsettling for being found in a form where we least expect it: characterisation being 'simple' rather than 'complex' in allegories.

Mary Shelley, *Frankenstein*: Discourses of Monstrosity

Some bastard forms are, of course, more fabulous than others, and few carry more resonance for literature since 1800 than Mary Shelley's *Frankenstein* (1818). In her brief 'Author's Introduction' to the 1831 Standard Novels edition, Shelley identifies the place occupied by fantasy in *Frankenstein*. She opens with an evaluation of two differing forms of 'invention': those of fiction and those of dream. Of her own narrative she is relatively dismissive, identifying its key characteristics as those of 'close imitat[ion]' in comparison with her dreams, which she considers 'more fantastic and agreeable.'[37] Clearly, 'agreeable' here means exciting and innovative rather than congenial or pleasant, as the apparent 'waking dream' she has while lying in her bed testifies:

> I saw the hideous phantasm of a man stretched out, and
> then, on the working of some powerful engine, show signs
> of life . . . His success would terrify the artist; he would
> rush away from his odious handiwork, horror-stricken . . .
> He sleeps; but he is awakened; he opens his eyes; behold,
> the horrid thing stands at his bedside, opening his curtains
> and looking on him with yellow, watery, but speculative
> eyes. (*F*, 59)

Here we notice Shelley's usage of the term *phantasm*, which, as we will recall from our discussion in Chapter 2, refers to 'memory working on itself' in tandem with imagination.[38] Also pertinent is the close alignment we can recognise between Coleridge's distinction between fancy and imagination and Shelley's distinction between night-dreaming (which seems to emanate from the unleashed imagination) and imitative daydreaming in fictive form (fancy, or as Shelley puts it, 'castles in the air' [*F*, 55]). Rather as in the case of the monster itself, however creative 'invention' might be, 'the materials must, in the first place, be afforded: it can give form to dark, shapeless substances, but cannot bring into being the substance itself' (*F*, 58). In drawing this direct parallel between her own text and the monster that her character, Victor Frankenstein, builds—itself constructed out of an amalgam of body parts and infused with 'new life'—she also, paradoxically, releases aspects of control over it. For, just as Victor creates the monster out of what he claims to be positive aspirations, so Shelley finds her own imagination, through dream, rises 'unbidden' as she is 'possessed' in return (*F*, 59).

In generic terms, Shelley tells us she is looking for the inspiration to write a ghost story. That this will be generically complex, however, can also be ascertained from the fact that the creator in this imagined scene is both an 'engineer' (i.e. the person operating this 'powerful engine' upon which the phantasm is laid out) and an 'artist.' Even taking into account the fact that nineteenth-century intellectual thought made far less of a rigid distinction between the work of the sciences and that of the arts than we do today, we can still recognise *Frankenstein* as a text that interrogates the subgeneric limits within fantasy rather than slavishly settling into any one of them. For instance, while Shelley's novel is today considered to be one of the key Gothic texts, it is equally seen as an early work of science fiction.

Thus we can add Shelley's voice to those we have already examined in considering the interface between dreaming and writing in the context of fantasy. There is, however, one clear difference between Shelley as the dreamer of her own Introduction and the dreamer in Freud's 'Creative Writing and Day-Dreaming' essay, which is that in Freud's case it is always a male child who is at play. Shelley's motivation for writing her retrospective Introduction is, as she herself acknowledges, to answer the question 'How I, then a young *girl*, came to think of and to dilate upon so very hideous an idea?' (*F*, 55; my emphasis). Her motivation is, then, primarily gendered as she adopts what is the typically apologetic stance of the early nineteenth-century woman writer, defending her own existence in print, let alone as the birth mother of such 'hideous progeny' (*F*, 60). Because of the controversy surrounding women writers of her age, it is inevitable that Shelley will privilege, in her account, a creative form deriving from a lack of consciously controlled influence, as opposed to one in which greater personal control is foregrounded. What her novel also did, and continues to do, is inspire an ongoing debate about the relationship between women writers and monstrosity, which often manifests itself, in fantasy writing, around the question of reproduction. As Anne K. Mellor puts it, 'From a feminist viewpoint, *Frankenstein* is a book about what happens when a man tries to have a baby without a woman.'[39]

Frankenstein's monster is a figure in transition, both anatomically and nominally. Anatomically speaking, of course, the monster is manufactured out of parts of the dead. Originally composed of fine ingredients ('His limbs were in proportion, and I had selected his features as beautiful' [*F*, 105]), the finished monster is hideous in its totality ('Beautiful! Great God! . . . [N]ow that I had finished, the beauty of the dream vanished, and breathless horror and disgust filled my heart' [*F*, 105]). Nominally, like its mother text, the genus to which the monster is attributed shifts. Irrespective of Shelley's claims in 1831, self-evidently her monster is not a 'ghost' in the accepted sense of the word, though certainly it haunts Victor as insistently as Shelley claims her idea 'possessed' her. Out alone on the icy wastes of the Alps, in a classic instance of the interface between the Gothic and the Romantic sublime, Victor strives to attain transcendence over the bounds of his environment by reminding himself of the power of the natural landscape, when suddenly that power of the gaze is infiltrated by this 'other':

> . . . I suddenly beheld the figure of a man, at some distance, advancing towards me with superhuman speed. He bounded over the crevices in the ice, among which I had walked with caution; his stature, also, as he approached, seemed to exceed that of man. I was troubled; a mist came over my eyes, and I felt a faintness seize me . . . I perceived, as the shape came nearer (sight tremendous and abhorred!) that it was the wretch whom I had created. I trembled with rage and horror . . . I recovered only to overwhelm him with words expressive of furious detestation and contempt.
> 'Devil,' I exclaimed, 'do you dare approach me?' (*F*, 144–145)

As here, rather than 'ghost,' Victor most commonly refers to the monster as a devil or 'daemon.' As Fletcher observes, the word *demon* itself has an intriguing etymology, 'meaning to distribute or to divide,' and what the demon traditionally distributes are 'destinies.'[40] To *distribute* is, of course, to take and apportion control of something, but when coupled with destiny, there is an instant irony in the fact that this monster, which has no clear relationship to origins and with an unfixed destiny of its own ('He sprang from the cabin window . . . [and] was soon borne away by the waves and lost in darkness and distance' [*F*, 265]) should decide Frankenstein's fate. Yet, to cite Fletcher again, an alternate etymological route for the term *demon* might cast light on this. Returning to the ancients, and reading the term through Lactantius, Fletcher suggests that the term *demon* may also carry the meaning 'skilled and learned, because "Grammarians say demons were gods by reason of their skill and their knowledge."'[41]

Lacking in traditional knowledge, such a judgment of Frankenstein's monster seems misplaced. And yet, the monster certainly learns quickly—not least how to mimic the traits of bad parenting. Treated hideously by his 'father,' the monster is rendered most hideous in his ability to turn that monstrosity back on his creator. Denied a family of his own, the illegitimate 'other' rebels against the family structures of the Frankenstein family, murdering Victor's young brother and, in also murdering his lover/sister Elizabeth, cutting off Victor's hopes of reproducing his kind as surely as Frankenstein does the monster's. Frankenstein's own family structures are, in fact, as 'monstrous' as his relations with his creation.

The first information we glean from Victor is the importance of origins to his sense of who he is: 'I am by birth a Genevese, and my family is one of the most distinguished of that republic' (*F*, 80). His father, a respected civic dignitary, marries late and becomes a parent only in later life. An only child for many years, Victor idealises his relationship to both parents:

> My mother's tender caresses and my father's smile of benevolent pleasure while regarding me are my first recollections. I was their plaything and their idol . . . the innocent and *helpless creature* bestowed on them by heaven . . . whose future lot it was in their hands to direct to happiness or misery, according as they fulfilled their duties towards me. (*F*, 82; my emphasis)

Yet threaded through this cloying sentimentality is the disingenuousness of the account. We recall that this is an account told in the first person and after Victor has committed his transgressions and paid the consequences for them. The 'telling' (which we hear in advance of the rest of the story) has therefore been repackaged by Victor to cast the greatest light on his own fate. Note, also, the way in which clear demarcations between relations and identities blur in the telling. Victor refers to his childhood self as an 'innocent and helpless creature' and, in so doing, uses the noun most often applied to the monster—his own bastard offspring. Compare, for instance, this childhood bliss with the monster's account of its own 'infancy':

> It is with considerable difficulty that I remember the original era of my being; all the events of that period appear confused and indistinct. A strange multiplicity of sensations seized me, and I saw, felt, heard, and smelt at the same time

> . . . Darkness then came over me and troubled me, but
> hardly had I felt this when, by opening my eyes, as I now
> suppose, the light poured in upon me again. I walked . . .
> and then lying down, was overcome by sleep. (*F*, 148)

In comparison with the meticulously documented, orderly nature of Victor's own early memories, the monster's are what we would expect from an artificial creation born in adult form. Whereas the monster is denied an infancy, Victor's own childhood appears exaggeratedly heightened. His father's wife, Caroline, was the daughter of his father's best friend, Beaufort, whom Victor's father, Alphonse, took in after his friend's death. There is therefore a rather eccentric coupling in the marriage, Alphonse being simultaneously father and husband to Caroline. That eccentric dynamic is then passed on in the circumstances surrounding Victor's own boyhood. Taking in Elizabeth by adoption, Victor's mother tells him ' "I have a pretty present for my Victor . . ." [and] presented Elizabeth to me as her promised gift . . . No word, no expression could body forth the kind of relation in which she stood to me—*my more than sister*, since till death she was to be mine only' (*F*, 84; my emphasis). As if this were not strange enough, on the death of Victor's mother, Elizabeth is asked to take her place, being simultaneously daughter and wife to Alphonse, as well as simultaneously sister and fiancée to Victor. Sealing these intergenerational twists with a speech act, in a supreme instance of deathbed manipulation, Caroline joins the hands of Victor and Elizabeth and asserts 'my firmest hopes of future happiness were placed on the prospect of your union. This expectation will now be the consolation of your father' (*F*, 91). Surely, it is through unravelling these overly possessive, overly controlling parental dynamics that we best understand how Victor's own monstrosity is inherited as well as passed on through blood.

In considering to what extent Shelley's monster holds a typical relationship to familial inheritance, we might turn to the words of Kathryn Hume:

> Monsters . . . have an ancestry that links them to a total
> network of divine and demonic powers. In dragon stories, a
> dragon may not have a genealogy, yet western dragons share

family resemblances which give them predictable powers (such as breathing fire) and predictable weaknesses (soft underbellies). Evil or unpleasant such monsters may be for a hero, but at least the hero knows himself to be in touch with something more than an ad hoc obstacle; the monsters have significance beyond the fight itself . . . [42]

The nature of the 'significance beyond the fight' is, in this case, to some extent revealed through a consideration of a family resemblance between Frankenstein's monster, in the early decades of the nineteenth century, and Bram Stoker's eponymous protagonist, Dracula, at its end. At first sight, these creatures bear little fraternal resemblance to each other; in fact, Franco Moretti goes further, describing each of the two as '*totalizing* monsters' in their own right.[43] Nevertheless, a comparison between the two is useful for our purposes. Moretti identifies Shelley's monster with the proletariat, born out of William Blake's 'dark satanic mills' of the early decades of the Industrial Revolution.[44] As such, its illegitimate relationship to familial inheritance is crucial, for without that the monster represents the threat of a new order with, at the time Shelley was writing, as yet unspecifiable consequences. Hence, while traditional Gothic monsters could be considered containable, 'Frankensteins's [sic] monster sows devastation over the whole world, from the Alps to Scotland, from Eastern Europe to the Pole . . .'[45] In the process, it must become more than a specific monster and take on form as the embodiment of a wider threat: here the newly emergent industrial capitalism.

In order to best emphasise the inherent danger of this new ideology, Shelley divorces production from capital by making Victor's monster literally useless, and this she achieves by creating a landscape in which there is nothing for him to do: '[T]here is no way of utilizing [the monster] because there are no factories. And there are no factories . . . because for Mary Shelley the demands of production have no value in themselves, but must be subordinated to the maintenance of the moral and material solidity of the family . . .'[46] Implicit in this critique is the realisation that, if Shelley favours the family unit over the community, she does so by refusing to acknowledge inheritance to be as much a capitalist notion as it is one of biology. Marriage is, as any reader of Jane Austen will tell us, predominantly an economic contract dressed up as love and romance, and the role of any father of daughters is to make as economically favourable a match for them as possible in order to secure a future for his own wealth. Victor's father knows and practices exactly this, as did Beaufort. Frankenstein's real flaw, therefore, in economic terms, is that he 'wastes' family assets such as Elizabeth and William in favour of an offspring who usurps lineage.

Contrast this with Dracula, who, as Moretti sees it, is a fully motivated killer: 'he *needs* blood . . . His ultimate aim is not to destroy the lives of others according to whim . . . but to use them.'[47] Where Shelley's monster severs bloodlines in an act of self-destructive spite, Dracula calculatedly uses them for his own ends. Where Shelley's monster retreats into 'the wastes,' Dracula wastes nothing: 'Like capital, Dracula is impelled towards a continuous growth, an unlimited expansion of his domain: accumulation is inherent in his nature.'[48] This comparison requires us to return to Tolkien's the Lord of the Rings, for Moretti's argument does much to shed new light on two of Middle Earth's 'monsters,' the Orcs on the one hand and the Black Riders on the other.

The Monsters of Middle Earth

Like Frankenstein's monster, the Orcs are a physical mutation, but unlike him they do have a traceable lineage. A member of the species of Goblin, which Carole Silver defines as 'small, hostile, unattractive, grotesque, and almost exclusively male,'[49] we can also see them as a hideous mutation of two otherwise distinct species, the Dwarf and the Elf. Silver uses the terms *Goblin* and *Dwarf* almost interchangeably in her book *Strange and Secret Peoples*, while at the same time recognising that the term *Dwarf* itself is not easily placed: 'actual dwarfs already inhabited a borderland between the natural and the supernatural, and had always been perceived as "freaks" or "others."'[50] The connection with the Elves takes us straight to the question of origins for, as Treebeard the Ent informs Merry, Orcs and Trolls are 'counterfeit' species, 'made by the Enemy in the Great Darkness, [Trolls] in mockery of Ents, as Orcs were of Elves' (*TT*, 101). Hence, as each mutation takes effect, the question of evolution becomes less clear. Much like the process of worker alienation, the relationship between the end product and the precise raw ingredients comprising it starts to dim. In Tolkien's trilogy, there is more than a hint, reinforced by Peter Jackson's recent cinematic version of *The Lord of the Rings: The Fellowship of the Ring* (New Line Cinema, 2001), that the Orcs are in some manner 'manufactured' at Isengard: mass-produced rather than reproduced. So, just as Frankenstein's involvement is necessary if there is to be a mate (hence a race and a future) for the monster, so Saruman is necessary to the future of the Orcs. Furthermore, though one or two Orcs are singled out by name, on the whole their significance is collective or tribal rather than individual, their deaths remaining statistical in significance and their passing never mourned. In that sense, the Orcs are actually, in my opinion, a more apt example of a trend Moretti identifies in Shelley's novel, and as such, I have replaced Moretti's use of the name *Frankenstein* in the following quotation with *Saruman*:

> [Saruman's] invention is thus a pregnant metaphor of the process of capitalist production, which forms by deforming, civilizes by barbarizing, enriches by impoverishing—a two-sided process in which each affirmation entails a negation. And indeed the monster . . . is always described by negation . . . [51]

The impact of Saruman's hideous instance of manufacturing industry is heightened by the fact that, elsewhere in Tolkien's trilogy, there is precious little manufacture of anything at all, enabling Isengard to reign supreme as an industrial chimera:

> Many houses there were . . . Thousands could dwell there . . . Shafts were driven deep into the ground . . . The shafts ran down by many slopes and spiral stairs to caverns far under; there Saruman had treasuries, store-houses, armouries, smithies, and great furnaces. Iron wheels revolved there endlessly, and hammers thudded. At night plumes of vapour steamed from the vents, lit from beneath with red light, or blue, or venomous green. (*TT*, 191–192)

Despite these occasional glimpses of a post-industrial consciousness, as I have already suggested, 'progress' in Middle Earth is distinctly medieval and relates primarily to journeys. Travel is on foot, long-distance travel on horseback, and the word *engine* is used only to refer to the type of contraption one found on a medieval battlefield. Take, for instance, the following scene from *Volume III, The Return of the King*, in which bestiality, fantasy monsters, and the monstrosity of manufacture combine:

> There came great beasts, like moving houses in the red and fitful light, the *mûmakil* of the Harad dragging through the lanes amid the fires huge towers and engines . . . Great engines crawled across the field; and in the midst was a huge ram, great as a forest-tree a hundred feet in length, swinging on mighty chains. Long had it been forging in the dark smithies of Mordor, and its hideous head, founded of black steel, was shaped in the likeness of a ravening wolf . . . Grond they named it, in memory of the Hammer of the Underworld of old. Great beasts drew it, orcs surrounded it, and behind walked mountain-trolls to wield it. (*RK*, 111–112)

Perhaps this pre-capitalist identification explains Hume's dismissal of the lack of a sound economic basis upon which Tolkien's Shire is based:

> It reflects a child's understanding of the world: food is delivered, put into the pantry, and eaten, but not paid for. The labor goes into its production and the problems of isolated agricultural communities are ignored. The wealthy families have money but no source for it in tenant peasantry or stock-exchange investments.[52]

Turning now to the second monster of Middle Earth, in considering where Tolkien's version of Stoker's Dracula is to be found, we need look no further than the Black Riders. Though somewhat like the Orcs in their relative lack of individuality, being only nine in number they are immediately seen as a higher chain of being. Described by Gandalf as 'the Ringwraiths' (*FR*, 289), they are as ruthlessly motivated in their pursuit of Frodo as Moretti claims Dracula is in his desire for capital advantage, hence Dracula's desire for gold, here shaped into the 'One Ring.' Like vampires, the Black Riders track by blood, sharing their wraith-like corporeality and horror of broad daylight, the oral drive so dominant among vampires remaining satisfied by the presence of 'The Black Breath' (*FR*, 229) and the hissing that accompanies the Black Riders' sense of smell as they hunt their prey. When Frodo is stabbed with the Morgul-Knife, he compares the pain to 'a dart of poisoned ice [that] pierce[d] his left shoulder' (*FR*, 258), much like the vampire's conventional 'bite.' Similarly, just as the vampire's bite passes on vampirism by contagion, so the knife wound in Frodo's shoulder will never fully heal, and as Gandalf informs him, had they succeeded in piercing his heart, 'you would have become like they are, only weaker and under their command' (*FR*, 291).

Adolescent Monsters: Harry Potter

Of course, Tolkien is not alone in drawing on vampire mythology as a basis for spawning new fantasy monsters, and while the Black Riders are certainly among the most chilling of recent fantasy adversaries, even they almost meet their match in the surprisingly horrifying dementors, introduced in the third volume of J. K. Rowling's Harry Potter series, *Harry Potter and the Prisoner of Azkaban* (1999). Though written for a child reader, as one progresses through the volumes one is struck by the accumulation of a distinctly sinister tone, which, from *Volume III, The Prisoner of Azkaban* onwards, transforms what begins as a series based in fantasy into one with clear episodes of Gothic horror:

> Standing in the doorway . . . was a cloaked figure that towered to the ceiling. Its face was completely hidden beneath its hood. Harry's eyes darted downwards, and what he saw made his stomach contract. There was a hand protruding from the cloak and it was glistening, greyish, slimy-looking and scabbed, like something dead that had decayed in water . . .
> And then the thing beneath the hood . . . drew a long, slow, rattling breath, as though it was trying to suck something more than air from its surroundings.[53]

Like the traditional vampire, here the dementor pauses on the threshold (in this case of a railway carriage), awaiting right of entry. Where, in the case of the typical vampire, one finds distended teeth and nails, symbolic of its desires to penetrate the flesh of others, here the phallic element of penetration is replaced entirely by the oral drive. Bearing in mind the child readership of this series, this shift might be interpreted as a means of playing down the sexual dimension often accompanying fantasy monsters (even at the hands of Tolkien's Orcs, Pippin and Merry squirm at the repulsive memory of 'the pawing hands' and 'hot breath' of Grishnákh, the Northern Orc [*TT*, 203]), were it not for the fact that the horrifying 'dementor's kiss,' used to suck the victim's soul from the body, comes as close to a rape scene as one is ever going to find in children's fiction:

> . . . [A] pair of strong, clammy hands suddenly wrapped themselves around Harry's neck. They were forcing his face upwards . . . he could feel its breath . . . it was going to get rid of him . . . he could feel its putrid breath . . . his mother was screaming in his ears . . . she was going to be the last thing he ever heard. (*HPPA*, 281)

What readers unfamiliar with the Harry Potter series will not realise in reading this passage is that Harry's mother has been dead since he was a baby. The dementors bring death with them and, in inflicting oral contagion upon their soulless victim, leave him or her in a similarly undead state to that of the vampire. Harry's relationship to his dead parents is one of the most intriguing aspects of Rowling's series, in that it combines a complex combination of desire, fear, guilt, and misery. As Harry ages with every volume, the emotions become increasingly complicated, presumably much like those of his readers who, as they age along with him, will find their own emotions to their (usually) living parents similarly complex and incomprehending. Here we have the last similarity between the vampire and ruthlessly motivated sucking: through Meredith Skura's reading of the relationship between narrative horror and the adolescent memories of infantile need.

According to Skura, all fantasy texts facilitate the ability of the young person to negotiate changing relationships with his or her own family. So, in the 'toothy monster' of 'Little Red Riding Hood,' she finds the typically contradictory response many teenagers have to their parents, Skura reading the wolf as a direct replacement for the mother the child has outgrown, a figure 'the child is both drawn to and repelled by . . . But it is not so much that she wants to be hurt as that she wants someone strong enough to take care of her, even if that means someone strong enough to devour her.' In the case of vampire monsters such as those discussed above, we find an outward projection of the child's now ambivalent response to what was, as an infant, instinctual, '[t]he child [having been] tied down, moved, filled, and emptied by someone too strong to resist . . .' Thus, in Gothic fantasy, '[t]he mother welcomes the child—and then turns on him with open jaws.'[54] In the context of the Harry Potter series, this last observation carries particular weight, for in dying, Harry's mother has also abandoned him to a damaged existence, of which the scar on his forehead is a visual reminder. This takes us to the last aspect of the fantasy monster, its existence as outward projection of our internalised fears and desires, stored in the unconscious since our first days in the womb.

In her book *Powers of Horror: An Essay in Abjection*, Julia Kristeva examines our response to the role of the scapegoat, the foreigner, the stranger (all of which are qualities the fantasy monster simply embodies, in more extreme form), and argues that, in order to understand the loathing we project outwards onto this 'other,' we need also to take it back to our own relationship to bodily waste products. Our repulsion at excrement, blood, and sweat is, she claims, testimony to our existence 'at the border of [our] condition as a living being. My body extricates itself, as being alive, from that border.'[55] What threatens us in loathing (be it loathing of the self or loathing of the other) is a kind of fear of contamination or infiltration. The splinter in my finger, the speck of dust in my eye, the asylum seeker, the fantasy monster: all can be summarised in the one phrase: the *foreign body*. It is this aspect of the fantasy monster that is always best explored through that mode of fantasy writing known as space/science/speculative fiction (*sf*); in fact, one might argue such to be one of *sf*'s key raison d'êtres.

H. G. Wells: *The First Men in the Moon* and *The Time Machine*

In *The First Men in the Moon*, there is an almost anthropological exploration of alternative species, be they vegetable or animal. The first encounter with alien life-forms is vegetative, and rather like in John Wyndham's *The Day of the Triffids* (1951), it takes on beastly proportions. So, on arriving on the surface of the moon, Bedford, the central protagonist, observes to his companion, Cavor, 'These things are less like earthly land plants than the things one imagines among the rocks at the bottom of the sea. Look at that yonder! One might imagine it a lizard changed into a plant.'[56] As the vegetation proliferates with the rising sun, it increasingly takes on the form of a mass antagonist as it quickly conceals the location of the sphere by which they travelled to the moon: 'All about us on the sunlit slopes frothed and swayed the darting shrubs, the swelling cactus, the creeping lichens . . . North, south, east, and west spread an identical monotony of unfamiliar forms'(*FMM*, 61).

The first animal the men encounter is a mooncalf, a dinosaur-like species, 'the girth of [whose] body was some fourscore feet, its length perhaps two hundred . . . its gigantic, flabby body . . . [being] of a corrugated white, dappling into blackness along the backbone' (*FMM*, 66–67). Next, as if moving up a Darwinian chain of being, come the Selenites, the species attributed—as so often in *sf*—with humanoid characteristics and the moon's superior race. The first of these is described thus:

> By contrast with the mooncalves he seemed a trivial being, a mere ant, scarcely five feet high. He was wearing garments of some leathery substance, so that no portion of his actual body appeared, but of this, of course, we were entirely ignorant. He presented himself, therefore, as a compact, bristling creature, having much of the quality of a complicated insect, with whip-like tentacles and a clanging arm projecting from his shining cylindrical body case. (*FMM*, 67)

This initial description alternates between a sense of awe, inspired by difference, and a sense of derision, inspired by a desire to perceive this 'Other' as an inferior version of the self. The combination is typical of *sf* narratives and again reflects the fears and paranoia of the human race. In narratives such as this, where we leave Earth to infiltrate other cultures, our apparent desire for new experience is always compromised by a need to assert familiarity at all costs. When taken captive by this species, however, fear comes to the fore and, along with it, a determination to reassert difference. As a Selenite enters the room in which Bedford and Cavor are imprisoned, it does so from behind them. As they are chained to the floor, they are unable to immediately place it within their line of vision, with the result that Bedford initially allows his imagination to 'suppl[y] features to [its] very human outline' (*FMM*, 77). As it moves fully into view, however, the reader is taken, step by step, through a journey of uncertainty, Bedford delaying a full description for as long as possible, Wells knowing we can only 'see' as quickly, or otherwise, as Bedford allows:

> For a moment my eyes sought him in the wrong place, and then I perceived him standing facing us both in the full light. Only the human features I had attributed to him were not there at all!
> Of course I ought to have expected that, only I didn't. It came to me as an absolute, for a moment an overwhelming, shock. It seemed as though it wasn't a face, as though it must needs be a mask, a horror, a deformity, that would presently be disavowed or explained. There was no nose, and the thing had dull bulging eyes at the side—in the silhouette I had supposed they were ears. There were no ears . . . I have tried to draw one of these heads, but I cannot. There was a mouth, downwardly curved, like a human mouth in a face that stares ferociously . . . (*FMM*, 77)

Throughout this passage, the Selenite's description fully confirms Moretti's earlier observation that 'the monster . . . is always described by negation.' First it is there, then it is not; it looks like a human/it does not look like a human. Bedford hints at the presumed presence of a nose, only to dismiss it; eyes are ears (or are ears eyes?). In evoking his own inability to draw the Selenite, Bedford accentuates the sense of 'difference' in saying, in effect, that what he is giving us is a poor and potentially misleading description, thereby leaving us with a presiding sense of 'space' between what we imagine and what might prove to be the case. Only the mouth can be described with any clarity, being 'like a human mouth in a face that stares ferociously' (though of course it is eyes, not mouths, that stare).

In *The Time Machine*, Wells provides us with more speculative anthropology, introducing us to two different species: the fair, daylight Eloi and the nocturnal, predatory Morlocks. Like the Selenites, the Morlocks live beneath the ground. Where the Selenites are set up, at first, as the highest form of civilization on the moon, however, the Morlocks are introduced as being 'strange creatures in the black shadows.'[57] Yet the Selenites and the Morlocks turn out to have more in common than we at first realise and, as in *Frankenstein* and the Lord of the Rings, this derives from their shared association with mechanised labour.

In both *The First Men in the Moon* and *The Time Machine*, we are presented with industrial subterranean landscapes. The first clue Bedford has of the presence of the Selenite race is not through their appearance, but through the noise of their industry. As he and Cavor cower on the moon's surface in the face of the rising sun, they hear 'Boom . . . Boom . . . Boom,' a sound they compare to 'the sound of some gigantic buried clock' (*FMM*, 62). Gradually, this sound develops into 'the clanging and throb of machinery' (*FMM*, 65), and once they are taken beneath the lunar surface, they find another instance of manufacturing industry, though what it produces remains unclear. Once again, worker and the thing produced are shown to have only an indirect relationship to each other, hence the characters' confusion over what it is they are looking at:

> . . . a vast mass of machinery [was] in active movement, whose flying and whirling parts were visible indistinctly over the heads and between the bodies of the Selenites who walked about us . . . The meaning and structure of this huge apparatus we saw I cannot explain, because we neither of us learnt what it was for or how it worked . . .
>
> Thud, thud, thud, thud, came the sweeping arms of this unintelligible apparatus . . . At first the thing seemed only reasonably large and near to us, and then I saw how exceedingly little the Selenites upon it seemed, and I realised the full immensity of cavern and machine. I looked from this tremendous affair to the faces of the Selenites with a new respect. (*FMM*, 87)

Though the purpose of the machinery is indistinct, it casts a clearer reflection, we notice, on the faces of those who work it. Unlike Shelley's monster, the Selenites do have a clear function, and unlike the Orcs, this function is constructive. So utilitarian are they, in fact, that their bodies have evolved to take on their required role: 'Some, who I suppose deal with bell-striking mechanisms, have enormously developed auditory organs; some whose work lies in delicate chemical operations project a vast olfactory organ; others again have flat feet for treadles with anchylosed joints; and others— who I have been told are glass-blowers—seem mere lung-bellows' (*FMM*, 169). What becomes clear in Wells's novels is that culture is always superior to nature, a point also made in relation to species identity in *The Time Machine*.

Like Bedford, the Time Traveller of Wells's later novel initially explores only the surface of future Earth, with the result that he first meets the Eloi, whom he considers to be 'pretty little people . . . so frail that I could fancy myself flinging . . . them about like ninepins' (*TM*, 21). In terms of fantasy narratives, the Eloi are more the creatures of folklore than science fiction. Like the fair folk, their activities are ruled by diurnal light patterns, and their world is understood in terms of fears connected with the uncanny: 'To me there is always an air of expectation about that evening stillness . . . Well, that night the expectation took the colour of my fears' (*TM*, 53). In traditional fairy lore, certain times of the day, particularly those associated with the half-light of dawn and dusk, are those most closely associated with fairy activity. Here, this is reversed, as the Eloi retreat indoors with the onset of dusk, fearing the nocturnal wanderings of the Morlocks.

Where the Eloi are fair, the Morlocks evoke an abject response in the Time Traveller: 'I felt a peculiar shrinking from those pallid bodies. They were just the half-bleached colour of the worms and things one sees preserved in spirit in a zoological museum' (*TM*, 46). Again, as he gains a better view of their 'great, lidless, pinkish-grey eyes' (*TM*, 50), we are reminded of Kristeva's loathing for the filmy skin on warm milk: 'harmless, thin as a sheet of cigarette paper, pitiful as a nail paring—I experience a gagging sensation and, still farther down, spasms in the stomach . . .'[58] Nor is this repulsion restricted to their physical form, for, in true abject tradition, dietary issues intervene, their preference for flesh being put into relief by the Eloi's strict vegetarianism. This results in a surprising degree of repulsion in the reader, who translates that craving straight into cannibalism. Immediately, Wells allows the Gothic to add a further 'skin-crawling' element to the plot, this time of the same kind that Shelley employed in describing the effect she desires to produce in her reader. Just as Shelley describes herself lying in bed, pondering the dilemma of a creator who gives life to monstrosity, abandons his offspring to what he hopes will be certain death, then wakes to find 'behold, the horrid thing stands at my bedside' (*F*, 59) so, in *The Time Machine*, monstrosity shadows the Time Traveller unknown until he 'wakes' to the reality of the existence of the Morlocks. After that, 'I felt I could never sleep again until my bed was secure from them. I shuddered with horror to think how they must already have examined me' (TM, 52).

Nevertheless, though repulsed by the Morlocks, the traveller gradually has to realise that abjection can play us false: 'The Upperworld people might once have been the favoured aristocracy, and the Morlocks their mechanical servants . . . Ages ago, thousands of generations ago, man had thrust his brother man out of the ease and the sunshine. And now that brother was coming back—changed!' (*TM*, 52) On some level, therefore, Wells seems to trace out a tentative line more robustly pursued later on in the twentieth century by identity politicians such as Mary Russo: 'Grotesque realism present[s] a dynamic, materialist, and unflinching view of human bodies in all stages and contours of growth, degeneration, anomaly, excess, loss, and prosthesis.'[59] In other words, perfection (such as is reflected in the Eloi's form) is 'closed' and, in the process, 'finished'—like the society they collectively comprise. It is usually the case that body imagery has a collective symbolic rather than merely individualistically mimetic application in fantasy texts, particularly those taking a futurist perspective. At its most fundamental level, *sf* relegates 'normality' or 'sameness' to the point of view character, the one who does the looking, not the one who is seen. Its major importance is therefore to demonstrate what happens when we embrace abjection, for in doing so one also embraces the 'other.' Not all such transformations have an instantly progressive result, as Bedford in *The First Men in the Moon* reveals: 'My mailed hand seemed to go clean through him. He smashed like—like some softish sort of sweet with liquid in it! He broke right in! He squelched and splashed. It was like hitting a damp toadstool . . . I was incredulous that any living thing could be so flimsy' (*FMM*, 95).

This physical and grotesque individual transformation of the Selenite certainly works to diffuse Bedford's former sense of considered repulsion. Nevertheless, what replaces it reveals a matching fragility in terms of Bedford's own sense of self. In all space fiction, the alien functions, in part, to hold up a mirror to who we are. Once that opposition implodes, we turn back inside ourselves for definition. Bedford's response is, we notice, purely sensory and regressive. Contemplation immediately gives way to the oral pleasures of childhood ('some softish sort of sweet') combined with a similarly childish euphoria—that of the toddler who discovers, for the first time, how easy it is to destroy another's sandcastle. In fact, such childish games epitomise Bedford's relationship with aggression elsewhere, too:

> I seem to remember a kind of stereotyped phrase running though my mind: 'Zone of fire, seek cover!' I know I made a dash for the space between two of the carcasses, and stood there panting and feeling very wicked . . .
>
> I felt an enormous astonishment at the evaporation of the great fight into which I had hurled myself, and not a little of exultation. It did not seem to me that I had discovered the Selenites were unexpectedly flimsy, but that I was unexpectedly strong. I laughed stupidly. This fantastic moon!
>
> I glanced for a moment at the smashed and writhing bodies that were scattered over the cavern floor, with a vague idea of further violence, then hurried on . . . (*FMM*, 112–114, passim)

Wells was frequently praised for the compelling 'otherness' of his fictive environments. As C. S. Lewis said of *The First Men in the Moon*,

> The first glimpse of the unveiled airless sky, the lunar landscape, the lunar levity, the incomparable solitude, then the growing terror, finally the overwhelming approach of the lunar night—it is for these things that the story . . . exists.[60]

In equal measure, however, Wells was criticised for the limitations of his character construction across his oeuvre. There is perhaps always a sense in which the 'other' world, as much as its inhabitants, is the main protagonist in *sf*, and it is primarily when in communication with that presiding otherness that Bedford learns most about himself. In this sense, Wells makes a particular virtue of his adoption of the first person, for this prevents a more coherent 'prepackaged' sense of his character from forming too early, the reader relying entirely on Bedford's relationship with others in making character judgments. Finally, having lost Cavor and fled the Selenites, while suspended halfway between the moon and Earth, Bedford learns he has become a stranger to himself:

> I became, if I may so express it, dissociate from Bedford; I looked down on Bedford as a trivial, incidental thing with which I chanced to be connected. I saw Bedford in many relations—as an ass or as a poor beast, where I had hitherto been inclined to regard him with a quiet pride . . . But at the time the thing was not in the least painful, because I had that extraordinary persuasion that, as a matter of fact, I was no more Bedford than I was any one else, but only a mind floating in the still serenity of space. Why should I be disturbed about this Bedford's shortcomings? I was not responsible for him or them. (*FMM*, 135)

Only once he again feels the pull of the earth's atmosphere can he assert 'that I was quite certainly Bedford after all' (*FMM*, 137), identity being shown to be determined by the precarious maintenance of external boundaries, including that outward projection of foreignness masking an inward sense of cultural dispossession.

'Other' Desires: Homoeroticism and the Feminine

While we have contemplated the role abjection plays in the construction of the self through antipathy (what one is not), what we have not yet considered is the role fantasy writing plays in relation to desire: commonly seen as the articulation, through substitution, of what it is that one lacks. *The First Men in the Moon* is, like so many traditional space fiction narratives, a narrative about competing visions of masculine identity. Though Bedford does make fleeting reference to the existence of Selenites who might be feminine, the action deals only with stereotypically masculine forms of escapism: adventure, experiments with gadgetry, violence, the manufacturing industry. Through having a masculine travelling companion, the need for Bedford to have an encounter with a female 'other' is reduced (as opposed to in *The Time Machine*, where the isolation of the Time Traveller inevitably requires the development of a relationship with Weena, one of the Eloi, in order to enhance the revelation of anthropological issues).

As such, *The First Men in the Moon* falls within a far longer established tradition than merely that of space fiction. As suggested in Chapter 1, science fiction is, in many ways, the twentieth- and twenty-first-century equivalent of the quest myth, and as Hume observes, the common absence of women in this subgenre of writing is part of what she calls a typical 'subtraction and erasure' paradigm.[61] A reader who allows him- or herself to act complicitly with this code will, she claims, employ it to avoid the type of meaningful resolutions in one's own life that precisely depend on the forging and development of personal relations. In other words, though quest narratives obviously have important allegorical applications to all of our everyday lives, the irony is we will refuse to sanction these if we abide too willingly by the internal desire mechanisms within the texts.

What happens, however, when readers refuse to abide so complicitly? For instance, when I read the Lord of the Rings, one of the first questions that came to me was 'Where are all the women?' And though there is close camaraderie between the group of travellers, the abiding emotion of the trilogy is not resolution through the evading of feminine encounters, but a desperate loneliness and isolation, which Sam desperately tries but fails to fill. Sam and Frodo's quest is characterised by profound disquiet from start to finish, and Frodo's inability to forge relationships beyond his quest leads him simply to an early 'offstage' death. This lack of fulfilment is one of the key means by which Tolkien's trilogy departs from populist writing such as the Western genre, another descendent of the heroic tradition. Here, too, we find lone or lonely quests based upon all male conflict and combat, women only fleetingly moving in and out of the narrative as punctuation marks to a more compelling male world. However, these texts tend to privilege resolution, and where that includes death, our hero will usually die centre stage, perhaps even having time for an accompanying dramatic oration.

Like all quest narratives, the Lord of the Rings is a trilogy about desire, but it is a desire continually tainted by loss, the most obvious illustration of which is the story of the disappearance of the Entwives in *Volume II, The Two Towers*. This episode could be read as an allegory for the general schism between the masculine and the feminine in the entire trilogy. As Treebeard tells Merry and Pippin, while the Ents maintained their love for the wilderness, the Entwives yearned for order and cultivation. Moving across the river to till their gardens, the Entwives found cultivation increasingly difficult in the face of Sauron's warring forces and gradually disappeared from view. Treebeard's abiding desire is that they will be found once again, though:

> . . . now the Entwives are only a memory for us, and our beards are long and grey . . . We believe that we may meet again in a time to come, and perhaps we shall find somewhere a land where we can live together and both be content. But it is foreboded that that will only be when we have both lost all that we now have. And it may well be that that time is drawing near at last. (*TT*, 89)

What replaces male/female desire in Tolkien's trilogy is an increasing feminisation of the Sam/Frodo relationship. Looking into Frodo's face as he sleeps, later on in *Volume II, The Two Towers*, Sam's contemplation of it is more characteristic of a long-married wife watching her elderly husband than it is of a travelling companion:

> . . . [his] face was peaceful . . . but it looked old, old and beautiful, as if the chiselling of the shaping years was now revealed in many fine lines that had before been hidden, though the identity of the face was not changed. Not that Sam Gamgee put it that way himself. He shook his head, as if finding words useless, and murmured: 'I love him. He's like that, and sometimes it shines through, somehow. But I love him, whether or no.' (*TT*, 321)

As the general absence of women becomes increasingly marked, the feminisation of Sam's desire for Frodo develops into homoeroticism and, with it, an increasing possessiveness. Hence, though Sam mistrusts Gollum/Sméagol for a variety of reasons, one of them is undoubtedly resentment at having to share Frodo with him. A second resides in the fact that Gollum, who is elsewhere described as one 'who pried into all dark holes' (*TT*, 415), is also suggested to be sexually predatory.

Frodo himself has concerns about Gollum's deviance, as becomes clear when they cross the Dead Marshes in *Volume II, The Two Towers*. Warning them both of the dangers lurking beneath the surface, Gollum's prior knowledge of the terrain implies, he has tried to make 'contact' with the corpses underlying the mere: 'You cannot reach them, you cannot touch them. We tried once, yes, precious . . . Only shapes to see, perhaps, not to touch . . .' (*TT*, 289). In response, Frodo 'looked darkly at him and shuddered . . . thinking that he guessed why Sméagol had tried to touch them' (*TT*, 289). Such inferences give Sam the perfect excuse to develop an increasingly protective relationship with Frodo. So, while Gollum is out of range, Sam insists Frodo should lie in his lap and go to sleep, assuring him that 'no one could come pawing you without your Sam knowing it' (*TT*, 403). We have encountered this word *paw* before: it is used by Pippin and Merry as they shudder at their own recollections of 'rough handling' by the Orcs. Nor are Sam's fears unfounded, for as Gollum returns to find both of them asleep, he cannot stop himself: '[S]lowly putting out a trembling hand, very cautiously he touched Frodo's knee—but almost the touch was a caress' (*TT*, 403).

As if to affirm that Sam's desire for Frodo is no fleeting crush, the second book of *Volume III, The Return of the King* opens with Sam searching for Frodo in the depths of the Orcs' fortress. As he does so, we read that he 'longed only for his master, for one sight of his face or one touch of his hand' (*RK*, 216). Certainly, his persistence is rewarded, for when he finally finds him, Frodo is naked and alone. And yet, as if to prove he is no predatory Gollum, rather than taking sexual advantage, Sam's maternal instincts take over, 'and [Frodo] lay back in Sam's gentle arms, closing his eyes, like a child at rest when night-fears are driven away by some loved voice or hand' (*RK*, 218).

So acute and convincing is the feminised nature of this relationship between Sam and Frodo that, by the end of the trilogy, it takes what can only be seen as a brutal contrivance to sever the bond. This comes in the form of Rosie Cotton, the girl left behind in the Shire, whom Sam suddenly remembers as he returns, though she seems to have slipped his mind for the best part of two and a half volumes. On the one hand, this is a common feature of the quest element of the trilogy, not just in the sense that the returning warrior deserves his 'prize,' but also in the sense that 'There is usually a paradoxical suggestion that by leaving home the hero can return to another better "home."'[62] Nevertheless, that the homosocial bond between the two men is directly challenged by this realisation is made clear in the need to (here, literally) accommodate it *within* the dominant parameters of the Sam/Frodo match and, in the process, rob Sam of the chance of this 'better' home:

> 'When are you going to move in and join me, Sam?
>   Sam looked a bit awkward . . . and he went very red.
>   'It's Rosie, Rose Cotton' . . .
>   'I see,' said Frodo, 'you want to get married, and yet you want to live with me in Bag End, too? But my dear Sam, how easy! . . . There's room enough in Bag End for as big a family as you could wish for.' (*RK*, 369–370)

In fact, the hurried and unpredictable nature of this wedding almost emphasises, rather than dispels, the homoerotic dimension of the Sam/Frodo bond, because it occurs as an obviously contrived means by which Tolkien can assure his readers of the restoration of heterosexual 'normality.' Without this, it would be difficult to assure Tolkien's middle-class readers of the (largely) homophobic 1950s that all could ever again be 'well' in the Shire.

As we have seen, the Lord of the Rings can be read as one response to an inhuman war from a man who had served in the trenches, whose friends and comrades had died in the trenches, and for whom the horror of war was the ultimate monster. Like those men conscripted into battle, the central protagonists of the trilogy are ordinary in their gifts and talents, albeit that they take part in extraordinary events, meet extraordinary characters—villainous and heroic—and return transformed, wounded, and simultaneously magnified in stature, if physiologically impaired. The absence of one's family and of women is part of that legacy, as is the threat to male bonding posed by the women whom they do meet on their travels. For, on the rare occasions women do appear, this is the inevitable result. Take, for instance, the Lady Galadriel, who polarises opinion and whose honour Gimli threatens to fight and die for. From their first encounter with her, the group of travellers are left with a sense of unease mingled uncomfortably with desire:

> 'What did you blush for, Sam?' said Pippin . . .
>
> 'If you want to know, I felt as if I hadn't got nothing on, and I didn't like it. She seemed to be looking inside me . . .'
>
> 'That's funny,' said Merry. 'Almost exactly what I felt myself; only, only well, I don't think I'll say any more,' he ended lamely.
>
> All of them, it seemed, had fared alike . . .
>
> And as for Frodo, he would not speak, though Boromir pressed him with questions. 'She held you long in her gaze, Ring-bearer,' he said.
>
> 'Yes,' said Frodo; 'but whatever came into my mind then I will keep there.' (FR, 469–470)

In this otherwise profoundly sexless narrative, this isolated vision of penetrative desire echoes particularly resonantly. Though it is the Lady Galadriel whose character is called into question by their responses, we are aware that this is merely an outward projection of masculine guilt. 'Woman,' at least as embodied by the Lady Galadriel, takes on an almost talismanic property—not unlike the One Ring itself in her ability to provoke ambivalence of intent in otherwise 'virtuous' men. In essence, the greatest fear she evokes resides in her power to enchant (in the sense both of seduction and of casting a spell). When those such as Sam jump to her defence, a question remains about the wisdom of doing so:

> 'Beautiful she is, sir! Lovely! Sometimes like a great tree in flower, sometimes like a white daffadowndilly, small and slender like. Hard as di'monds, soft as moonlight. Warm as sunlight, cold as frost in the stars. Proud and far-off as a

snow-mountain, and merry as any lass I ever saw with daisies in her hair in springtime. But that's a lot o'nonsense, and all wide of the mark.'

'Then she must be lovely indeed,' said Faramir, 'Perilously fair.'

'I don't know about *perilous* . . . It strikes me that folk takes their peril with them into Lórien, and finds it there because they've brought it. But perhaps you could call her perilous, because she's so strong in herself. You, you could dash yourself to pieces on her, like a ship on a rock; or drownd [sic] yourself, like a hobbit in a river. But neither rock nor river would be to blame. Now Boro————' He stopped and went red in the face. (*TT*, 357)

The irony here, of course, is that it proves to be Sam who 'takes [his] peril with [him]' in his unguarded eulogy of Galadriel. As if to prove Faramir right, it leads him to confess the nature of Frodo and Boromir's rivalry, and perhaps it is also through such elven enchantment that Frodo, though present here, has otherwise inexplicably 'fallen deep into his own thoughts for a while, and came out of them suddenly and too late' (*TT*, 357).

Though she is beautiful, it is the strangely mellifluous cadence of the Lady's voice that is most often stressed. When we first encounter her, it is described as 'clear and musical, but deeper than woman's wont' (*FR*, 466), and even when silent it is as if the absence of that voice is a presence in itself: 'with that word she held them with her eyes, and in silence looked searchingly at each of them in turn' (*FR*, 468). As they leave Lórien, Frodo is conscious of her singing as they go: 'But now she sang in the ancient tongue of the Elves beyond the Sea, and he did not understand the words: fair was the music, but it did not comfort him' (*FR*, 495–496). Mingled, then, is a powerful sense of danger ravelled in a complex knot of loss. But, where these travellers refuse to acknowledge anything threatening about her, the potential 'danger' of this siren presence is voiced more strongly by others on several occasions.

For instance, despite her beauty, the Lady Galadriel is directly or implicitly set up as a nemesis for the monstrous Shelob, firstly in the Orcs' nickname for the latter, 'Her Ladyship,' and secondly in the manner in which Galadriel's description, in Éomer's eyes, at the start of *Volume II*, *The Two Towers*, prophesies Shelob's appearance towards the end of it: 'Then there is a Lady in the Golden Wood, as old tales tell! . . . Few escape her nets, they say . . . But if you have her favour, then you also are net-weavers and sorcerers, maybe' (*TT*, 30). Ironically, therefore, as Sam and Frodo are faced by Shelob in her lair, their only hope of escape is to outdo her monstrous potency by fighting fire with fire:

> The bubbling hiss drew nearer, and there was a creaking as of some great jointed thing that moved with slow purpose in the dark. A reek came on before it. 'Master, master!' cried Sam . . . 'The Lady's gift! The star-glass!' . . . 'Galadriel!' [Frodo] called, and gathering his courage he lifted up the Phial once more. The eyes halted . . . Then Frodo's heart flamed within him . . . [and] holding the star aloft and the bright sword advanced, Frodo, hobbit of the Shire, walked steadily down to meet the eyes. (*FR*, 410–412 passim)

The stereotypically perceived connection between female charms, enchantment, and a specific form of 'beautiful monstrosity' renders woman the most monstrous of all fantasy villains. In *Frankenstein*, for instance, though it is the male monster that seemingly bears the brunt of his creator's fear and hatred, it is the idea of creating a female counterpart that Victor simply cannot bear. So much is this the case that he aborts the 'girl-child' he has embarked upon, fleeing from and then returning to that scene of carnage in order to witness 'The remains of the half-finished creature . . . scattered on the floor . . . as if I had mangled the living flesh of a human being' (*F*, 215). Similarly, in *Beowulf*, though it is Grendel who is couched in the role of the monstrous other, it is Grendel's mother who forms the epitome of evil personified, being described variously as 'a ghoul, drooling at her feast of flesh and blood,' a 'wandering, murderous monster,' a 'sea-monster' and a being 'vindictive [and] fiercely ravenous for blood.' In these varying and shape-shifting descriptions, two constants remain: her fascination for blood and her own determination (which any mother would share) to avenge the death of her son.[63] In essence, then, what the Beowulf poet draws attention to here is how 'familiar' such maternal monstrosity is to this world of men. The Lord of the Rings is not so very different in its treatment of female monstrosity except for the fact that Shelob is 'clever': she has learnt that survival requires her to 'go underground,' and, whereas the Orcs are slaves to the master Saruman (much as the monster becomes the slave to Frankenstein), 'Her Ladyship' Shelob 'served none but herself' (*TT*, 414).

According to the film critic Barbara Creed, the preponderance of female monsters or monstrous women in cinema testifies to a patriarchy 'haunted' by powerful women. And though this may manifest itself in the many faces of an archetype that spans the vampire, the witch, and 'the woman as possessed body,' it is when related to 'her mothering and reproductive functions' that such monstrosity finds its epitome.[64] As fantasy monsters go, the spider is one of the most archetypally feminine and equally archetypally associated with monstrous and cannibalistic mothering.[65] Shelob is certainly arachnid in form, and yet, like all 'good' monsters, she is more shape-shifting than that species identity may suggest:

> Most like a spider . . . but huger than the great hunting beasts . . . great horns she had, and behind her short stalk-like neck was her huge swollen body, a vast bloated bag, swaying and sagging between her legs; its great bulk was black, blotched with livid marks, but the belly underneath was pale and luminous and gave forth a stench. Her legs were bent, with great knobbed joints high above her back, and hairs that stuck out like steel spines, and at each leg's end there was a claw. (*TT*, 417)

In the bodily markings identified here, which, with their 'black, blotched . . . livid marks' imply disease even if they are simply superficial hues of pigment, we can see that it is the lower body that is associated most clearly with a kind of putrifying abjection. In the case of such monsters as these, Creed argues for a kind of fascinated response from the reader:

> . . . On the one hand . . . they fill the subject—both the protagonist in the text and the spectator in the cinema [or, in our case, the reader of the book]—with disgust and loathing. On the other hand they also point back to a time when a 'fusion between mother and nature' existed; when

bodily wastes, while set apart from the body, were not seen as objects of embarrassment and shame.[66]

It is difficult, at first glance, to consider how the presence of Shelob testifies to our own sense of a lost mother. Certainly, however, it might testify to the evident absence of any sense of mothering in the text. Physical intimacy between men—either in Sam's overly protective fascination with Frodo, or in the hand-to-hand combat of the battle scenes, or in that filthy 'pawing' of the Orcs— replaces the meaningful intimacy of the mother-child bond. What Sam might come face-to-face with, therefore, in the guise of his horror of Shelob, is the horror he has of female intimacy in general. Significantly, it is as she fells Frodo that, as far as Sam is concerned, her hideous abjection reaches its peak and must be avenged:

> She yielded to [Sam's knife-]stroke, and then heaved up the great bag of her belly high above Sam's head. Poison frothed and bubbled from the wound. Now splaying her legs she drove her huge bulk down on him again . . .
> Sam had fallen to his knees by Frodo's head, his senses reeling in the foul stench . . . (*TT*, 421)

No reader can miss the fact that the source of the 'foul stench' here derives from the 'splaying' of the legs, itself a slur against the sexual woman. The sexual dimension of Sam's own motivations is implied in the narrator's comparison between him and a 'desperate small creature armed with little teeth, alone, [who] spring[s] upon a tower of horn and hide that stands above *its fallen mate*' (*TT*, 420; my emphasis). Phallic potency (even if, as here, diminished to the level of 'little teeth') must come out on top, and Sam knows 'it's what you do with it that counts.' So, as the monstrous feminine bears down on Sam, something he has already called 'horrible beyond the horror of an evil dream' (*TT*, 417), he penetrates the orifice in her lower belly right up to the hilt.

We have seen that, in *Powers of Horror*, Kristeva claims we unconsciously associate those aspects of the 'foreign' we most fear in those elements of our bodies we consider to be waste: 'The body's inside . . . shows up in order to compensate for the collapse of the border between inside and outside. It is as if the skin, a fragile container, no longer guaranteed the integrity of one's 'own and clean self' but . . . gave way before the dejection of its contents.'[67] For men, Kristeva argues, never is this more apparent than in their fearfully desirous relation to the all-consuming mother, whose excesses they continue to sublimate in confrontations with the 'other.' So 'man, frightened, crosses over the horrors of maternal bowels,' but only in order to 'immers[e]' himself within 'the bad object that inhabits the maternal body.'[68] One of the most grotesque aspects of Shelob is that we learn she 'drink[s] the blood of Elves and Men, bloated and grown fat with endless brooding on her feasts' (*TT*, 414). A number of grotesque associations cluster around this image. The first is parasitism: like the louse, her body is a bag full of blood, sucked directly from the body of another. The second is demonic: she is vampiric in her desire to suck and, in a trilogy in which blood and the sacrament are frequently connected, she 'takes and eats' in order to drain life rather than give it. The third, connected with sucking, is an explicit articulation of her role as the bad mother. Note the wordplay of the phrase 'brooding on feasts,' which, in part by using the word *brooding* (suggestive of a *brood*), also evokes the echo 'feeding on breasts.'

Mothers and Mirrors: Harry Potter

Rowling's Harry Potter series takes, as one of its central preoccupations, the manner in which desire is initially shaped in relation to our experiences of good and bad parenting. So the treatment of basic familial structures in the series is more typical of nineteenth-century rather than contemporary fiction. Like Pip or Oliver Twist, Harry Potter is an orphan who is brought up by bad surrogate parents, in the form of Vernon and Petunia Dursley (his maternal aunt), and tormented by their grotesque son, Dudley. Amalgamating that traditional, canonical British narrative of childhood with another, popular twentieth-century mode, the boarding school story as perfected by Enid Blyton in the St. Clare's (1941–45) and Malory Towers (1946–51) series, the original element of J. K. Rowling's work lies in her use of magic. And yet, though original, this again returns us to an earlier convention of children's writing: the traditional fairy tale in which children oppressed by hostile or forbidding environments are saved by fairy godmothers and, in the process, stamped with that icon of special status only a parent can normally endow upon his or her child. Harry is saved in precisely this manner, though perhaps his 'fairy godmother' is rather less than conventional:

> The door was hit with such force that it swung clean off its hinges and with a deafening crash landed flat on the floor.
>
> A giant of a man was standing in the doorway. His face was almost completely hidden by a long, shaggy mane of hair and a wild, tangled beard, but you could make out his eyes glinting like black beetles under all the hair.
>
> The giant squeezed his way into the hut . . . bent down, picked up the door and fitted it easily back into its frame . . .
>
> 'Couldn't make us a cup o' tea, could yeh? It's not been an easy journey . . .'[69]

Though aimed at children, Harry Potter involves a philosophical and emotional complexity more typical of adult Gothic. It is, overall, a series about melancholia—hence desire always returns us to loss—and, through the Gothic environment of Hogwarts school, it also becomes a series about haunting and the manner in which we remain driven by the traumas we try but fail to leave behind. As such, it contains a number of the elements of adult fantasy narratives we have already identified elsewhere in this book, including its use of enchanted mirrors. At times these mirrors take on a relatively complex philosophical dimension, one of the most intriguing of which is the pensieve Harry finds in the office of the headmaster, Professor Albus Dumbledore, in *Volume IV, Harry Potter and the Goblet of Fire* (2000), an object sharing similar characteristics to Tolkien's Mirror of Galadriel.

As the word *pensieve* implies, this is a mirror retaining the same wordplay on cognitive reflection inherent in any mirrored surface, but here with a twist deriving from a sieve's permeability. As Harry spies the basin, he is aware that he is looking at something with which he should not interfere, but curiosity gets the better of him:

> He could not tell whether the substance was liquid or gas. It was a bright, whitish silver, and it was moving ceaselessly . . .

> He wanted to touch it . . . but nearly four years' experi-
> ence of the magical world told him that sticking his hand
> into a bowl full of some unknown substance was a very stu-
> pid thing to do . . .
>
> Harry bent closer . . . The silvery substance had become
> transparent; it looked like glass. He looked down into it,
> expecting to see the stone bottom of the basin—and saw
> instead an enormous room into which he seemed to be
> looking through a circular window in the ceiling.
>
> . . . Lowering his face so that his nose was a mere inch
> away from the glassy substance, Harry saw that rows and
> rows of witches and wizards were sat around every wall . . .
> An empty chair stood in the very centre of the room. There
> was something about the chair that gave Harry an ominous
> feeling . . . [70]

As Harry peers even closer, the tip of his nose touches the 'mirror'
and instantly he is thrown through it into the alternative reality he
perceives. In the process, he answers, through action, the implicit
question that remains unanswered (through inaction) in Lord of
the Rings, for in Tolkien's narrative each gazer heeds the Lady
Galadriel's reiterated warning: 'Do not touch the water!' (FR, 475).

One difference, however, between these two scenes is the nature
of the substance in the bowl in each case. In the mirror of Galadriel,
the basin is filled with pure stream water, whereas Dumbledore's
pensieve is filled with a kind of ectoplasmic substance resembling
strands of hair but turning out to be thoughts in material form (the
metaphorical connection between hair and thoughts presumably
lying in phrases such as 'losing the thread of what I was saying'). So
it takes on the abject connotations of offal or 'brain matter,' a feature that becomes more repulsive in *Volume V, The Order of the
Phoenix*, when Professor Snape, the sinister Potions Master, who has
been charged with giving Harry extra lessons in Occlumency ('The
magical defence of the mind against external penetration'[71]),
employs a pensieve to remove the thoughts he wishes to conceal
from Harry during the lesson. As Snape places a wand to the roots
of his notoriously greasy hair and withdraws the 'silvery substance
. . . like a thick gossamer strand' (HPOP, 471) it is the grease that
stays with us, not the reference to (flower-fairy) gossamer.

In scenes such as those employing the pensieve, we find desire taking on a contemplative, intellectual quality in a highly controlled manner (even if Harry does find himself 'pitched headfirst' [*HPGF*, 508] into and through it when his nose touches its surface). This aspect of them is reminiscent of the medieval dream vision structure discussed in Chapter 3, for it is only through Harry's encounter with this substance and the vision he finds on the other side of the surface that he is endowed with a heightened perspective on events. This is unusual, however, and, in the first and far more characteristic instance of mirror imagery in *Volume I, Harry Potter and the Philosopher's Stone* (1997), we find the Mirror of Erised (think backwards) and a different kind of 'take' on the Mirror of Galadriel. We recall that, in Tolkien's trilogy, the Lady cautions the travellers thus: 'many things I can command the Mirror to reveal . . . But the Mirror will also show things unbidden, and those are often strange and more profitable than things which we wish to behold' (*FR*, 475). In Harry Potter, the Mirror of Erised promises much: '*Erised stra ehru oyt ube cafru oyt on wohsi*' ('*I show not your face but your heart's desire*' [*HPPS*, 152]), but rather like Galadriel's cautionary words, our 'heart's desire' may carry a darker echo.

Harry's encounter with the Mirror of Erised occurs at night, while he is hiding from Snape and Filch the caretaker. Concealed by one of his treasures, the invisibility cloak he inherited from his dead father, Harry slips into an adjoining room to allow them to pass. It is here, where he believes himself to be both alone and undetectable, that the mirror reveals the falsity of these assumptions. Glancing at the mirror with the playful anticipation of both seeing and not seeing his own image,

> He had to clap his hands to his mouth to stop himself screaming. He whirled around. His heart was pounding . . . for he had seen not only himself in the mirror, but a whole crowd of people standing right behind him.
> But the room was empty . . .
> He looked in the mirror again. A woman standing right behind his reflection was smiling at him and waving. He reached out a hand and felt the air behind him. If she really was there, he'd touch her, their reflections were so close

> together, but he felt only air—she and the others existed
> only in the mirror . . .
>   Harry was so close to the mirror now that his nose was
> nearly touching that of his reflection.
>   'Mum?' he whispered. 'Dad?' . . .
>   . . . He had a powerful kind of ache inside him, half joy,
> half terrible sadness. (*HPPS*, 153)

This is the first of many occasions in the series when Harry comes
face to face with his dead parents, but in this case what the mirror
specifically achieves is to remind us that this image is 'ghosted' in a
dual sense. Where the reflections perpetually emphasise the manner in which these 'echoes' resemble Harry, they approach the status of a 'ghosted' image (as on a television screen). What Rowling
achieves time and again is to provoke, perhaps particularly in adult
readers, the genuinely profound sense of longing such images inspire
in Harry.[72]

So powerful are these instances of melancholic ghosting that we
long, with him, for what Harry can never have: a true reuniting with
his mother and father. Those who, like me, are reading Harry Potter
before Rowling completes the series as a whole find themselves
willing her to satisfy Harry's needs in the final volume. Using the
philosophical basis set up within the first five volumes currently
available, it is clear that any such ending relies, absolutely, on some
form of beyond-death reincarnation. Haunting, in a traditional
sense, is ruled out in *Volume V, Harry Potter and the Order of the
Phoenix* (2003), for, following the death of Sirius Black (Harry's substitute father), Harry accosts Headless Nick, one of the spectres
haunting Hogwarts, and demands to know the likelihood of Sirius
returning. As a means of prolonging readerly desire for resolution,
on each occasion when Harry's hopes are raised on this subject, various well-meaning characters crush them in turn. Usually, this role
falls to Albus Dumbledore, but here it is given to Headless Nick,
who cautions Harry in terms that again evoke melancholia: 'Wizards
can leave an imprint of themselves upon the earth, to walk palely
where their living selves once trod . . . But very few wizards choose
that path . . . [Sirius] will not come back . . . He will have . . .
gone on' (*HPOP*, 758–759).

If haunting offers no positive answer, however, one alternative possibility is explored in *Volume III, Harry Potter and the Prisoner of Azkaban* and is again prompted by the desire to save Sirius—this time from the threat of the dementors' kiss. Hermione, the class swot and one of Harry's two best friends, has taken lessons enabling her to effect time travel in order to attend two different classes at once, and it is suggested to her, by Dumbledore, that she might surreptitiously employ the technique to alter the 'fate worse than death' that has otherwise already befallen Sirius. However, where, in Wells's *The Time Machine*, the Time Traveller employs a machine comprising two levers (one effecting progress, the other regress, and a seat whereon one sits astride), Hermione employs 'a tiny, sparkling hour-glass' pendant from a very long chain about her neck (*HPPA*, 288). Also, where Wells's Time Traveller disappears into another room and makes a solitary sojourn into time, Hermione throws the chain about both Harry's and her own necks so that they might journey together. The results, nevertheless, are closely comparable. Where the Time Traveller experiences an 'excessively unpleasant [sensation] . . . of a helpless headlong motion . . . [and] the same horrible anticipation, too, of an imminent smash . . . [he] had a dim impression of scaffolding, but . . . was already going too fast to be conscious of any moving things' (*TM*, 17), Harry experiences 'the sensation that he was flying, very fast, backwards. A blur of colours and shapes rushed past him . . . He tried to yell but couldn't hear his own voice—' (HPPA, 288).

The question is whether the underlying narrative motivation for the time travel is the same in *sf* novels such as *The Time Machine* as it is in supernatural/magical fantasy. At face value, it appears not: in *The Time Machine*, the Time Traveller is a very self-contained man whose motivations appear to fasten upon a desire to *elongate* the real, hence the extension of the narrative present into the future. In Harry Potter, the central character is physically branded with an involuntary mark of specialness in response to which his desire is to retreat into *reduction*: ' "I DON'T CARE!" Harry yelled . . . "I'VE HAD ENOUGH, I'VE SEEN ENOUGH, I WANT OUT, I WANT IT TO END, I DON'T CARE ANY MORE—" '(*HPOP*, 726). By association, and as we will discuss in more detail in Chapter 5, Harry Potter eschews futurism (including its technologies) at all costs and replaces it with atavistic visions of the past, complete with Latinisms.

This broader cultural retreat into the past is, however, the backdrop to a more specific piece of time travel for which Harry most longs and that is most clearly denied him: reunion with both dead parents. Twisted in relation to this desire, what replaces his dream is a kind of Gothic horror scene: their murder replayed on an endless loop, which, in psychoanalytic terms, can be read as a kind of distorted originary phantasy. According to Freud, the originary phantasy is an imprint made upon an infant by unwitting and incomprehending exposure to the parental sex act. This image, which the infant misinterprets as the father's 'attack' upon the mother, a violent assault, imprints upon the infant's unconscious an inherent desire to protect and desire the mother and reject the father as a violent rival, coupled with a simultaneous awareness of the child's own impotence to effect either act. In every case when this originary phantasy is evoked as a kind of 'trace memory' in Harry Potter (and only the most traumatic incidents have this effect upon him), what Harry always hears in his mind is his mother 'screaming, terrible, terrified, pleading screams. He wanted to help [her], he tried to move his arms, but couldn't . . .' (*HPPA*, 66). Also accompanying these horrors, at times, is a similarly infantile regressive fixation upon the oral drive, which, in the absence of the mother, cannot be assuaged: 'He felt drained and strangely empty, even though he was so full of chocolate' (*HPPA*, 180).

In contrast to Tolkien's Lord of the Rings trilogy, as we progress through the Harry Potter series the potency of maternal desire becomes ever stronger. In *Volume V, Harry Potter and the Order of the Phoenix*, Dumbledore informs Harry that what makes him so invincible, even to Lord Voldemort, is the power of his mother's love for him, a potency that Rowling invests with an especial 'magic.' This, the headmaster explains, is why he delivered Harry into the hands of the Dursleys, despite his realisation that their treatment of the boy might prove less than satisfactory:

> . . . I knew . . . where Voldemort was weak . . . You would be protected by an ancient magic of which he knows, which he despises, and which he has always, therefore, underesti-

mated—to his cost. I am speaking, of course of the fact that your mother died to save you. She gave you a lingering protection he never expected, a protection that flows in your veins to this day. I put my trust, therefore, in your mother's blood. I delivered you to her sister, her only remaining relative. (*HPOP*, 736)

Here we have an impressive antidote to the Beowulf poet's, Shelley's, and Tolkien's monstrous maternity, though notice that it again comes down to that key abject fluid, mother's blood. Rowling's identity, not only as a woman but also as a relatively recent mother, might lead us to expect her to valorise motherhood more than Tolkien does, though it does not, of course, explain Mary Shelley's own self-destructive treatment of the theme in *Frankenstein*. Nevertheless, this is not the only view of motherhood on offer in Harry Potter and, in the same volume, not only does Ron's mother (and part maternal substitute in Harry's mind) slip from her former reified status, becoming hectoring, fussy, and overly critical, but we also have the Gothic vision of Sirius's mother to contend with in Number 12 Grimmauld ('Grim Old') Place:

> For a split second, Harry thought he was looking through a window . . . behind which an old woman in a black cap was screaming and screaming . . . then he realised it was simply a life-sized portrait, but the most realistic, and the most unpleasant, he had ever seen in his life.
> The old woman was drooling, her eyes were rolling, the yellowing skin of her face stretched taut as she screamed . . . (*HPOP*, 74)

Where Harry's mother is his adored other, Sirius's mother is her son's greatest enemy. Not satisfied with spurning her own son, she inflicts a double sense of punishment upon him, 'put[ting] a Permanent Sticking Charm on the back of the canvas' (*HPOP*, 76) to prevent him from ridding himself of her. In the vision offered of 12 Grimmauld Place, with its need for decontamination in order to make it once again habitable and rid it of the various infestations of magical species and supernatural monsters that have settled in following Sirius's mother's death a decade ago, we have more than an individual instance of a kind of living crypt. According to Jan Relf, this is the typical environment of the 'terrible mother, who presides over a dreadful, claustrophobic nursery world for which nostalgia and idealization are clearly inappropriate terms.'[73] Much as Mrs. Weasley sets out to purge this House of Black, so Relf calls on us to look for transformative possibilities in our own readings of the maternal, whereby we can create 'a shape-shifting, disorderly house . . . in which . . . much "work need[s] to be done" to make it "habitable," but which nevertheless is "full of possibilities, or alternatives."'[74] In turning, now, to some of the main subgenres of fantasy writing, we will begin with that drive for what Relf calls 'the Good Breast,' 'the authentically utopian impulse.'[75]

Notes

1. At the time of writing, only five of the projected seven volumes in the Harry Potter series have been published.

2. This was the consensus of several independent polls, including a collaborative poll in 1996 between Waterstone's, the British bookseller, and the BBC Channel 4 programme *Book Choice*; a second poll in the *Daily Telegraph* newspaper in the same year; a third by the Folio Society, also in 1996; and a fourth, in 1997, for the British television programme *Bookworm*. For a fuller account, see Tom Shippey, *J. R. R. Tolkien: Author of the Century* (London: HarperCollins, 2001), xx–xxii.

3. Rosemary Jackson, *Fantasy: The Literature of Subversion* (London: Routledge, 1981).

4. Lewis Carroll, 'Alice in Wonderland,' in *The Annotated Alice*, Martin Gardner, ed. (Harmondsworth: Penguin, 1970), 17–164 (p. 134). Further quotations from this story will be referenced within the main body of the text, accompanied by the abbreviation *AW*.

5. Lewis Carroll, 'Through the Looking-Glass and What Alice Found There,' in *The Annotated Alice*, Martin Gardner, ed. (Harmondsworth: Penguin, 1970), 165–345 (p. 191). Further quotations from this story will be referenced within the main body of the text, accompanied by the abbreviation *LG*.

6. Jean-Jacques Lecercle, *Philosophy of Nonsense: The Intuitions of Victorian Nonsense Literature* (London: Routledge, 1994), 203.

7. Susan Stewart, *On Longing: Narratives of the Miniature, the Gigantic, the Souvenir, the Collection* (Durham, NC: Duke University Press, 1993), 182–183.

8. John Tenniel based his illustrations of Alice on a photograph of one of Dodgson's child subjects. By the time *Alice in Wonderland* came to publication, Dodgson's schism with the Liddell household had already taken place.

Consequently, the photograph Tenniel was sent was not one of Alice Liddell, but of 'the waspish-looking' Mary Hilton Badcock, a subject whom Hendrik van Leeuwen refers to as 'a mixture of an imp and a finely dressed doll,' whose face is characterised by a paradoxical sullenness combined with 'its pout and . . . doll's eyes . . . It allures us and yet keeps its distance at the same time' (Hendrik van Leeuwen, 'The Liaison of Visual and Written Nonsense' in *Explorations in the Field of Nonsense*, Wim Tigges, ed. (Amsterdam: Rodopi, 1987), 61–96 (p. 69).

9. J. R. R. Tolkien, 'On Fairy-Stories,' in *Tree and Leaf* (London: HarperCollins, 2001), 1–81 (p. 39).

10. Vivien Noakes, *Edward Lear 1812–1888: The Catalogue of the Royal Academy of Arts Exhibition (1985)*, 14. Cited in *Edward Lear: The Complete Verse and Other Nonsense*, Vivien Noakes, ed. (Harmondsworth: Penguin, 2001), xxiii. All further quotations from this volume will be referenced within the main body of the text, accompanied by the abbreviation *EL*.

11. Lecercle, *Philosophy of Nonsense*, 20.

12. Lecercle, *Philosophy of Nonsense*, 202.

13. John Lehmann, *Edward Lear and His World* (London: Thames and Hudson, 1977), 62.

14. Lecercle, *Philosophy of Nonsense*, 184.

15. Lecercle, *Philosophy of Nonsense*, 221–222.

16. Lecercle, *Philosophy of Nonsense*, 56.

17. Lecercle, *Philosophy of Nonsense*, 42.

18. Lecercle, *Philosophy of Nonsense*, 72.

19. Verlyn Flieger, *A Question of Time: J. R. R. Tolkien's Road to Faerie* (Kent, OH: Kent State University Press, 1997), 88.

20. J. R. R. Tolkien, *The Lord of the Rings, Volume I: The Fellowship of the Ring* (London: HarperCollins, 1999), 12. Further quotations from this novel will be referenced within the main body of the text, accompanied by the abbreviation *FR*.

21. Louis Marin, 'The Frontiers of Utopia,' in *Utopias and the Millennium*, Krishan Kumar and Stephen Bann, eds. (London: Reaktion Books, 1993) 7–16 (p. 13).

22. George Orwell, *Animal Farm* (1945; Harmondsworth: Penguin, 1951), 19; my emphasis.

23. Jonathan Swift, *Gulliver's Travels* (1726; Harmondsworth: Penguin, 2001), 30. Robert Demaria, Jr., editor of this edition notes that 'half a stang' equates with a quarter of an acre (p. 276n).

24. Stewart, *On Longing*, 37 and 38.

25. J. R. R. Tolkien, *The Lord of the Rings, Volume II: The Two Towers* (London: HarperCollins, 1999), 398–399. Further quotations from this novel will be referenced within the main body of the text, accompanied by the abbreviation *TT*.

26. J. R. R. Tolkien, *The Lord of the Rings, Volume III: The Return of the King* (London: HarperCollins, 1999), 22–23. Further quotations from this novel will be referenced within the main body of the text, accompanied by the abbreviation *RK*.

27. Angus Fletcher, *Allegory: The Theory of a Symbolic Mode* (Ithaca: Cornell University Press, 1964), 253.

28. Ibid.

29. Stewart, *On Longing*, 147.

30. Sigmund Freud, 'Mourning and Melancholia,' in *The Standard Edition of the Complete Psychological Works of Sigmund Freud, Vol. 14, On the History of the Psycho-Analytic Movement, Papers on Metapsychology, and Other Works*, James Strachey, ed., in collaboration with Anna Freud (London: Hogarth Press, 1957), 237–258 (pp. 243–244, 245, and 246 respectively).

31. Maureen Duffy, *The Erotic World of Faery* (London: Hodder and Staughton, 1972), 312.

32. Flieger, *A Question of Time*, 7.

33. Lewis Spence, *The Fairy Tradition in Britain* (London: Rider and Company, 1948), 116.

34. Flieger, *A Question of Time*, 97

35. Compare Dorian's view of his own painted image: 'Morning after morning he had sat before the portrait wondering at its beauty . . . Was it to alter now with every mood to which he yielded? Was it to become a monstrous and loathsome thing . . . ?' Oscar Wilde, *The Picture of Dorian Gray* (1891; Oxford: Oxford University Press, 1974), 105.

36. Fletcher, *Allegory*, 160.

37. Mary Shelley, *Frankenstein, Or, the Modern Prometheus* (1818; Harmondsworth: Penguin, 1985), 55.

38. Mark Philpott, 'Haunting the Middle Ages,' in *Writing and Fantasy*, Ceri Sullivan and Barbara White, eds. (London: Longman, 1999), 48–61 (p. 53).

39. Anne K. Mellor, *Mary Shelley: Her Life, Her Fiction, Her Monsters* (New York: Routledge, 1989), 40.

40. Fletcher, *Allegory*, 42–43.

41. Fletcher, *Allegory*, 43.

42. Kathryn Hume, *Fantasy and Mimesis: Responses to Reality in Western Literature* (New York: Methuen, 1984), 67.

43. Franco Moretti, 'Dialectic of Fear,' in *Signs Taken for Wonders: Essays in the Sociology of Literary Forms* (London: Verso, 1983), 83–108 (p. 84).

44. William Blake, 'Jerusalem' (1804–10): 'And did the Countenance Divine / Shine forth upon our clouded hills? / And was Jerusalem builded here, / Among those dark Satanic Mills.'

45. Moretti, 'Dialectic of Fear,' 84–85.

46. Moretti, 'Dialectic of Fear,' 90.

47. Moretti, 'Dialectic of Fear,' 91.

48. Ibid.

49. Carole G. Silver, *Strange and Secret Peoples: Fairies and Victorian Consciousness* (New York: Oxford University Press, 1999), 117.

50. Ibid.

51. Moretti, 'Dialectic of Fear,' 87–88.

52. Hume, *Fantasy and Mimesis*, 47.

53. J. K. Rowling, *Volume III, Harry Potter and the Prisoner of Azkaban* (London: Bloomsbury, 1999), 65–66. Further quotations from this novel will be referenced within the main body of the text, accompanied by the abbreviation *HPPA*.

54. Meredith Skura. *The Literary Use of the Psychoanalytic Process* (New Haven, CT: Yale University Press, 1981), 105 and 104.

55. Julia Kristeva, *Powers of Horror: An Essay in Abjection* (New York: Columbia University Press, 1982), 3.

56. H. G. Wells, *The First Men in the Moon* (1901; London: J. M. Dent, 1993), 56. Further quotations from this novel will be referenced within the main body of the text, accompanied by the abbreviation *FMM*.

57. H. G. Wells, *The Time Machine* (1895; London: J. M. Dent, 1995), 33. Further quotations from this novel will be referenced within the main body of the text, accompanied by the abbreviation, *TM*.

58. Kristeva, *Powers of Horror*, 2–3.

59. Mary Russo, *The Female Grotesque: Risk, Excess and Modernity* (New York: Routledge, 1994), 78.

60. C. S. Lewis, 'On Science Fiction,' in *Of This and Other Worlds*, Walter Hooper, ed. (London: Collins, 1982), 80–96 (p. 86).

61. Hume, *Fantasy and Mimesis*, 92.

62. Fletcher, *Allegory*, 151.

63. 'Beowulf,' in *The Anglo-Saxon World: An Anthology*, Kevin Crossley-Holland, ed. and trans. (Oxford: Oxford University Press, 1984), 69–154 (pp. 107, 112, and 111 respectively).

64. Barbara Creed, *The Monstrous Feminine: Film, Feminism, Psychoanalysis* (London: Routledge, 1993), 1 and 7.

65. This figurative identification does, in part, have a 'natural' origin. Spiders are carnivorous, the female of the species such as the black widow spider or certain subspecies of tarantula being known to consume the male after mating and the infant offspring of some species consuming the weaker young.

66. Creed, *The Monstrous Feminine*, 13.

67. Kristeva, *Powers of Horror*, 53.

68. Kristeva, *Powers of Horror*, 53–54.

69. J. K. Rowling, *Volume I, Harry Potter and the Philosopher's Stone* (London: Bloomsbury, 1997), 39. Further quotations from this novel will be referenced within the main body of the text, accompanied by the abbreviation *HPPS*.

70. J. K. Rowling, *Volume IV, Harry Potter and the Goblet of Fire* (London: Bloomsbury, 2000), 507. Further quotations from this novel will be referenced within the main body of the text, accompanied by the abbreviation *HPGF*.

71. J. K. Rowling, *Volume V, Harry Potter and the Order of the Phoenix* (London: Bloomsbury, 2003), 458. Further quotations from this novel will be referenced within the main body of the text, accompanied by the abbreviation *HPOP*.

72. Interestingly, if my nieces' views are typical, children are far more emotionally affected by the death of Sirius Black in Volume V than by Harry's feelings for his dead parents, taking the philosophical view that he cannot miss 'what he has never known.'

73. Jan Relf, 'Utopia the Good Breast: Coming Home to Mother,' in *Utopias and the Millennium*, Krishan Kumar and Stephen Bann, eds. (London: Reaktion Books, 1993), 107–128 (p. 123).

74. Relf, 'Utopia the Good Breast,' 124.

75. Relf, 'Utopia the Good Breast,' 128.

Chapter Five

The Utopia as an Underlying Feature of All Major Modes of Fantasy

Utopia (1516)

Gulliver's Travels (1726)

A Connecticut Yankee at King Arthur's Court (1889)

The Time Machine (1895)

The First Men in the Moon (1901)

Herland (1915)

Animal Farm (1945)

Neuromancer (1984)

The Harry Potter books (1997–2003)

The PowerBook (2000)

Life of Pi (2002)

Introduction

Where the previous chapter examined a range of texts in detail as exemplars of some of the best that fantasy writing has to offer, here we take a single urge or impulse within fantasy writing more generally, namely the utopia, and examine what happens to it over time. It seems to me that the utopian impulse—the desire to go 'beyond'—underlies all fantasy writing, even, paradoxically, of the darkest kind. In fact, Louis Marin goes further, reminding us there is something intrinsically utopian in the act of *all* writing: 'All narrative is a space narrative . . . All narrative is a travel narrative; all travel consists in going from a place to a no-place, a route to U-topia.'[1] On this journey, then, from 'place to no-place,' we will examine a variety of different modes of fantasy writing on the way, beginning with the classic utopia before moving on to examine allegory, space fiction, fairylore, the ghost story, animal fable, magic, and cyberpunk. In the process, we cross the space of four centuries and plot a path from Thomas More's *Utopia* (1516) to William Gibson's *Neuromancer* (1984). I have long deemed the desire to subclassify fantasy into different boxes to be anathema to the texts' innate creativity. What this chapter sets out to show, therefore, is the affinity these texts share (despite their obvious differences in style, content, and setting) as one single continuum of fantasy writing.

Thomas More, *Utopia*

Like most types of fantasy writing, utopia can be traced back to classical antiquity. Paul Turner identifies utopian trappings in the various versions of originary paradise constructed by differing cultures, as well as in the Elysian Fields of Homer's *Odyssey* and, in its political aspect, in Plato's *Republic*.[2] In the modern age, however, the 'father' of the utopia is typically identified as being Sir Thomas More, whose own work *Utopia* gave the name to this mode of writing. The word *utopia* itself is originally taken from the Greek *ou-topia* ('non-place'), put through a connotative shift to incorporate a celebratory dynamic, *eu-topia* ('good place').[3] In that semantic impulse to reach beyond the horizon, we are instantly in the world of fantasy and, in so being, it is no surprise that the majority of subsequent utopias (if not More's itself) are written employing the trappings of fantasy.

Angelika Bammer's definition of utopia is as succinct and compelling as any: 'A utopia is the fictional representation of an ideal polity. It is political in nature, narrative in form, *literary only in part*.'[4] That final, potentially damning last clause suggests that the literary quality of utopian writing must always, to some extent, become compromised by the communication of ideas, which ultimately are given precedence in the work. In essence, a utopia critiques the society in which we live, for in suggesting that the ideal lies elsewhere one is, by inference, already casting negative judgement upon the 'here and now.' Because of this, a utopian writer is typically anti-establishment and usually has subversive intent. Both of these characteristics are, to a surprising degree, in evidence in More's *Utopia*, a feature that made More's presence at court in real life already potentially controversial, despite the apparent courtesy he enjoyed from King Henry VIII at that time.

One can summarise the political content of More's *Utopia* as being anti-aristocracy, anti-church, and pro–the ordinary masses, but More is careful to appear to disparage these opinions by putting them into the mouth of a character called Raphael Nonsenso. In More's Latin original, most of the proper names in the text (of both people and places) are of Greek derivation; hence Nonsenso is Turner's translation of the Greek term *Hythlodaeus*, the River Nowater his translation of the term *Andryus*, and the Nopeople his translation of the term *Ademus* (*U*, 8). Where, in the Latin original, a sense of strangeness (and, Turner argues, significance) would be maintained in More's inclusion of the Greek, the original meaning would be apparent to most classically educated early modern readers. However, in observing that 'modern education very seldom includes Greek' (*U*, 8), Turner's choice to translate brings to the fore (if rather more clumsily than More's original) the satirical distance inherent in the text.

In addition to the names, however, also undermining the apparent criticisms in the text are the presence of two epistles at the start of it: one from More to his publisher, Peter Gilles, and one from Gilles to his patron, Busleiden. In these, both More and Gilles describe the book as a mere transcript of a conversation they both had with Raphael Nonsenso, who has now conveniently disappeared. Gilles writes: 'I've heard several different stories about him. Some people say that he has died somewhere on his travels. Others that he has gone back to his own country. Others again that he has returned to Utopia . . .' (*U*, 34). Purportedly divorced from its original context, the following is typical of the type of opinions More puts into Nonsenso's mouth:

> . . . to tell you the truth, my dear More, I don't see how you can ever get any real justice or prosperity, so long as there's private property, and everything's judged in terms of

money—unless you consider it just for the worst sort of
people to have the best living conditions, or unless you're
prepared to call a country prosperous, in which all the
wealth is owned by a tiny minority . . . The rich will be
greedy, unscrupulous, and totally useless characters, while
the poor will be simple, unassuming people whose daily
work is far more profitable to the community than it is to
them. (*U*, 65–66)

More's disagreement is worded thus:

I don't believe you'd ever have a reasonable standard of living under a communist system. There'd always tend to be
shortages, because nobody would work hard enough. In the
absence of a profit motive, everyone would become lazy,
and rely on everyone else to do the work for him. Then,
when things really got short, the inevitable result would be
a series of murders and riots, since nobody would have any
legal method of protecting the products of his own labour
—especially as there wouldn't be any respect for authority
. . . (*U*, 67)

Nevertheless (and Turner's clumsy choice of the word 'communist'
apart), while More apparently disagrees with Nonsenso, he continues to give him the lion's share of the narrative, intervening only at
particular moments. Inevitably, in a narrative in which *I* becomes *he*
and *he* becomes *I* (further emphasised, as Turner indicates, by More
making *he* the Utopian word for *I* [*U*, 10]), the distinction between
the two gradually blurs.

The global political context surrounding More's writing of
Utopia is more important to his book than to any of the others we
are looking at, not least because it helps explain the comparative
absence of fantasy in it. Where *Gulliver's Travels* (1726), Charlotte
Perkins Gilman's *Herland* (1915), or Yann Martel's *Life of Pi* (2001)
rely on the use of fabulous yarn-spinning or larger-than-life claims,
More can benefit from the fantastic dreams *really* associated, in the
sixteenth century, with even the idea of travelling to the New
World, coupled with the simple adoption of a hearsay structure: 'I
don't know whose fault it was . . . but we never thought of asking,
and he never thought of telling us whereabouts in the New World

Utopia is' (*U*, 30–31). Furthermore, though it is usual, as Northrop Frye argues, for utopian texts to be 'constructed as a guided tour: a visitor from another time and place visit[ing] the utopian world, [being] shown around, and in the end return[ing] home,'[5] More can afford to play down the travelogue aspect of his narrative. Along with this downplaying comes an attendant reduction in the need for exotica: hence More's own fictive double inside the text, in describing his initial encounter with Raphael, casually observes, 'We did not ask him if he had seen any monsters, for monsters have ceased to be news' (*U*, 40).

Nevertheless, More's island Utopia sets the standard for all others, its location simultaneously suggesting it to be set apart from the rest of the world, while only precariously holding on to its own form, swamped as it is by the ocean around it:

> . . . the island is broadest in the middle, where it measures about two hundred miles across. It's never much narrower than that, except towards the very ends, which gradually taper away and curve right round, just as if they'd been drawn with a pair of compasses, until they almost form a circle five hundred miles in circumference. So you can picture the island as a sort of crescent, with its tips divided by a strait approximately eleven miles wide. Through this the sea flows in, and then spreads out into an enormous lake . . . Thus practically the whole interior of the island serves as a harbour, and boats can sail across it in all directions . . . (*U*, 69)

What we have here, in visual form, is a sense of the precarious means by which utopias in general (like the horizon) struggle to maintain their boundaries. Though the island seems to have its own captive water supply, water flows in and out of the harbour at will. Less easily navigable are the straits to sea voyagers: 'the harbour mouth is alarmingly full of rocks and shoals . . . Only the Utopians know where the safe channels are . . .' (*U*, 69). Again, on the face of it this physical feature favours the inhabitants of Utopia, until we read that the entrance to the harbour 'would be risky enough even for the local inhabitants, if it weren't for certain landmarks erected on the shore—and by simply shifting these landmarks they could lure any number of enemy warships to destruction' (*U*, 69). At that point, we recognise such landmarks could also be shifted to prevent inhabitants of the island from leaving, thus implying an underlying possibility of dystopia.

One other geographical feature impacts on our reading of the island: More draws attention to the fact that a utopia is always an unnatural community by describing the means by which this island was created:

> They say . . . and one can actually see it for oneself, that Utopia was originally not an island but a peninsula. However, it was conquered by somebody called Utopos, who gave it its present name—it used to be called Sansculottia—and was also responsible for transforming a pack of ignorant savages into what is now, perhaps, the most civilized nation in the world. The moment he landed and got control of the country, he immediately had a channel cut through the fifteen-mile isthmus connecting Utopia with the mainland, so that the sea could flow all around it. (*U*, 69–70)

Hence culture is continually given priority over nature and, in the process, 'civilization' comes to be viewed similarly to an artificial—indeed untenable—society. By extension it takes on a fantasy identification: the outward projection of our collective inner desires.

Jonathan Swift, *Gulliver's Travels*

Gulliver's Travels (1726)[6], or, to give it its proper title, *Travels into Several Remote Nations of the World, in Four Parts, by Lemuel Gulliver*, shares this element of being an outward projection of collective inner desires, in the sense that it was published at a time when, as we have just seen, a number of European sea voyages were undertaken as journeys into the unknown, inspired by fantasies of what exotica one might discover across the horizon and bring back as plunder. As already noted in Chapter 4, maps play a key function in these texts, each part being punctuated by a new chart of territory visited. Once they are compared with a modern atlas of the world, one discovers that Swift's fantasy lands map directly onto 'real' territory (the islands and coastlines border the Pacific Ocean) and the timescale for journeys is as meticulously plotted as it is in the Lord of the Rings.[7]

In combining realist cartography with a feasible timescale, what Swift also offers us here is a view of the arbitrary manner in which realism frames its own axes of space and time, marrying 'framework,' here, with perspective. For instance, in the case of the Lilliputians, the globe has a circumference of only twelve miles and miniaturism leads to introspection. Gulliver assures us, 'they see with great exactness, but at no great distance' (*GT*, 55). In the correspondingly expansive Brobdingnag, on the other hand, the extent of Gulliver's travels around the metropolis follows a circumference of 2,000 miles, this being seen to be well within the limits of the kingdom for, as Gulliver observes, 'The whole extent of this Prince's Dominions reacheth about six thousand Miles in Length, and from three to five in Breadth' (*GT*, 103). Here the inhabitants are shown to have 'large Optics [that] were not so acute as [Gulliver's] in viewing smaller Objects' (*GT*, 102). Stature is also seen to have an impact on self-perception: ' . . . while I was in [Brobdingnag] I could never endure to look in a glass after my eyes had grown accustomed to such prodigious Objects, because the Comparison gave me so despicable a conceit of myself' (*GT*, 137). All of these shifts in perspective, however, are set in a wider context by Gulliver's early observation, quickly passed over, that he has a 'weakness of [the] Eyes' (*GT*, 38). Considering that so much of what follows reads as a playing with optics and the effect of lens distortion, this directly impacts on the relationship between 'reality' and its representation.

This question of shifts and distortions of vision must affect larger questions of perspective, not least when Gulliver's own view is seen to be at odds with how others see the world:

> . . . [R]epeating my voyage early in the Morning, I arrived in seven Hours to the *South-East* Point of *New Holland*. This confirmed me in the opinion I have long entertained, that the *Maps* and *Charts* place this Country at least three Degrees more to the *East* than it really is; which Thought I communicated many Years ago to my worthy Friend Mr. *Herman Moll*, and gave him my Reasons for it, although he hath rather chosen to follow other Authors. (*GT*, 260–261; original italics)

As Robert Demaria Jr. points out, this issue relates to real questions of relevance in cartography at the time. Herman Moll was a Dutch geographer and author of the *New and Correct Map of the Whole World* (1719), which Swift is known to have read.[8] His aim, here, is as hyperbolic as the society of Brobdingnag; by using Gulliver, Swift briefly endows him with the ability to transcend the parameters of his own text in order to claim precedence—on Swift's behalf—as the source for Moll's information. In the process Gulliver offers a joke at realism's expense, namely that, as Lilian R. Furst puts it, in fiction '*All is true*' while still remaining 'an illusion.'[9]

The positioning of early utopias in that literary shadowland where realism and fantasy meet is, in part, reflected in the frequency with which claims for truth-telling preface any narrative action. Swift's version is no exception to this rule. Like More, he allows fact and fiction to mingle in order to more carefully persuade the reader that what appears to be larger than life may actually exist.[10] Hence, just as More opens his *Utopia* with several peritexts: 'The Utopian Alphabet,' 'A Specimen of Utopian Poetry' (first as transliteration, then as translation), 'Lines on the Island of Utopia by the Poet Laureate, Mr Windbag Nonsenso's sister's son,' then the two letters formerly mentioned, so Swift opens *Gulliver's Travels* with an advertisement, a letter to the publisher (purportedly written by Gulliver himself), and a further letter, this time from that publisher to the reader. All 'establish' the veracity of Gulliver's account, while simultaneously conveying (as we shall see also in *Life of Pi*) the typical tall-tale status of the sailor's yarn, the potency of the text *lying* in the realm of fable, not fact.

The asymmetrical nature of the relationship between plot and structure becomes clear once one pays attention to the mirroring that works as a foundation to the text. Voyages begin and end, to be followed by new ones, which also begin and end. Once the traveller comes ashore in new territory, encounters with alien beings always follow. In the first mirror they are miniaturised, in the second magnified, as if the places visited have not changed, only the lens through which they are viewed. Each time, however—and here comes the skewed vision upon the 'real' that fantasy offers—those encounters 'reflect' upon Gulliver's home. Hence, though the surface layer of these encounters relies on variety, there are very few genuine surprises in store. In that sense, the novel tracks Angus Fletcher's ornamented tree model discussed in Chapter 2, the bare trunk representing, as it were, the utopian travelogue, while the variety within those encounters with alien peoples and creatures foliates the branches. Fletcher, in particular, draws attention to the overly repetitive instance of shipwreck in *Gulliver's Travels* and the fact that this is the sole determinant of destination. He continues,

> Allegories are codes . . . Their enigmatic surfaces are known not to be random and accidental . . . [A]s each successive shipwreck occurs . . . [it becomes clear that] to be shipwrecked for him is always to experience a violent exclusion from safety, from social comfort and friendship. With each successive appearance of the figure there is an increased degree of human malevolence toward Gulliver.[11]

In other words, Fletcher implies, each time Gulliver 'runs aground,' so do our feelings for him as a literary character. In part, this effect is enhanced by his overdetermination to assert his status as 'truth-teller.' As we will see later, in a utopian text such as *Life of Pi*, the truth status of the tale matters because it directly affects the way in which we derive meaning from the novel. Here its effect is less integral, and as Gulliver continues to insist, even at the end, that 'I have not been so studious of Ornament as of Truth' (*GT*, 266), we become tired of his protestations and dismiss him for these more than anything else.

In fact, within the travels themselves there is an implied critique of overemphasising empiricism at the expense of speculation, in the example offered by the Houyhnhnms. Their determination to cling only to those aspects of mimesis they can objectively verify leads to inevitable limitations in geographical and scientific terms. Even the concept of sea travel is beyond them (in both senses of the phrase), as they cannot fathom how one could construct a vessel in which one could float across the surface of the sea. As with all exotic travelogues, therefore, the relationship between the tangible and the speculative underlies the whole rationale for Swift's text. In essence, this is typical of all fantasy literature, whether it deals in outer space, the sea voyage, myths and legends, or ghost stories. Fantasy positions itself within that space/place at which the two come adrift and, in the process, encourages us to lose, question, and reorientate our-selves in relation to the real. Swift offers us a particularly intriguing example of this in the flying island of Balnibarbi (Figure 5.1).

A strange hybrid encapsulating Western fascinations with the exoticism of the Middle Eastern flying carpet and the utopian pos-sibilities of every tropical isle, what 'grounds' this hyperbolic piece of fantasy writing are the geometrical principles upon which its nav-igation is based:

> To explain the manner of its Progress, let *A B* represent a Line drawn cross the Dominions of *Balnibarbi*, let the Line *C D* represent the Loadstone, of which let *D* be the repelling end, and C the attracting end, the Island being over C; let the Stone be placed in the Position *C D* with its repelling end downwards; then the Island will be driven upwards obliquely towards *D*. When it is arrived at *D*, let the Stone be turned upon its Axle till its attracting end points towards *E*; where if the Stone be again turned upon its Axle till it stands in the Position *E F*, with its repelling

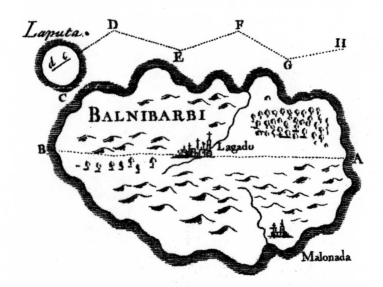

Figure 5.1 *Balnibarbi* from Jonathan Swift, *Gulliver's Travels* (Harmondsworth: Penguin, 2001), p. 157.

> Point downwards, the Island will rise obliquely towards F,
> where by directing the attracting end towards G, the Island
> may be carried to G, and from G to H, by turning the
> Stone, so as to make its repelling Extremity point directly
> downwards. And thus by changing the Situation of the
> Stone as often as there is occasion, the Island is made to rise
> and fall by turns in an oblique Direction, and by those alter-
> nate Risings and Fallings (the Obliquity being not consid-
> erable) is conveyed from one part of the Dominions to the
> other. (GT, 157–158)

Hence, though Swift's novel lacks the fascination with gadgetry one finds in the work of writers such as H. G. Wells, scientific specula-tion remains an important aspect of his vision. One could even go further and suggest that, to a twenty-first-century reader, the man-ner in which Gulliver ascends to Balnibarbi could be interpreted as an instance of eighteenth-century UFO abduction:

> They made signs for me to come down from the Rock, and
> go towards the Shore, which I accordingly did; and the fly-
> ing Island being raised to a convenient height, the Verge
> directly over me, a Chain was let down from the lowest
> Gallery, with a Seat fastened to the Bottom, to which I
> fixed myself, and was drawn up by Pullies. (GT, 147)

However, and as this method of 'abduction' implies, the alterna-tive vision science affords in *Gulliver's Travels* is, on the whole, a kinder, more holistic one than we typically expect to find in *sf*. So, though Swift's vision of the eccentric scientific Academy of Lagado can be read as a bare parody of the Royal Society,[12] one can hardly object to the members' efforts to try and extract 'sunbeams from Cucumbers' (GT, 167) or replace silkworms with spiders because they 'underst[and] how to weave as well as spin' (GT, 169).

The same certainly cannot be said for aspects of the sociological and anthropological visions of the text, most particularly Swift's vision of women. Take, for instance, his journey to Brobdingnag, where Gulliver encounters beings 'as tall as an ordinary Spire-steeple, and [who] took about ten Yards at every stride . . .' (GT, 82). Here, Gulliver's disgust for women reaches its climax in the guise of a nursing mother:

I must confess no Object ever disgusted me so much as the sight of her monstrous Breast . . . The Nipple was about half the Bigness of my Head, and the Hue both of that and the Dug so varified with Spots, Pimples and Freckles, that nothing could appear more nauseous . . . This made me reflect upon the fair Skins of our *English* Ladies, who appear so beautiful to us, only because they are of our own size, and their Defects not to be seen but through a Magnifying Glass, where we find by Experiment that the smoothest and whitest Skins look rough and coarse, and ill coloured. (*GT*, 87)

By the end of the book, this has extended to a dislike for his own wife (whom he refers to as 'that odious Animal') and his children, whom he forbids to stand in his presence, eschewing their collective company in preference for 'two young Stone-Horses . . . and next to them the Groom is my greatest Favourite; for I feel my Spirits revived by the Smell he contracts in the Stable' (*GT*, 265–266).

It is predominantly in response to this kind of misogyny, coupled with a desire to speculate more positively on woman's position within culture, that feminist utopian writing developed as a separate, if related, tradition. According to Bammer, the first feminist utopia can be identified as Christine de Pizan's *The Book of the City of Ladies* (1405), which precedes More's by 110 years. This work she describes as 'a collection of exemplary tales about women . . . depict[ing] a perfect otherworld deeply steeped in and loyal to the hegemonic class and religious values of its time.'[13] Rather than fastening, as most male-authored texts do, upon 'a state, a polity, a commonwealth . . . new institutions or new forms of government, it presents new ways of thinking about women and history: what they have been and could be.'[14] In the process, we see the beginnings of the establishment of alternative visions of the masculine and feminine as they exist within cultures and the manner in which society is shaped by gendered conditioning. A tradition of feminist utopian writing continues with us throughout history, Lady Mary Wroth's *The Countess of Montgomery's Urania* (1621), Margaret Cavendish's *The Blazing World* (1666), and Aphra Behn's *Oronooko, Or The Royal Slave* (1688), all borrowing from the utopian tradition in the period between More's *Utopia* and Swift's *Gulliver's Travels*.

Nevertheless, it is in the later twentieth century, accompanying the various advances within the women's movement, that feminist utopian writing really begins to gather pace. Though Naomi Mitchison's *Memoirs of a Spacewoman* was published as early as 1962, the zenith of this movement was arguably during the post-'68 second wave of feminism, when texts such as Monique Wittig's *Les Guérillères* (1969), Joanna Russ's *The Female Man* (1975), Marge Piercy's *Woman on the Edge of Time* (1976), Sally Miller Gearhart's *The Wanderground* (1978), and Suzette Elgin's *Native Tongue* (1984) all used science fiction as a means of exploring political change.

Accompanying these fictional works, a burgeoning cluster of feminist criticism developed and, along with it, a debate regarding how genuinely transformative such fictions could be. One of the problems raised by utopian writing is, as I have previously argued elsewhere, that '[i]t takes more than revolutionary content to revolutionize form . . . [S]peculative fictions, however progressive in ideological terms, always remain at least partially compromised by the generic enclosures which give them their voice.'[15] Nevertheless, the visions these texts offer work, in themselves, as a kind of 'fictive history,' less because of what they contain and more because the impulse to write utopia tends to accompany existing advances in women's position within present society. Such is true of Charlotte Perkins Gilman's early twentieth-century feminist utopia, *Herland* (1915), which builds directly on what was then the ongoing campaign for American women's suffrage.[16]

Charlotte Perkins Gilman, *Herland*

One of the intriguing paradoxes of Perkins Gilman's novel is that it offers us a vision of a feminist society named and framed through phallocentrism, hence the third-person perspective of '*her*-land,' coupled with the overtly penetrative approach to its exploration: 'No place for men? Dangerous? [Terry] looked as if he might shin up the waterfall on the spot.'[17] Where Gulliver looks to expand knowledge of unknown geography, the three central protagonists of this text—Terry O. Nicholson, Jeff Margrave, and the primary narrator, Vandyke Jennings—look to expand knowledge of 'virgin

territory' in more permissive ways. All three are scientists, perpetu-
ating the theme of science as speculation, though questioning what
Swift largely suggests are its benevolent motivations.

Bammer, who shares my view that 'Conventional utopias thus
embody an inherent contradiction . . . they tend to reinforce established ways of thinking even as they set out to challenge them,' also
has her criticisms of Perkins Gilman's text:

> Obviously, it would be absurd to suggest that *Herland* is
> simply ideology in utopian guise. I believe, however, that it
> puts the relationship between utopia and ideology in par-
> ticularly sharp relief and could thus be regarded as an
> experiment to see how far the utopian dimension of an oth-
> erwise ideological construct like motherhood can be
> *pushed*.[18]

The inference of Bammer's words here implies that where 'pushing'
has its advantages, it also involves risk. Intriguingly, though the form
of Perkins Gilman's novel works through rather conventional means
(she employs what Tolkien later refers to as competing Primary and
Secondary Worlds, the Primary setting being the world of everyday
reality and the Secondary 'World' a 'closed' and imprecisely located
region of it), the parameters of that embedded world of storytelling
(told by Vandyke Jennings) are structured with far more risk-taking
in mind and return us to Bammer's 'pushing' terminology: 'I haven't
said where it was for fear some self-appointed missionaries or
traders, or land-greedy expansionists, will take it upon themselves
to *push in*' (*H*, 1; my emphasis). As we saw in the case of *Gulliver's
Travels*, we can forgive structural rigidity where the content is sufficiently engaging, and Perkins Gilman introduces a more enticing
'hearsay' structure to her otherwise unambitious narrative structure
by introducing the Secondary World not as fact, but as legend. In
the process, she introduces a third layer of storytelling: '[A]s we got
farther and farther upstream, in a dark tangle of rivers, lakes,
morasses, and dense forests . . . I noticed that more and more of
these savages [local guides] *had a story about* a strange and terrible
Woman Land in the high distance' (*H*, 2; my emphasis).

Though maternity is *Herland*'s main theme (one of the ways in
which it offers an attractive antidote to Swift's misogyny), it

remains a text rooted very clearly in the early twentieth century, which Ernest Mandel identifies as the era of the 'machine production of electric and combustion motors.'[19] Though we never see a car in Herland, Terry's admiration for the quality of the roads seems to imply they (or similar modes of conveyance) exist and, though again we are never given clear illustrations of what they may be, we are told the women have 'mechanical appliances for disseminating information almost equal to ours at home' (*H*, 65). In instances where there is a lack of what we would consider to be advanced science, we are told it is due to cultural redundancy, not a lack of technological know-how: 'Physiology, hygiene, sanitation, physical culture—all that line of work had been perfected long since. Sickness was almost wholly unknown among them, so much so that a previously high development in what we call the "science of medicine" had become practically a lost art' (*H*, 71). Nevertheless—and from a feminist perspective this is the most controversial aspect of the novel—where all three men, and in particular Terry, assume that a culture populated entirely by women must lack something, so, it turns out, do the women themselves. One might even go so far as to suggest that, to a degree, the inhabitants of Herland appear to be suffering from what Sigmund Freud defined as penis envy.

In his essay 'On Narcissism' (1914), published one year previously to *Herland*, Freud argues that male sexuality alone is determined by 'complete object-love,' a paradigm inherited from an infantile investment in 'two sexual objects—himself and the woman who nurses him.' It is this that drives him towards the choice of an 'other' as sexual partner, for without this substitute for the originary object choice, he remains unfulfilled. In the case of women, however, they 'develop a certain self-contentment which compensates them for the social restrictions that are imposed upon them . . . Strictly speaking, it is only themselves that such women love . . .'[20] *Herland* provides us with a society that, in eradicating the male of the species, demonstrates the ease with which women can become self-satisfied in these terms. Indeed, as Perkins Gilman evades issues of sexual frustration, sublimating them solely into questions of maternity, it is also the case that she offers us an all-women society in which, as Freud also argues, the mother's love operates as a surrogate for penis envy: 'Parental love . . . is nothing but the parents' narcissism born again . . .'[21] Though the women claim to wish to return to a bisexual nation-state, this is because their perception of what men might offer them is entirely determined by what they love about their own society, a fact revealing their own thinking about men to be as flawed as Terry's phallocentric conceptions of women:

> They're all old maids—children or not. They don't know the first thing about Sex.
> When Terry said *Sex*, sex with a very large *S*, he meant the male sex, naturally; its special value, its profound conviction of being 'the life force,' its cheerful ignoring of the true life process, and its interception of the other sex solely from its own point of view. (*H*, 134)

So, while we never go so far as to empathise with the discredited Terry, there are certainly moments at which Herland seems a very tame place, not least for the static vision it offers.

Such difficulties are inevitable in any 'closed vision' and will always increase with the widening passage of time between the date of publication and the date when a text is read. Nor is it only the tamer aspects of *Herland* that unsettle its readers: the women's ecological practice also strikes us as flawed. For instance, as Elladaor proudly tells the story of what inspired her to become a forester, she talks of finding, as a child, 'a big purple-and-green butterfly on a low flower.' Taking it to her teacher to identify the species, she discovers she has found 'a female of the obernut moth . . . We have been trying to exterminate them for centuries . . . I was shown the history of the creature, and an account of the damage it used to do . . .' (*H*, 100–101). Despite the lack of any precise geographical location being specified, the nature of the terrain, its comparative proximity to North America (home to all three men), and the ancient mythical associations of the Amazon with a single-breasted tribe of warrior women all suggest *Herland* is set in the South American rainforest. Then note that from the moment the men arrive, they notice nature having been replaced, wholesale, with culture: 'These towering trees were under as careful cultivation as so many cabbages' (*H*, 14) and the inhabitants' relationship with that environment is compared to the care of 'a florist . . . for his costliest orchids' (*H*, 18). Aside, therefore, from the irony of Ellador's 'dangerous butterfly' displaying traditional suffragette colours (an inherent ideological contradiction within Perkins Gilman's own vision, and a gift to any patriarchal countercritic wishing to draw attention to the negative symbolism inherent in this oxymoron), we also recognise that the nature of the inhabitants' horticultural and zoological policies spells death to their idyllic surroundings.

H. G. Wells, *The First Men in the Moon* and *The Time Machine*

It is perhaps for this reason that most science/speculative fiction (*sf*) narratives combine certain elements of utopianism with a counter-balancing flavour of nightmare and monstrosity. This also makes them more unashamedly exploitative than the traditional utopia. In H. G. Wells's *The First Men in the Moon*, for example, the same sense of adventure and ambition we saw in Perkins Gilman's male protagonists characterises Bedford, its hero. Bedford is a failed businessman and hence, at least metaphorically if not literally, a gambler: 'Nowadays even about business transactions there is a strong spice of adventure. I took risks.'[22] In that sense, he is worth directly comparing with the eponymous adventurer of that 'characteristic [English] Utopia of the early eighteenth century,' *Robinson Crusoe* (1719).[23] As Crusoe tells his mother at the start of Defoe's novel,

> I was now eighteen years old, which was too late to go apprentice to a trade, or clerk to an attorney; [and] I was sure if I did, I should never serve out my time, and I should certainly run away from my master before my time was out, and go to sea . . . [24]

In fact, Bedford is an intriguing hybrid whose phraseology slides between disciplines, almost as if he cannot bear to 'settle.' For instance, in straddling the divide between arts and sciences, Bedford refers to his own interest in Cavor in mercantile terms. Cavor, Bedford assumes, is 'in pursuit of a valuable invention' (*FMM*, 9), while this is actually more true of himself. As an aspiring playwright, his aim is financial rather than artistic: his play will, he hopes, become precisely such a 'valuable invention,' removing the need—again like Crusoe—to 'drudge for my living as a clerk' (*FMM*, 4). Cavor, in fact, pursues science for 'purely' scientific concerns—something Bedford fails to comprehend.

Elements of utopianism also occur in Wells's most famous *sf* novel, *The Time Machine* (1895). As the central protagonist watches the earth spin across the centuries, buildings and civilizations appearing and disappearing before his very eyes, he notes that 'Even through the veil of my confusion the earth seemed very fair.'[25] Later he observes, 'There were no hedges, no signs of proprietary rights, no evidences of agriculture; the whole earth had become a garden' (*TM*, 27). As in *Herland*, far from being an image of idealism, this leads the Time Traveller to dystopian contemplation. 'I had always anticipated that the people of the year Eight Hundred and Two Thousand odd would be incredibly in front of us in knowledge, art, everything . . . A flow of disappointment rushed across my mind. For a moment I felt that I had built the Time Machine in vain' (*TM*, 22). As the garden analogy suggests, though we have seen the clear structural similarities between *Herland* and earlier utopian narratives such as More's (not least in the way in which documentary anthropology renders fantasy modes of writing subordinate once we are inside Herland itself), the women in *Herland* are most similar to the Eloi of Wells's novel. Though the Eloi are sexed male and female, the traveller notes a tendency towards feminisation in the gendering of the species, each person having 'the same soft hairless visage, and the same girlish rotundity of limb' (*TM*, 26) that Wells inevitably interprets as negative proof of innate indolence.

Again, in *Herland* we remember the absence of men translating into a different relation to occupation, despite all three male visitors falling foul of the same assumptions as Wells. So convinced is Terry of the ineptitude of women that he adamantly refuses to believe in the total absence of men, for he cannot conceive of advancement in an all-female world: 'The road was some sort of hard manufactured stuff, sloped slightly to shed rain, with every curve and grade and gutter as perfect as if it were Europe's best. "No men, eh?" sneered Terry' (*H*, 18). Where advancement plays these women false, nevertheless, is in the realisation that '[t]he years of pioneering lay far behind them. Theirs was a civilization in which the initial difficulties had long since been overcome. The untroubled pace, the unmeasured plenty, the steady health, the large good will and smooth management which ordered everything, left nothing to overcome' (*H*, 99). Hence, just as the Eloi become so comfortable they lay themselves open to attack by the savage and avaricious Morlocks, by implication a similar danger faces Perkins Gilman's women, here in their welcome of the male 'invaders' who find their complacency so boring.

In fact, Wells regresses further than Perkins Gilman in rendering technology anathema to rural living. The Eloi inhabit a post-technological landscape in which, though they are unaware of the fact, the selective breeding of horticultural breeds has eradicated all irritants and disease. In this vision of their society, the Time Traveller recognises the natural extension of his own:

> We improve our favourite plants and animals . . . gradually by selective breeding . . . We improve them gradually, because our ideals are vague and tentative, and our knowledge is very limited . . . Some day all this will be better organized, and still better . . . things will move faster and faster towards the subjugation of Nature. In the end, wisely and carefully we shall readjust the balance of animal and vegetable life to suit our human needs. (*TM*, 27–28)

At first sight, as we have seen, the effects appear utopian: 'The air was free of gnats, the earth from weeds or fungi; everywhere were fruits and sweet and delightful flowers; brilliant butterflies flew hither and thither' (*TM*, 28). Only gradually do the hidden dangers of this new rural idyll become apparent. What Wells offers us here is proof of the dangers of genetically modified (GM) crops, except that the dangers he foresees are not those we foresee ourselves: where we invest them with the label 'Frankenstein foods,' what Wells shows us is a perfection so absolute it will kill us.

In relation to the impact such utopian visions can be seen to have upon our sense of present community, we need to remember the drawbacks of the closed vision. In essence, and as *The Time Machine* demonstrates, futurist writing offers a shortcut, and as Nick Bingham suggests, shortcuts can be dangerous when applied to political thinking. On the other hand, our own 'alarm-bell' response is a similar shortcut: one based on blind fear of the alien. Bingham poses the possibility that cautious progress may offer a route forward in the GM debate, and in doing so he suggests, not a time machine, but the more conventional transportation offered by the railroad or even the space race as examples of previous technological advances giving 'access . . . to a whole new world.'[26] Nor are Bingham's words of value only to the reader beyond the text; when he argues for a need for us all to be 'made to participate' and assures us that 'collective responsibility means becoming more and not less involved,'[27] we are made uncomfortably cognisant of the apathy of the Eloi. Though, on one level, they have embraced 'collective responsibility' (indeed, one of the first words to form in the Time Traveller's consciousness on his arrival is 'Communism' [*TM*, 26]), on another they are wedded to precisely the type of 'them' and 'us' thinking that Bingham also identifies with a philosophical 'blind alley, taking us two steps back for every one forward.'[28] It is this determination to treat the Morlocks as absolute 'other' that has transformed their enemy into their monster.

The Time Machine is, however, more than just a futurist vision; though propelling its protagonist headlong into the future, it never loses its sense of being anchored in the Primary World of the Victorian era. In fact, in terms of the fantasy genre more generally, the closest literary kin the Eloi have are the fair folk, or more precisely, fairies, as they appeared in their most sentimental guise—as a rural antidote to Victorian fears surrounding industrial expansion. In her book *Fairies in Nineteenth-Century Art and Literature*, Nicola Bown situates fairy culture at the apex of the tensions provoked by the shifting trends of Victorian society: 'The Victorians thought of themselves as makers and masters of the modern world: that is the self-image they were most anxious to pass on to posterity. But they also felt oppressed by their responsibilities, fearful of the future and doubtful of the unalloyed benefits of progress.'[29] As a response, she claims, 'They shaped fairyland into the negative image of their own disenchanted world, and saw their own disappointed forms transfigured in the shape of a fairy.'[30] Certainly, we can recognise, in Wells's Eloi, this kind of collective embodiment of disappointment and, accompanying it, the same connections between an overly assertive technophobia and the resultant threat of species extinction. J. R. R. Tolkien joins forces with this kind of Victorian thinking in praising what he describes as the 'enchantment of distance' offered in Wells's novel, while dismissing 'the preposterous and incredible Time Machine itself' (*Tree and Leaf*, 13). Certainly, whether we like it or not, the Eloi's world, with its 'tangled waste of beautiful bushes and flowers, a long-neglected and yet weedless garden' (*TM*, 23), offers a version of what John Ruskin saw as a vestige otherwise only left behind in fanciful children's stories. In those, he observes,

> There are no railroads . . . to carry the children away . . . No tunnel or pit mouths to swallow them up . . . There are only winding brooks, wooden foot-bridges, and grassy hills without any holes cut into them! . . . And more wonderful still,—there are no gasworks! No waterworks, no mowing machines, no sewing machines, no telegraph poles, no vestiges, in fact, of science, civilization, economical arrangements, or commercial enterprise!!!.[31]

Where the Eloi are most seen to resemble the fair folk is in their shared relationship to festive allure. The traveller associates them with 'amorous sport,' witnessing a couple running past him, '[t]he male pursu[ing] the female, flinging flowers at her as she ran' (*TM*, 42). Here, in their frugivorous abundance ('Transvers[ing] the length [of the hall] were innumerable tables . . . and upon these were heaps of fruits. Some I recognized as a kind of hypertrophied raspberry and orange, but for the most part they were strange' [*TM*, 23]), we can hear echoes of Christina Rossetti's earlier Victorian poem 'Goblin Market' (1862):

> *Morning and evening*
> *Maids heard the goblins cry:*
> *'Come buy our orchard fruits,*
> *Come buy, come buy:*
> *Apples and quinces,*
> *Lemons and oranges,*
> *Plump unpecked cherries,*
> *Melons and raspberries,*
> * . . . Come buy, come buy.'*
> (lines 1–8 and 31)

However, what is missing in Wells's book is the predatory masculinity of Rossetti's Goblins:

> *Lashing their tails*
> *They trod and hustled her,*
> *Elbowed and jostled her,*
> *Clawed with their nails,*
> *Barking, mewing, hissing, mocking,*
> *Tore her gown and soiled her stocking,*
> *Twitched her hair out by the roots,*
> *Stamped upon her tender feet,*
> *Held her hands and squeezed their fruits*
> *Against her mouth to make her eat.*
>
> (lines 398–407)

What we come to realise, in Wells's use of fairylore within what is otherwise *sf*, is the manner in which even those works of fantasy having an apparently straightforward relationship to a particular subgenre, frequently borrow from the structures or trappings of others. Hence folkloric allusions are not the only means by which the supernatural intervenes in this novel of science: in fact, the opening of *The Time Machine* borrows direct from the ghost story.

Inter-Generic Texts: *The Time Machine* and *A Connecticut Yankee at King Arthur's Court*

Before the Time Traveller embarks on his journey, he calls together a group of knowledgeable friends to witness his experiment. As we shall see in Chapter 6, the typical ghost story opening follows just such a format: usually a predominantly masculine social gathering in which the assembled men meet to tell stories. Here, '[t]he fire burn[s] brightly, and the soft radiance of the incandescent lights in the lilies of silver [catch] the bubbles that flashed and passed in [their] glasses' (*TM*, 3). The primary narrator is one of the assembled friends, but not the main protagonist—this being another typical ghost story technique. His role is to play primary storyteller, drawing the reader into an implied setting of shared confidences, the central character only being introduced later. As in *The First Men in the Moon*, doubt is cast upon which type of inventor the Time

Traveller is, gadgeteer or phoney. Later on in the text, in a kind of theatrical wink to the reader detailing the dance of joy he executes on discovering the dry matches in the museum, he continues: 'In part it was a modest *cancan*, in part a step-dance, in part a skirt-dance . . . and in part original. For I am naturally inventive [i.e. with the truth?], as you know' (*TM*, 61). As part of this narrative sleight of hand, the preliminary demonstration carried out by the Time Traveller is told using the lexis not of science, but of conjuring tricks:

> . . . [He] held in his hand . . . a glittering metallic frame-work, scarcely larger than a small clock . . . He took one of the small octagonal tables . . . [and o]n this table he placed the mechanism . . . I sat in a low arm-chair nearest the fire, and I drew this forward so as to be almost between the Time Traveller and the fireplace . . . 'This little affair,' said the Time Traveller . . . 'is only a model . . . Now I want you clearly to understand that this lever, being pressed over, sends the machine gliding into the future, and this one reverses the motion . . . Presently I am going to press the lever, and off the machine will go. It will vanish, pass into future Time, and disappear. Have a good look at the thing. Look at the table too, and satisfy yourselves there is no trickery.' . . . Then the Time Traveller put forth his finger towards the lever. 'No,' he said suddenly. 'Lend me your hand' . . . So it was the Psychologist himself who sent forth the model Time Machine on its interminable voyage. (*TM*, 7–8)

This is only one aspect of what Wells sets up as a preliminary narrative involving Victorian debates about the natural, the super-natural, and the unnatural. What follows the 'trick' (and the disappearance of the model) is not a debate about magic, but a brief hiatus in which the assembled guests are subjected to an apparent encounter with the supernatural, as if these men are attending a séance rather than a scientific demonstration: 'There was a breath of wind, and the lamp flame jumped. One of the candles on the mantel was blown out, and the little machine suddenly swung round, became indistinct, [and] was seen as a ghost for a second . . .' (*TM*, 8). Of course, the relationship between ghosts and science fiction is not as strained as we might presume: though time travel is commonly associated with science fiction, we are similarly aware that ghosts travel through time, and certainly this protagonist has a reputation for associating with ghosts: '"Look here," said the Medical Man, "are you perfectly serious? Or is this a trick—like that ghost you showed us last Christmas?"' (*TM*, 10).

Nor is the generic hybridity between speculative fiction and the ghost story unique to *The Time Machine*. A similar combination can also be identified in Mark Twain's *A Connecticut Yankee at King Arthur's Court* (1889), a fantasy narrative also dealing in time travel, in this case primarily between sixth-century Arthurian Britain and nineteenth-century Connecticut, although, as we shall see, the novel begins and ends in neither of these chronotopes. As in *The Time Machine*, there are atavistic elements to Twain's narrative. At face value, since the novel is a hybrid of science fiction and old-fashioned romance myth, drawing (loosely) on the legends of King Arthur and the Knights of the Round Table, we could alternately brand it a work of 'sword and sorcery' or, to use one of Kathryn Hume's categories of writing, 'outsider-pastoral':

> [This] internalizes a sophisticated perspective. Characters from city, court, or any complex sector of society enter the green and pleasant land, but self-consciously and temporarily . . . the logic of this mode [being] romance . . . Many of the authors who use outsider-pastoral to revisit their age of innocence remain fully aware of the adult knowledge that makes the idyllic world unobtainable to them now.[32]

However, the beginning and ending of the narrative further complicate its identity. The opening, taking the form of a 'Word of Explanation' by the author, is set in the famously haunted Warwick Castle[33] and involves a 'strange encounter' between the implied author (or, at least, a framing storyteller in the guise of the author) and an otherwise unidentified visitor. Though no official expert, the 'curious stranger' becomes almost a kind of alternative tour guide: 'We fell together . . . in the tail of the herd . . . he at once began to say things which interested me.'[34] So attracted is the frame storyteller by the voice of this man, that he forms an easy rival to 'the droning voice of the salaried cicerone' (*CY*, 33). As the attraction grows, the central protagonist emerges as a ghost: ' . . . and so he gradually wove such a spell about me that I seemed to move among the spectres and shadows and dust and mould . . . holding speech with a relic of it!' (CY, 33).

Retiring, later, to his room at the Warwick Arms, the narrator begins to read an extract from Malory's *Le Morte d'Arthur*. We expect him to drift off into sleep as he does so, thus setting up the conventional dream structure of fantasy narratives such as *Alice in Wonderland* (which precedes Twain's novel by twenty-four years). However, while this interpretation remains a possibility, it is further complicated by the fact that the narrator (who has already told us it was past midnight when he started reading) now claims to put down the book, hear a knock, and find this visitor once more at the door. In a realist text, the obvious question a reader might have would be, 'How does he know where the narrator is staying and what is he doing coming to his room after midnight?' Here our response may take one of two forms, depending on the generic identity we impose on the text. Either this stranger is an outward projection of the storyteller's ego, manifest as dream—which makes it a kind of psychological allegory—or he is a ghost, and this is therefore a ghost story. This generic uncertainty is maintained by the story the visitor/ghost/one who is dreamed tells.

We discover the stranger is the eponymous Yankee and he tells us, first through verbal reportage, then through a manuscript (for as he starts to drift off to sleep he tells our primary narrator, 'I've got it all written out, and you can read it if you like' [CY, 38]), all about his life in Connecticut. He was, he tells us, 'head superintendent' at an arms factory, but became involved in a fight 'conducted with crowbars' with one of the men whom he was supervising:

> He laid me out with a crusher alongside the head that made everything crack, and seemed to spring every joint in my skull and make it overlap its neighbour. Then the world went out in darkness, and I didn't feel anything more, and didn't know anything at all—at least for a while.
>
> When I came to again, I was sitting under an oak tree, on the grass, with a whole beautiful and broad country landscape all to myself . . . (CY, 36–37)

There are a number of barriers between Primary and Secondary Worlds here. First we are reading, over the shoulder of our narrator as it were, one text (an extended extract from Malory's *Le Morte d'Arthur*), then, after that reading is interrupted by a piece of oral storytelling, a secondhand version of the account the Yankee could have given us more directly, had he chosen not to leave us to read the written version instead. Reading and writing are, then, foregrounded as the entry points to the fantasy world and, as the medievalist Janet Cowen observes, Twain's narrative—for all its popular appeal—is deceptively 'literary' (in its most value-laden sense), in that 'Malory's idiom pervades the text . . . [but is augmented by] features from several centuries, including Middle English forms predating Malory, though not used by Malory himself, and extending to Romantic fiction in the nineteenth century.'[35]

Twain's is, then, a narrative about the power of storytelling and the means by which levels of consciousness can work in an allegorical manner to replicate the different layers of literary history being overlaid upon each other in the text. Layers of storytelling are also overlaid, one upon another, on the level of character, for who is telling us this story? The account is purportedly the Yankee's, though we are reading it over the primary narrator's shoulder. And just who is this primary narrator? As he is introduced within a peritext to the main narrative, headed 'A Word of Explanation,' he would appear to be the implied author himself. But of course the author cannot be within the text, and so we must assume it either to be a character called Mark Twain (though in actuality unnamed), or an unnamed storyteller who (as in the typical ghost story) stands in to provide an additional hearsay layer further enabling the fabulous aspect of the novel. However, a further question remains, which directly impacts upon our unpeeling of layers of consciousness within the text, and this revolves around whether this is actually a story framed through *loss* of consciousness. Perhaps the whole text, including the visit from the Yankee, is a dream of the anonymous reader in the text. Or is it the fault of the blow to the Yankee's head? If so, what we read is a narrative recalling the aftereffects of a concussion, and not a novel of time travel at all.

If, as here, the precise means by which we move into the fantasy world is unclear, one might hope the manner in which we retreat from it may prove to be less so. However, the ending of the text is equally unresolved. The novel concludes with an apocalyptic battle and, on the verge of victory, the protagonist's assertion, 'But how treacherous is fortune! In a little while—say an hour—happened a thing, by my own fault, which—but I have no heart to write that. Let the record end here' (CY, 405). After that, the narrative is concluded in brief by Clarence, the page whom the Yankee encounters when he first arrives in sixth-century Camelot. He implies that, while he and the rest of the army die from a plague contracted from the bodies of those by whom they are surrounded, the Yankee is put into an enchanted sleep by a witch who claims to be Merlin. As our primary narrator puts the manuscript to one side, he then goes to listen at the door of the stranger's room and hears him raving in his sleep about 'such dreams! Such strange and awful dreams . . .' (CY, 409). Hence we are again unclear about whether these 'dreams' belong to the ghostly Yankee or the storyteller—who could be dreaming the Yankee into autonomous existence here, too.

Yann Martel, *Life of Pi*

Generically hybrid narratives are far more common than many fantasy critics would have us believe, and they are usually more interesting precisely for being so. One of the most recent, and certainly one of the more intriguing, is Yann Martel's Man Booker Prize–winning second novel, *Life of Pi* (2002), a novel that is unusual in straddling the subgenres of utopia and the rather less common contemporary narrative mode of animal fable. *Life of Pi* is not, in the conventional terms I formerly laid down in Chapter 1, a fantasy novel, though it definitely shares much of the outlook of narratives such as More's. It is set in a series of 'real' locations (the Indian town of Pondicherry in Madras, the Canadian city of Toronto, the Pacific Ocean, the Mexican town of Tomatlán) and is told in a clinical, documentary style with no clear reference to dreams, madness, or hallucination (albeit that doubts are raised about the credibility of the protagonist's tale at the end). These competing locations outlined above, however, are not just settings; they are chronotopes ('slices' of space/time forming alternative realities). In opening with the Pondicherry Zoo, the original home of the animals with which the central human protagonist, Piscine Molitar Patel (Pi), finds himself cast adrift later on, the novel acquires a type of fabular 'feel' in the tradition of Aesop, and this despite recurrent warnings about anthropomorphism being threaded throughout that first section of the novel:

> . . . though I may have anthropomorphized the animals till they spoke fluent English, the pheasants complaining in uppity British accents of their tea being cold and the baboons planning their bank robbery getaway in the flat, menacing tones of American gangsters, the fancy was always conscious. I quite deliberately dressed wild animals in tame costumes of my imagination. But I never deluded myself as to the real nature of my playmates.[36]

In fact, one of the key themes of this book is the complex nature of human and bestial relations. For instance, when Pi tells us, 'I learned the lesson that an animal is an animal, essentially and practically removed from us, twice; once with Father and once with Richard Parker' (*Pi*, 31), we naturally assume Richard Parker to be another human acquaintance. This is even more of a natural assumption as he continues to crop up, throughout the first section of the book, as an extension to the family group:

> *[Pi] shows me family memorabilia. Wedding photo first . . .*
> *On the same page there's another group shot, mostly of schoolchildren. He taps the photo.*
> *'That's Richard Parker,' he says.*
> *I'm amazed. I look closely, trying to extract personality from appearance. Unfortunately, it's black and white again and a little out of focus. A photo taken in better days, casually. Richard Parker is looking away. He doesn't even realize that his picture is being taken.* (*Pi*, 86–87; original emphasis)

In fact, we only much later discover Richard Parker to be a three-year-old Bengal tiger, presumably photographed here as part of the background—and caged. His significance lies in the fact that it is ultimately with this tiger, a zebra, an orangutan, a hyena, and a 'scrawny brown rat' (*Pi*, 152), that Pi navigates his passage across the Pacific. During the course of the crossing, Pi's survival depends upon his own ability to understand how a tiger communicates with others: *aaonh* (the roar), *woof* (anger at having been taken by surprise), *meow* (pleasurable satisfaction), and most significant of all, *prusten* ('the quietest of tiger calls, a puff through the nose to express friendliness and harmless intentions' [*Pi*, 163–164]). In the process, he narrows the distance between human and beast, and becoming increasingly aware that, as he tames the tiger sufficiently to prevent it from tearing him to pieces, it is only at the expense of him becoming bestial in return: 'I ate like an animal . . . [T]his noisy, frantic, unchewing wolfing-down of mine was exactly the way Richard Parker ate' (*Pi*, 225). So close do the two become, during this unlikely journey, that when both Pi and the tiger go blind through malnourishment, and Pi hears another voice suddenly conversing with him in the darkness, he (and we) make the natural assumption that it must be the voice of Richard Parker:

> The carnivorous rascal. All this time together and he had chosen an hour before we were to die to pipe up. I was elated to be on speaking terms with a tiger . . .
> But something was niggling at me . . .
> 'Excuse me?'
> 'Yes?' came Richard Parker's voice faintly.
> 'Why do you have [a French] accent? . . .' (*Pi*, 246–248)

In fact, it transpires, truth is even less likely than talking animals, here. Having been cast adrift on the Pacific Ocean for months, at the moment of approaching death this other voice turns out to belong to another human castaway on the ocean, also blind from poor nutrition. It is as if, no longer able to see, this voice takes the place of Pi's own reflection in the ocean. Hence, on one level, we obviously have to ask how 'real' this other is. On another level, and precisely like the rest of the animals with which Pi is cast adrift earlier in the novel, his appearance—however unlikely—does have the 'real' effect of saving Pi's life for, like the zebra, orangutan, and hyena, he turns out to be the sacrificial lamb offered up to an equally starving Richard Parker. As soon as this other man places one foot on the bottom of the boat (Richard Parker's territory), the tiger kills him instantaneously. Furthermore, in providing food for Richard Parker he also provides food for Pi, for onboard his craft, Pi finds provisions and, on eating them, regains his own sight. As he does so, what he sees is again a kind of double in death:

> Richard Parker had amply supped on him, including on his face, so that I never saw who my brother was. His eviscerated torso, with its broken ribs curving up like the frame of a ship, looked like a miniature version of the lifeboat, such was its blood-drenched and horrifying state. (*Pi*, 255–256)

Much of the early stages of the adventure read as a study in abjection, Pi's terror at the close-up view of nature, red in tooth and claw, being repeatedly stressed. So the hyena tears at the zebra's flesh, 'pulling out coils of intestines and other viscera . . .' (*Pi*, 125), the hyena tears its jaws through the orangutan's neck in order to behead her, and Richard Parker devours the hyena with 'a noise of organic crunching as windpipe and spinal cord were crushed' (*Pi*, 150–151). Once we realise that all this has been fabricated, and the 'real' antagonists are human, such details can be—at least in part—assumed to be the product of Pi's imagination. As Julia Kristeva questions, 'does not fear hide an aggression, a violence that returns to its source, its sign having been inverted?'[37]

For Kristeva, this source is always the mother, to whom we are eternally bound in death, in that she propels us into mortality. Pi is, at least superficially, persistently devoted to his mother, and on the level of animal allegory, one of Pi's greatest senses of loss accompanies his belief that his mother failed to escape from the sinking ship and drowned. Only at the end of the novel is it finally revealed (to an incredulous audience of two Japanese civil servants from their Ministry of Transport) that the whole book is a narrative trick, Pi posing the question, 'Which is the better story, the story with animals or the story without animals?' (*Pi*, 317). Like *Animal Farm*, though written using animal protagonists, *Life of Pi* should be read as a story about human relationships. Orange Juice, the orangutan, turns out to be more than an unusually maternal pet—she is actually Pi's mother in bestial guise, the two of them escaping the sinking ship together, only to be joined in the lifeboat by a murderous and cannibalistic cook (the hyena) and a young sailor (the zebra). The sailor, like the zebra, breaks his leg jumping into the lifeboat and has it amputated by the cook for fishing bait. He, like the zebra, dies a slow, agonising death. Pi's mother is also killed and beheaded by the cook, while the devastated Pi (Richard Parker in the original), kills the cook as an act of retribution for the death of his mother.

However, can we perhaps see, in this determination to conceal the death of the mother through allegory, evidence of some kind of devious counterdesire? After all, why save her once only to ensure a more brutal version of her killing? It is as if Pi hopes to be doubly sure of his mother's death, for only then can he be equally sure that he is saved. To put it in Kristeva's terms again, he is guilty of what she calls 'syntactical passivation' or, to put it another way, 'the subject's ability to put himself in the place of the object' as a means towards 'the constitution of [one's own] subjectivity.'[38] Pi stops short of devouring his own mother's flesh, but he does ingest 'small pieces, little strips' of the body of his 'brother' (*Pi*, 256), the other man also cast adrift on the ocean. As we have seen, we can read this (br)other as a double for Pi, but he is only one of what turn out to be three possible doubles. The second of these is Richard Parker himself, for at the end of the novel Pi tells the officials that the tiger represented him on the level of allegory. The obvious question is, if Richard Parker is really Pi, then who is the other Pi—the one who travels *with* Richard Parker in the boat? Perhaps, like some of the other authors we have considered in this chapter, it is Yann Martel who cannot stay out of his own book and so tussles for alpha status with his own hero. For, in constructing that fictive version of the self who is simultaneously 'other' in the text and, like the story with animals, more interesting in that guise than he is 'in reality,' the author cannot help but write himself in. That, of course, explains Pi's apparent supremacy as storyteller in Section Two: what appears to be Pi is actually Martel here, telling Pi's story. Therefore Richard Parker's sudden disappearance as they land on the Mexican coast, though mourned by Pi, is required; only in this way can Pi (in his authorial, storytelling guise) once more take centre stage.

Martel's method of blurring the boundaries between his hero as adventurer and himself as adventurous storyteller is aided by the narrative purportedly existing as the account of an account. According to what we have, by now, come to recognise as the obligatory peri-textual claim for truth status, the author suggests his novel to be a transcript of a story the 'real' Pi divulges to him while Martel is in India, researching a different book:

> [Mr. Patel] showed me the diary he kept during the events. He showed me the yellowed newspaper clippings that made him briefly, obscurely famous. He told me his story. All the while I took notes. Nearly a year later, after considerable difficulties, I received a tape and a report from the Japanese Ministry of Transport. (*Pi*, xi)

That this type of blurring between the narrative subject as hero and the narrative subject as storyteller is reciprocally motivated becomes clear, in part, during Pi's own version of his crossing, in which he makes numerous references to 'yarn spinning.' The first is taken from the survival manual discovered onboard, which lists storytelling as one of several options for keeping ' . . . the mind . . . occupied with whatever light distraction may suggest itself' (*Pi*, 166). In other words, Pi reveals himself to be as self-consciously aware of the power of storytelling as Martel (and vice versa). This elision is further facilitated by the use of first-person narrative, so that when Pi tries to convince us of the truth value of his extraordinary tale in Chapter 81, he does so in the first person: 'Proof: I remained alive day after day, week after week. Proof: he did not attack me, even when I was asleep on the tarpaulin. Proof: *I am here to tell you this story*' (*Pi*, 223; my emphasis). It is pointless for us to step back from our identification with Pi and complain—'but it's Yann Martel who's telling us this story, not you'—because, as we have seen, Martel uses this narrative to establish not distance, but proximity with Pi.

According to the Author's Note, the other book the implied author is researching while in India is not, surprisingly, about India at all, but about Portugal: 'This is not so illogical if you realize . . . that a novel set in Portugal in 1939 may have little to do with Portugal in 1939' (*Pi*, vii). Indeed, if we return to Louis Marin's stance on More's *Utopia*, neither India nor Portugal may prove quite the red herrings Martel implies:

> When Peter Giles, More's friend, introduces Raphaël, the traveller and narrator-descriptor of Utopia, to Thomas

More, he narrates precisely Raphaël's travels; he tells More of Raphaël's motivation to travel, his desire to visit the world . . . his departure from Portugal, his participation to Amerigo Vespucci's expeditions. Raphaël's travels, in fact, would have been very similar to Vespucci's if, during the fourth journey, instead of coming back to Portugal, he had not been one of the twenty-four men left at Cape Frio, on the Brazilian coast . . . And on this frontier [of the known world], which is also an initiating threshold, human aban-donment, the desire of travelling and the encounter with death merge together.[39]

Like Raphael's, Martel's journey begins with Portugal and moves out into the unknown and, as Pi himself remarks in response to his father's desire to follow in the footsteps of such great pioneers, when Columbus set sail, 'He was hoping to find India' (*Pi*, 88).

Sea, sky, and space, these three are always the backdrop to utopia. As Marin puts it, the function of the necessary shipwreck or storm at sea is to 'open a neutral space, one which is absolutely dif-ferent: a meteoric event, a cosmic accident, which eliminates all beacons and markers in order to make the seashore of a land appear at dawn, to welcome the human castaway.'[40] In the early stages of Pi's navigation, such 'cosmic accident[s]' might prove a blessing, providing a sense of conclusion to something otherwise irresolvable: 'My whole being tended towards the spot on the horizon that would appear and save me. It was a state of tense, breathless bore-dom' (*Pi*, 118). Later on, such 'solutions' are greeted less satisfacto-rily, as when he is almost mown down by an oil tanker:

The bow was a vast wall of metal that was getting wider every second. A huge wave girdling it was advancing towards us relentlessly . . . Its engines rumbling loudly and its propellers chopping explosively underwater . . . In less than twenty minutes a ship of three hundred thousand tons became a speck on the horizon. (*Pi*, 235–236)

In other words, just as elsewhere Pi longs for 'A long book with a never-ending story' (*Pi*, 207), so Pi's own narrative journey requires a lack of clear resolution for effect. Recalling our previous discus-sion in Chapter 1, Marin puts it thus: 'My semantic journey adrift on the term *lisière* (edge, fringe, selvage), points out a notion I will call *a neutral place*, a locus whose characteristics are semiotically negative, whose specificity consists in being neither the one nor the other, *neither* this edge *nor* the other . . .'[41]

For much of Martel's novel, the lifeboat and attached improvised raft *are*, in Marin's terms, the *lisière*, the 'edge, fringe, selvage,' originally part of the sunk cargo ship on which Pi and his family were travelling and hence metonymically wedded to, even in its absence. However, without the ship, the improvised raft has no meaning and so—in isolation from that originary partner-ship—it becomes what Marin calls that 'neutral place . . . whose characteristics are semiotically negative.' It is in seeming recognition of this fact that Pi observes, 'To be a castaway is to be a point perpetually at the centre of a circle. However much things may appear to change . . . the geometry never changes. Your gaze is always a radius. The circumference is ever great' (*Pi*, 215–216). This does, however, change in Chapter 92, when land finally hoves into view in the form of a floating island. It is similar to the floating island of Balnibarbi in *Gulliver's Travels*, except insofar as, where Balnibarbi floats through air, this unnamed island floats on the surface of the ocean. In addition, where Balnibarbi is fully civilised (in both positive and negative senses of the word), one part of it inhabited by people who 'walked fast, looked wild, their Eyes fixed, and were generally in rags' (*GT*, 164), another by a palace with 'Fountains, Gardens, Walks, Avenues, and Groves . . . all disposed with exact Judgement and Taste' (*GT*, 165), Pi's apparently idyllic isle is entirely uninhabited except, it transpires, by the teeth of the dead. These are all that remain once the corpses have been consumed by the carnivorous vegetation—the ultimate instance of being identified by one's dental records alone. Pi's island utopia, it seems, is both self-consuming and self-regenerating: as structurally unstable, in other words, as his narrative.

The concept of allegory can be interpreted very broadly to refer to the type of fantasy narrative that 'says one thing and means another,'[42] though such a definition immediately reminds us of the nonsense literature discussed in Chapter 4. Fletcher goes further, however, in stressing what he refers to as a 'doubleness of intention.'[43] The animal fable is another of those subgenres of fantasy of which Tolkien disapproves: 'Men dressed up as talking animals may achieve buffoonery or mimicry, but they do not achieve Fantasy.'[44] Though Tolkien is imprecise about the actual reason for his disapproval, Fletcher's argument may well offer a partial answer. For him, the strength of allegory is also its weakness in that, like the utopia or the sea voyage, the defamiliarising landscape it offers risks leaving itself 'open to the inroads of excessive intentional control.'[45]

George Orwell, *Animal Farm*

In the case of a novel such as *Animal Farm* (1945), one can clearly see how that doubleness functions. Indeed, the significance of the narrative relies on us reading everything from landscape to the naming of character metaphorically: 'Moses, who was Mr. Jones's especial pet, was a spy and a tale-bearer, but he was also a clever talker. He claimed to know of the existence of a mysterious country called Sugarcandy Mountain, to which all animals went when they died.'[46] Some, like Bammer, have identified *Animal Farm* as a satire on utopias.[47] Such judgments of Orwell's novel tend to be based on the fact that, as we have seen, the one major downside of the utopic drive lies in its insistence on consensus at all costs, and certainly *Animal Farm* places greatest emphasis on the shortcomings of naive idealism. Though this is true, that is not to say Orwell offers no recognition of the harnessing power utopianism affords. At the beginning of *Animal Farm*, this positive impulse can be identified with old Major, 'the prize Middle White boar' (*AF*, 5), whose capacity to dream, coupled with his 'wise and benevolent appearance' (*AF*, 6), has the ability to 'thr[o]w the animals into the wildest excitement' (*AF*, 14). However, having associated that utopian dimension with night-dreaming, it is undoubtedly a savage twist on Orwell's part that old Major unexpectedly dies (albeit 'peacefully' [*AF*, 15]) in his sleep three nights later.

My own reservations about Orwell's novel are that it seems to have what Fletcher would call 'too much "message"' at the expense of 'the natural disinterest of art.'[48] To some extent, this problem can be alleviated by us taking a different perspective on the human/animal relations within it and linking metamorphosis, as Irving Massey does, with language. For Massey, metamorphosis gives corporeal shape to 'uninterpretable paradox,' a phenomenon he finds best expressed in the physical behaviour of pigs:

> . . . anyone who has spent time on farms has noticed the strange habit pigs have of gaping, or stretching their jaws . . . It makes them look as if they were laughing in some unnatural way. (Pigs always have a dead-alive look.) But it is, of course, the same position of the mouth that they fall into when they squeal or scream . . . Is it a mockery of human laughter? Is it the agonized shriek of the animal?[49]

We endow pigs, then, with an innate nuance of anthropomorphism, whilst at the same time having an uncanny suspicion that they may be the ones anthropormophising us. This is precisely the ambivalence Orwell plays with in *Animal Farm*. In linguistic terms, anthropomorphism can be succinctly summed up as 'adding (+ human) features to nonhuman things and activities' and, according to R. S. Sharma, every act of language is an anthropomorphising activity: 'language [being] specific to the human species.' Furthermore, because language is always at a stage of removal from reality (being a signifying system), so each act of linguistic communication is also an act of anthropomorphism, 'express[ing] human awareness of objects and not objects themselves.'[50] In Orwell's novel, the pigs *parade* anthropomorphism through their own act of mimicry, and yet in so doing, one has to question—as in Massey's quotation—who is the original model for the mime. Certainly, it seems difficult to endow such originary status upon Mr. Jones, for he seems little more capable of 'standing on his own two feet' than Squealer:

> It was [Squealer] walking on his hind legs.
> Yes . . . [a] little awkwardly, as though not quite used to supporting his considerable bulk in that position, but with perfect balance, he was strolling across the yard. And a moment later, out from the door of the farmhouse came a long file of pigs, all walking on their hind legs. (*AF*, 113)

Once we (and the other animals) take our eyes off those gaping pigs, we suddenly realise that behind this parade lies the one question we are not really encouraged to ask, namely the nature of the relationship between Mr. Jones, the evicted farmer, and the wider community of human beings—from which, presumably, he has also been expelled. In these terms, a brief reminder that language is an innately human activity will speak volumes about his presiding silence.

Quickly dispensed with as a drunkard and an incompetent, though we briefly hear of Mr. Jones sitting in the 'taproom of the Red Lion at Willingdon, complaining to anyone who would listen' (*AF*, 34), he is never given the power of direct speech in the text, unlike the animals that replace him. Certainly, the reported nature of his complaint (that he has been 'turned out of his property by a pack of good-for-nothing animals' [*AF*, 34]) accords with Sharma's definition of linguistic anthropomorphism, being the 'express[ion of] human awareness of objects and not objects themselves.' Nevertheless, despite being farmer of the inaptly named Manor Farm, Mr. Jones seems anything but privileged. Were *Animal Farm* to be written now, when the British farming industry is in such crisis, the reader would be much more likely to pose questions such as 'Why has he taken to drink?' and 'Why does he flee so readily from his farm?' not to mention 'Why does Orwell accord him so little presence in the text?' We would be also far more likely to examine the following of Fletcher's observations from the perspective of the farmer rather than from the animals: 'When a people is being lulled into inaction by the routine of daily life, so as to forget all higher aspirations, an author perhaps does well to present behavior in a grotesque, abstract caricature.'[51]

Any fantasy work that uses animals as its central protagonists will struggle to maintain the distinction between the animals themselves and the humans they represent. As Hume says of Richard Adams's *Watership Down* (1972), though it 'starts with an attempt to enter rabbits' minds, [it] quickly lets the lapine vocabulary—owlsa, sifflay, hraka—substitute for real strangeness, while the plot degenerates into the adventures of animals with human brains.'[52] This, in my opinion, is where *Life of Pi* comes into its own, for Martel's novel works not just from the stance of a 'doubleness of intention' but from a duplicity of intention and is, in my opinion, a far superior novel as a result. Unlike in *Animal Farm* or *Watership Down*, the reader reads *Life of Pi* 'straight,' right until Pi's own surprise revelation towards the end of the text, with the effect that both human and animal characters maintain their respective existence as humans and animals throughout. Only retrospectively do we recognise what Fletcher sees as a key facet of allegory, namely that it employs conflict between 'rival authorities' (including those governing truth status) as the basis for its very being: 'One ideal will be pitted against another, its opposite . . . The mode is hierarchical in essence . . .'[53]

Throughout Orwell's text, rival readings (and levels of interpretation) necessarily come into conflict. As we read, for instance, about Mollie the horse, who 'became more and more troublesome' (*AF*, 41), and who is suspected of fraternising with one of the farmworkers on the neighbouring farm, allowing her nose to be stroked and accepting sugar treats, part of us is dismayed by her disloyalty to the animals and part of us equally dismayed by the rigidity of the new order: 'Mollie! Look me in the face. Do you give me your word of honour that the man was not stroking your nose?' (*AF*, 41). As well as the positive and negative value judgments involved, the third reading we are carrying with us is the continual reality check that allegory involves. Here, we realise, we are reading about the manner in which human revolution quickly leads to a new dictatorship. To read an allegory, then, is an abrasive process, one in which we are never simply reading, but always interpreting, sometimes—like sandpaper—against the grain.

Perhaps this is why Orwell makes reading and its relation to interpretation one of the key themes in the book, for along with technology, this is where the ability to usurp power and knowledge are seen to be greatest. Hence, in *Animal Farm*, one of the first initiatives instilled by the pigs is the introduction of literacy classes for all, albeit with variable results. What this also enables is the synthesising of a new manifesto into a simple slogan: 'Four legs good, two legs bad' (*AF*, 31), which, following the above-mentioned metamorphosis among the pigs, becomes 'Four legs good, two legs *better*! Four legs good, two legs *better*!' (*AF*, 114; original emphasis). But literacy alone cannot effect a thorough social transformation—be that metamorphosis positive or negative: that requires additional input from technology. We have seen, in Chapter 4, that the manufacturing industry can be treated with grave suspicion in certain fantasy texts. In the Lord of the Rings, for example, quite aside from its association with Saruman and the Orcs, as the travellers return to the Shire after destroying the One Ring, they discover that, in their absence, the region has been taken over by 'ruffians,'[54] and that one of the acts of vandalism they impose upon it is to replace the old Saw-Mill, one of the few original instances of manufacturing, with 'a bigger one . . . full o'wheels and outlandish contraptions' (*RK*, 333), the primary output of which is, according to Farmer Cotton, 'a-hammering and a-letting out a smoke and stench . . . And they pour out filth a purpose' (*RK*, 334).

The manufacturing industry looms large on the landscapes of both *Animal Farm* and *A Connecticut Yankee at King Arthur's Court*, functioning simultaneously as a key landmark and site of progress, if also one of dispute. Among the first things Orwell's animals do, having acquired their freedom from the farmer, is to plan to build a mill that will supply power to the farm, thus making the animals independent of any reliance on human agency. However, though the animals are initially attracted by the visions of technology offered them by the pigs ('they listened in astonishment while Snowball conjured up pictures of fantastic machines which would do their work for them while they grazed at their ease in the fields or improved their minds with reading and conversation' [*AF*, 44]), the reality is that collectivism quickly gives way to inequalities, the pigs 'managing' the project while the other beasts struggle with labour beyond their physical and mental capabilities. In *A Connecticut Yankee*, two advantages afford the Yankee as he mulls over the means by which he will introduce technology to this preindustrial society. One is that, faced with no reasonable competitors, he can easily set himself up as the greatest entrepreneur and history-maker of all time. A second is that technology gives the Yankee a perfect opportunity to reveal Merlin's magic as a poor substitute for technical advancement; for if Snowball the pig is guilty of conjuring false images, Merlin, as far as the Yankee is concerned, is a 'maundering old ass' (*CY*, 64).

Technology Versus Magic: *A Connecticut Yankee* and Harry Potter

The interface between technology and magic is particularly interesting in *A Connecticut Yankee* because, where Fletcher perceives, in those narratives that work with magic as a central structural element, 'the principle of . . . contagion, by which characters . . . interact, infecting each other with various virtues or vices,'[55] here the fear of 'contagion' revolves around technology. Once forcibly introduced to a society lacking the infrastructure to support it, technology never quite abandons its status as alternative magic, and when it starts to turn against society, that magic takes on a black hue. Hamlin Hill argues that this aspect of Twain's novel has a biographical application. Samuel Langhorne Clemens, the man behind the Mark Twain pseudonym, had his own notorious fascination for gadgetry, particularly those aspects of technology that brought reading and writing to the masses in the form of print culture. As Hill puts it,

> As the decade of the 1880s began, Clemens committed himself ever more deeply to financial obligations in the field of publishing technology. In February, 1880, he purchased 80 percent of the stock in a printing process known as Kaolatype and immediately began spending additional amounts on 'a new application of this invention' . . . The following year he made his initial investment in the Paige Typesetter . . . [56]

Recalling that *A Connecticut Yankee* was first published in 1889, we realise that the protagonist within it is a form of comic self-caricature. For, not unlike his protagonist's own fame- and wealth-based motivations, 'Clemens was determined to become the publisher of his own books and to enjoy the profits made entirely by himself.'[57] But we also remember that, in *A Connecticut Yankee*, technology proves to be the Yankee's downfall, as indeed it did the author himself. Hill claims that as Clemens invested increasing amounts of his own capital in print-based technology, he effectively became part of his own machinery. Hence, once his machinery began to fail, there was no alternative outlet for his literary voice, and 'Typesetter and publishing house and Mark Twain all failed together.'[58]

Despite our own increasingly technological culture, it is still the case that the appetite for antidotes to the machine age remains strong, the most obvious recent example of such being J. K. Rowling's Harry Potter books (1997–present). Rowling's character

Arthur Weasley is a perfect illustration of this preference. An administrator in the Ministry for Magic, Arthur's job is to liaise with what are known, in the Harry Potter series, as Muggles (non-wizarding people) whose world exists in parallel—if obliviously so—to the magical one of Hogwarts. As an extension of his job, Arthur is teased for his hobby, which is his fascination with Muggle technology. So his office wall is covered in 'several posters of cars, including one of a dismantled engine; two illustrations of postboxes he seemed to have cut out of Muggle children's books; and a diagram showing how to wire a plug.'[59] As gadgets they are seen as quaint, testimony to Muggle limitations rather than (as in science fiction) human advancement. One only needs an aeroplane if one cannot fly on a broomstick (though Rowling makes it clear that flight by broomstick is a very chilly option at times) and postboxes are 'for the birds' when one has owls to make deliveries right into the recipient's hand.

In this sense, Rowling seems to be working within the same type of atavistic fantasy tradition dominated in the twentieth century by Tolkien. However, the two authors' attitudes towards technology are different. In Tolkien's case, technology is implied to be evidence of the dangers of the modern world, accruing a sense of grave moral suspicion. In Harry Potter, technology is used, but only for the purposes of disguise or as a last resort. Take, for instance, the Ford Anglia car Harry and his friend Ron Weasley (Arthur's son) use to fly to Hogwarts at the start of *Volume II, Harry Potter and the Chamber of Secrets* (1998). Bearing in mind that production of the Ford Anglia ceased in 1967, the Weasleys' choice of car is certainly eccentric. Where Muggles would usually choose the most modern car possible, Arthur chooses it much as an art dealer collects old masters. Nevertheless, the hierarchy of mechanical progress is not entirely disregarded: a Ford Anglia may be near obsolete, but it is certainly less so than a steam engine. Hence, once the boys are denied access to the Hogwarts Express, which leaves the imperceptible (to Muggles) platform 9¾ in London's Kings Cross station on the first day of the school year, their only alternative is to travel by car. Herein lies the major difference: where Muggles' cars travel on roads, the Weasleys' Ford Anglia flies through the air. As Ron himself puts it, 'All we've got to worry about now are aeroplanes.'[60]

A second similar example frames the means of entry to the Ministry of Magic, namely an old red telephone box first encountered in *Volume V, Harry Potter and the Order of the Phoenix* (2003). Harry, who is of course no stranger to Muggle living, demonstrates the typical scepticism of most twenty-first century British users of public services:

> 'Mr. Weasley, I think this might be out of order . . .'
> 'No, no, I'm sure it's fine,' said Mr. Weasley, holding the receiver above his head and peering at the dial. 'Let's see . . . six . . . two . . . four . . . and another four . . . and another two . . .'
> As the dial whirred smoothly back into place, a cool female voice sounded inside . . . as loudly and plainly as though an invisible woman were standing right beside them.
> 'Welcome to the Ministry of Magic.' (*HPOP*, 115)

Both episodes hold a kind of nostalgia for adult readers in Britain; the Ford Anglia was one of the 'classic' British family cars, and red telephone boxes one of the icons of post–World War II British culture. However, in this second example another more specifically fantasy-based nostalgia comes to mind in the use to which the police telephone box (or TARDIS, as it was known) was put in the popular British television crossover child/adult science fiction series *Doctor Who*.[61] This is, it seems, Rowling adding her own dose of intertextual 'magic.'

This anti-technological aspect of the mass appeal of Harry Potter is, in many ways, surprising, primarily because we (as adults) are repeatedly encouraged to believe our children to be continually—and en mass—hooked up to their computers to the total exclusion of all other forms of culture. In these terms, Rowling's achievement is not simply that she has succeeded in dragging them away from those computers and making them read books (books of 600–700 pages, at that), but also that those books openly reject technology as a poor substitute for the outmoded world of magic and spells. However, we must also remember that, although Rowling eschews technology within her texts, at the time of this writing the existence of at least the first three volumes in the Harry Potter series are readily available as virtual reality computer games (as, of course, is Tolkien's Lord of the Rings trilogy). Indeed, there are moments in this series—particularly in the later volumes—where Rowling appears to explicitly integrate passages adopting a 'computer-game' narrative style, as if directly gesturing towards the larger technological empire beyond. Take, for example, Harry's fascination for what is behind the door at the end of the corridor in the Ministry of Magic, a vision that repeatedly intercepts his dreams, and that draws him with the utopia possibility of what 'lies beyond.' As the image becomes more insistent, later in the text, Harry responds in the way in which a computer-game player would to the screen of a computer game at which he or she is 'stuck':

> He walked towards it with a sense of mounting excitement. He had the strangest feeling that this time he was going to be lucky at last, and find the way open . . . he was feet from it, and saw with a leap of excitement that there was a glowing strip of faint blue light down the right-hand side . . . the door was ajar . . . he stretched out his hand to push it wide and—
>
> Ron gave a loud, rasping, genuine snore and Harry awoke abruptly . . . (*HPOP*, 509)

So computer technology offers a window onto the literary world of fantasy, the screen becoming an updated version of the magical mirror. In Jeanette Winterson's *The PowerBook* (2000), she places this new technology at the heart of her novel.

Jeanette Winterson, *The PowerBook*

Winterson works, in most of her fiction, with a new type of time travel technique, one belonging to the polychronotopic possibilities of the postmodern. She shifts between centuries, spatio-temporal planes, and sometimes genders in her journeys into and through the mystery of the narrative subject in order to decentre assumptions about character construction, sexuality, and historical causality. Fantasy is her stock in trade: she is an unashamed storyteller of the kind one more typically finds in magic realism, though her narrative style is often far sparer than magic realism allows. *The PowerBook* is particularly spare in its narrative style, the plot being boiled down to sparse, staccato sentences and fractured paragraphs that in some ways fail to satisfy on first read. And yet, when one looks again, the enormity of the material compressed into so tight a form explodes off the page; in that sense, the e-mail, which her characters use as the main mode of communication in the book, also functions as a kind of narrative metaphor.

Take, for instance, the novel's opening. The main protagonist sits at her computer screen 'unwrap[ping]' an e-mail message. Immediately, that virtual connection opens out into a new space of desire— almost a pleasure dome in which the 'unwrapped' may wrap themselves up again in a variety of disguises and thereby unravel their core self-definition:

> Years ago you would have come to my shop . . . you would have found yourself alone . . . looking at the suits of armour, the wimples, the field boots, and the wigs on spikes like severed heads.
>   The sign on the shop says VERDE, nothing more, but everyone knows that something strange goes on inside. People arrive as themselves and leave as someone else. They say that Jack the Ripper used to come here.[62]

This is simultaneously a space of forbidden desire and a forbidding space of fantasy. Though a space in which 'anything becomes possible,' it is also an encaging space. Like the magic toyshop in Angela Carter's novel of the same name,[63] Winterson here takes virtual reality and gives it physical presence before endowing it with a temporal location. The quoted passage opens with the unspecified phrase 'years ago.' By the end of the passage, however, the number of years can be to some extent specified through the reference to Jack the Ripper (whose murders were committed in 1888). Looking up a storey to the original fascia of the buildings above shop level, Winterson's narrator wonders 'if time stacks vertically, and there is no past, present, future, only simultaneous layers of reality' (*PB*, 186).

Winterson is at her best when offering competing worlds, for it is in the interface between these versions of possibility that, in her hands, history becomes magic. In *The PowerBook*, the historical plot revolves around the larger-than-life narrative of a sixteenth-century female tulip smuggler, reputedly the first to bring tulips from Asia to Europe. As we journey across the boundaries between frame and inner fiction, we find a similar amalgam of fact and fancy that may well lead us to question the 'truth' of either. Should we do so, however, we will find that this narrator might well be speaking 'truth'—at least according to Sally Petitt, of Cambridge University Botanical Gardens:

> [Tulips were] first introduced into cultivation by the Ottoman Turks in the 15th century . . . From Constantinople, tulips . . . found their way into European gardens in the 1570s.
>
> There followed in the 17th century a wave of intense passion for tulip hybrids, and in the Netherlands 'tulip mania' resulted in ludicrous premiums for individual bulbs, along with the making and breaking of fortunes.[64]

As Winterson's tale unfolds, larger-than-life historical 'truth' gives way to the incredulity of fable. First our narrator informs us that 'It was the Key of Pleasure and Lover's Dream that I carried from Sulyman the Magnificent to Leiden in 1591.' In fact, the precise breeds carried to Europe are now unknown, and both cultivars mentioned here appear to be of Winterson's own invention. That matters less, however, than the further shift into comic fantasy, rooted in what comes next: 'To be exact, I strapped them under my trousers . . .' (*PB*, 9–10). Winterson's use of shifting modes of writing (from history to legend to the purely marvellous) is what makes her use of fantasy so powerful. The boundaries existing not only between dream and reality, fancy and imagination, but also between one of her books and another start to unravel, and we find ourselves immersed in the larger tapestry of Winterson's fictive world.

So, in *The PowerBook*, evocations of her other novels are everywhere, pulling together Winterson's two main themes, the flesh and its spiritual transcendence. On one level, *Written on the Body* and *The PowerBook* share a fascination for physiology; what is, in *Written on the Body*, 'I know the calcium of your cheekbones. I know the weapon of your jaw . . . Myself in your skin, myself lodged in your bones . . .'[65] becomes, in *The PowerBook*, 'What if skin, bone, liver, veins, are the things I use to hide myself?'(*PB*, 15). And, in *Sexing the Cherry*, where the huge physiognomy of Dogwoman is transcended by fantastic/supernatural means ('I was invisible . . . I, who must turn sideways through any door, can melt into the night . . .'),[66] so in *The PowerBook*, the tulip smuggler refers to herself as being 'So slender . . . and so slight, that I can slip under the door of a palace, or between the dirt and the floor of a hovel, and never be seen' (*PB*, 11). A further comparison between these two texts lies in the central role played by the sea voyage in both. Furthermore, though a real voyage on one level, on another it functions as a route into story:

> This is a world inventing itself. Daily, new landmasses form and then submerge. New continents of thought break off from the mainland. Some benefit from a trade wind, some sink without a trace. Others are like Atlantis—fabulous, talked about, but never found.
>
> Found objects wash up on the shores of my computer. Tin cans and old tyres mix with the pirate's stuff. The buried treasure is really there, but caulked and outlandish . . .
>
> That's why I trawl my screen like a beachcomber . . .
> (*PB*, 63–64)

Though Winterson frequently and fondly uses what we might consider to be a stereotypical 'women's' form of networking (legend, gossip, and hearsay), *The PowerBook* also capitalises on a newer type of network: the electronic variety. In the process, she maps legend onto those types of cybernetic models emerging out of the work of the feminist theorist Donna J. Haraway. Haraway's work embraces technology as a means of subverting the common phallocentric binary divide that, through the centuries, has relegated woman to biology, man to culture. Through technology, she claims, women are freed from their biological shackles of reproduction. Nevertheless, though her landmark essay, 'A Cyborg Manifesto,' offers a self-avowed utopian vision, it is not of the kind that accommodates traditional originary metanarratives: 'The cyborg would not recognize the Garden of Eden; it is not made of mud and cannot dream of returning to dust.' Instead, she offers the possibility of 'a world without gender, which is perhaps a world without genesis . . .

[and] outside salvation history.' The figure upon which she relies for this salutary role is that of the cyborg, 'simultaneously animal and machine,' who differs from the robot in having a non-originary relationship to humanity.[67] Where the robot mimics humanity, the cyborg's relationship to humanity is seamless: where does the distinction between nature and culture lie?

In looking at more traditional allegory, Fletcher repeatedly identifies science fiction as a new form of theology in which the demonic agent is replaced by a robot, or in which the automaton (in its ability to bridge the worlds of the human and the inhuman) almost functions in parallel to the former role adopted by angels. Such creations 'compartmentalize function. If we were to meet an allegorical character in real life . . . [i]t would seem that he was driven by some hidden, private force; or . . . controlled by some foreign force, something outside the sphere of his own ego.'[68] That such religious terminology is perfectly in keeping with the post-Christian ethos of Winterson's oeuvre does not surprise us; more unsettling, perhaps, is its application to Haraway's work, until we recall that she begins her own essay with a statement of faith, in her case to 'feminism, socialism, and materialism,' but she employs an inverted religious rhetoric to reinforce her stance: 'Perhaps more faithful as blasphemy is faithful, than as reverent worship and identification . . . Blasphemy protects one from the moral majority within, while still insisting on the need for community.'[69] Nevertheless, secular antecedents to the cyborg can also be found in other fantasy narratives, such as the knight on horseback of Arthurian myth, for whom the precise point at which 'technology' (the armour and weaponry) becomes nature (the man/the horse) is impossible to identify: separate them and the knight disappears, his function and identity relying on the commingling of forms.

The knight on horseback has remained a common theme in Winterson's writing from *Oranges Are Not the Only Fruit* (1985) onwards and is usually linked to a quest about sexuality. In *The PowerBook*, Winterson draws on the story of Lancelot coming to Guinevere's bedchamber and being betrayed to Arthur by Mordred and Agravaine, taken originally from the eighth tale of Malory's *Le Morte d'Arthur*. In the process, the narrator of *The PowerBook* is implicitly identified with Lancelot, the beloved with Guinevere, but here—as elsewhere in Winterson's writing—clear gender demarcations between lover and beloved break down:

> Your cock is in my cunt. My breasts weigh under your dress. My fighting arm is sinew'd to your shoulder. Your tiny feet stand my ground . . . When I see through your green eyes, I see the meadows bright with grass. When you creep behind my retina, you see the flick of trout in the reeds of the lake. (*PB*, 69)

Again we return to a vision of Haraway's cyborg, which 'has no truck with bisexuality,' instead being 'resolutely committed to . . . [a] perversity' under the terms of which 'the one can no longer be the resource for appropriation or incorporation by the other.'[70]

Winterson's *The PowerBook* is not, of course, in literal terms a novel about cyborgs in the manner of, for instance, Marge Piercy's *Body of Glass* (1991). Piercy takes a recognisably futurist *sf* landscape, combines it with the ancient Jewish mythology of the legend of the Golem, and follows her female character Shira as she forges a sensual relationship with the cyborg Yod, a creation with a masculine physique employed as a weapon to defend the Jewish community of Tikva, but with a largely feminine consciousness implanted in 'his' psyche.[71] Yet while *The PowerBook* is not populated by cyborgs, it does follow Haraway's larger cybernetic philosophy of how woman can use technology to re-establish a role for herself within what Haraway calls 'the integrated circuit,'[72] as opposed to the political (read patro-capitalist) globalised culture. Hence Winterson's protagonist Ali(x), online, becomes free of all biological determination, free to reconstruct subjectivity at will: 'Take off your clothes. Take off your body. Hang them up behind the door. Tonight we can go deeper than disguise . . . I can change the story. I am the story. Begin . . .' (*PB*, 4–5). By the end, nevertheless, she finds herself alone, this being another characteristic of Winterson's work.

William Gibson, *Neuromancer*

This solitariness also informs *Neuromancer* (1984), a dark, hard novel that updates the traditional cowboy genre to re-explore masculinity in a postmodern virtual landscape in which power means '[C]orporate power. The zaibatsus, the multinationals . . .'[73] According to Peter Stoneley, the traditional image of the cowboy is one that, despite appearing as the embodiment of 'a celebration of manliness,' defines himself primarily in relation to femininity: '[He] consciously attempts to evade and transcend the culture of women.'[74] Gibson's protagonist, Henry Dorsett Case, certainly shares this character profile, revealing his reluctance for intimacy in acknowledging that 'Cowboys didn't get into simstim . . . because it was basically a meat toy' (N, 71) and leaving behind his needy 'girl': 'Once he woke from a confused dream of Linda Lee, unable to recall who she was or what she'd ever meant to him. When he did remember, he jacked in and worked for nine straight hours' (N, 76). However, where, like the armoured knight, a traditional cowboy needs a horse, this aspect of the convention has become an anachronism: '"Hey, Christ," the Finn said, taking Case's arm, "looka that." He pointed. "It's a horse, man. You ever see a horse?" Case glanced at the embalmed animal and shook his head' (N, 112). Instead, Case substitutes nature for culture, Death Valley for Silicon Valley, for what he 'rides' is cyberspace, a new, technologised version of the 'deserts and windswept plains' that the traditional cowboy seeks out as 'an unsuitable locale for the niceties of womanly feeling.'[75] In that choice, however, Case makes a fatal error, for here he encounters Molly, his cybernetic other.

Neuromancer, as its opening sentence suggests ('The sky above the port was the color of television, tuned to a dead channel' [N, 9]), certainly depicts a world in which nature has become superseded by a bleak form of artifice and in which cyberspace has become the closest thing available to a lost utopia:

A year here and he still dreamed of [it], hope fading nightly. All the speed he took . . . and still he'd see the matrix in his sleep, bright lattices of logic unfolding across the colorless void . . . The Sprawl was a long strange way home over the Pacific now . . . But the dreams came on in the Japanese night like livewire voodoo, and he'd cry for it, cry in his sleep . . . temperfoam bunched between his fingers, trying to reach the console that wasn't there.' (N, 11)

As one might expect in a novel in which the central protagonist is called Case, the classic form of the human anatomy has also become an anachronism. Flesh is now meat and prosthetics routine, with the result that questions arise over the continued validity of something called 'full subjectivity.' Where, as we saw at the start of this chapter, More employs a reversal between first- and third-person pronouns in his *Utopia*, thus blurring the distinction between different characters' opinions, in *Neuromancer* Maelcum, Case's companion for part of his mission, uses only first-person pronouns in referring to them both ('I an' I mus' go' [*N*, 291]) as if neither he nor Case has autonomy from the other. Certainly, Case, though he has independence for us as a character in his own right, lacks a clear sense of who he is aside from what he is told: 'She recited the year and place of his birth, his BAMA Single Identification Number, and a string of names he gradually recognized as aliases from his past' (*N*, 189). Admittedly, he does have a form of narrative pre-existence: he was a cyber-thief, prior to his detection, and paid to use the software written by more senior criminals in order to access information for illicit purposes. Nevertheless, on being discovered by his own employers to have been attempting to defraud them, he is punished by being anatomically 'reprogrammed,' his nerve centres being attacked by a form of biological agent designed to render him incapable of working again. The process strips him of any connection with his own former self.

In a world where all is surface, there are inevitable repercussions for the psyche, too: instead of a personality, Case now has a 'profile' (*N*, 40). The mission upon which he is sent is orchestrated by Wintermute, a character who turns out to be a construct of artificial intelligence, thereby adding a new perspective on the aspects of anthropomorphism explored earlier through *Animal Farm*. Though dreams remain, memory bears only a fractured relationship to the self and can be physically removed by the cybernetically adept. So, as somebody skilled in illicit virtual access, it is ironic that Case's own memory banks become transformed into a kind of RAM 'lifted' by the Finn, a trafficker in stolen software, who retrieves elements of Case's memory while he is unconscious, extracting and visually confronting him with his own fears later on.

As Case 'jacks in' to his partner Molly's consciousness, using 'sim-stim' in order to trail her through the streets of the Sprawl, we are aware of the fact that, though he uses her dose of painkillers to dull his own headache, and reads the time through the digital display in her artificially enhanced optic nerve, he begins with some sense of flesh as original: 'He knew . . . the cyberspace matrix was actually a drastic simplification of the human sensorium . . .' (*N*, 71). As he moves into the next phase of tracking, his psyche becoming implanted into her own, this sense lessens, and with it his awareness of difference from Molly: 'Matrix gone, a wave of sound and color . . . Smells of urine, free monomers, perfume, patties of frying krill' (*N*, 71). This is not to say that Case and Molly, any more than Case and Maelcum, exist as one unified subject during simstim. A 'virtual' mimickry of the binding of bodies during intercourse, there are moments when Case's subjectivity comes adrift from Molly's, and at these moments it is clear that Molly is the one in control: 'He was thoroughly lost now; spatial disorientation held a peculiar horror for cowboys. But she wasn't lost, he told himself' (*N*, 249).

Despite these continual references to the postmodern cowboy, ultimately what *Neuromancer* gives us is a version of postmodern Gothic or, to put it more accurately, a vision of postmodern culture *as* Gothic. The title itself communicates that connection, as the eponymous character, a young boy on the beach found late in the novel, makes explicit in his explanation of its etymology: 'The lane to the land of the dead . . . Neuro from the nerves, the silver paths. Romancer. Necromancer. I call up the dead . . . But no, my friend . . . I *am* the dead, and their land' (*N*, 289; original emphasis). The difficulty is that in a land where living is a form of death, we are left asking what the status of death comprises and how it can, any longer, be meaningfully linked to loss. Furthermore, though corpses are frequently encountered, their identities shift—at least as far as Case is concerned, taking on different faces as the virtual technology is intercepted—with the result that death appears collectively inhabited and those who appear dead sometimes 'return.'

Neuromancer's explanation, given above, also evokes a clear sense of a cartography, one that can be mapped onto physical terrain. Where terrain usually deals in an expanse of space, however, here it deals in lack of space, and along with it comes a new form of claustrophobia. So Night City, like a ghoul, has only nocturnal existence: 'By day, the bars . . . were shuttered and featureless, the neon dead, the holograms inert, waiting, under the poisoned silver sky' (*N*, 13). Case, who lodges in temporary accommodation, rents a 'coffin' in which to sleep. Stacked one on top of another, six in a pile, and ten piles along a wall, these are nothing more than places to sleep and, their dimensions measuring 'three meters long, the oval hatches a meter wide and just under a meter and a half tall' (*N*, 30), claustrophobia would seem to be an essential given.

This reference to a 'shuttered and featureless' cityscape draws attention to another of the key themes of the novel, namely its compulsive focus on questions of perspective. As we have already seen in Chapter 4, through Tolkien's use of Legolas in the Lord of the Rings trilogy and, earlier in this chapter, Swift's use of shifting perspectives in *Gulliver's Travels*, perspective is a crucial marker of scale in fantasy narratives. Unlike realism, wherein the parameters of empiricism are ready-made, here we find them open to negotiation, and so, hand in hand with this, our vision expands and contracts in response. Gibson takes this to new lengths in his depiction of Molly, whose own mirror lenses 'were surgically inset, sealing her sockets. [They] . . . seemed to grow from smooth pale skin above her cheekbones . . .' (*N*, 36). As we progress through the text, we discover that eye imagery is particularly important, a feature one might expect when considering that Case's relationship to Molly is dependent upon a screen-based piece of technology that shows him only at what she is looking. And yet eyes are also repeatedly revealed to be wounded spaces: Molly, finishing off the suicidal Tessiere-Ashpool, kills him by pushing a poisoned dart through the lid of his closed left eye. In reply, his alter ego, Peter Riviere, boyfriend to Tessier-Ashpool's genetically cloned 'daughter' 3Jane, half-blinds Molly by smashing her left mirrored lens with a glass. Left without Molly at the end of the text, Case ponders the fact that 'I never even found out what color her eyes were' (*N*, 314). These eye images return us to Freud and his belief, as expressed in 'The "Uncanny,"' that a 'study of dreams, phantasies and myths has taught us that anxiety about one's eyes, the fear of going blind, is often enough a substitute for the dread of being castrated.'[76]

In terms of the aforementioned bodily punishment meted out on Case, castration becomes a metaphor for bodily breakdown, and perhaps it is therefore apt that the next occasion on which Case sees Molly she appears as the living dead. 'Something creaked, behind him, creaked again. 3Jane pushed Molly out of the shadows in an ornate Victorian bathchair . . . She looked very small. Broken. A patch of brilliantly white micropore covered her damaged lens; the other flashed emptily as her head bobbed with the motion of the chair' (N, 295). Where Molly's castration takes a physical manifestation, Case's takes a psychological track, channelling anxiety into a single phobic image, the one previously extracted from Case's memory by the Finn. The injury to the eye takes the form of a kind of visual goading as it is paraded before him: 'Remember this?' (N, 204). What Case recalls, and what the Finn holds up before him, is the image of a charred wasps' nest, one he destroyed nine years earlier, using a flamethrower. In the process of killing the wasps, Case turns the nest into a showpiece of horror, the force of the jet of fuel propelling it out of the open window and into the alleyway below. Running downstairs to finish the job, he is confronted with biology as nightmare: 'The spiral birth factory, stepped terraces of the hatching cells, blind jaws of the unborn moving ceaselessly, the staged progress from egg to larva, near-wasp, wasp' (N, 152). In a novel in which life exists as a form of living death, the 'natural' aspect of this ongoing metamorphosis seems particularly chilling because it confronts Case with an entomological version of what human life has become.

So, what is the main difference between *The PowerBook* and *Neuromancer*? Clearly, on one level, it resides in their respective treatments of gender politics. Though more potent than Case, Molly is, to a large extent, a fetish of male sadomasochistic sexual fantasy, with her surgically enhanced fingernails, incorporating 'four-centimeter scalpel blades' (N, 37), a fact rendered apparent in Riviera's 'spectacular' light show in which he conjures a simulacrum of himself engaged in sexual intercourse with her, a spectacle that begins with the construction of the staged space ('Lines of faint light began to form verticals and horizontals, sketching an open cube around the stage' [N, 166]), before filling with an accumulation of disconnected images of Molly's body ('A woman's hand,' 'the torso . . . white, headless, and perfect,' 'twitching limbs'). As it reaches its climax, 'the image slowly extended a clawed hand and extruded its five blades. With a languorous, dreamlike deliberation, it raked Riviera's bare back. Case caught a glimpse of exposed spine, but he was already up and stumbling for the door' (*N*, 168).

Certainly, where Gibson offers a highly masculinised vision of virtual technology, unequal relations between the sexes being made as evident in the 'women smiling as men made jokes' (*N*, 170) as they are in the gratuitous exploitation of images of the woman's body, Winterson's version is woman-centred. Nevertheless, the politics of her project are as complex as Gibson's, for where he draws attention to the exploitative treatment of women at the same time as he—on some level—revels in it, in Winterson's own treatment of the female beloved there is always a sense of that possessive objectification that only renders it different to Gibson's in terms of degree. In celebrating a technological advance that 'delivers me from the vestiges of biological constraints,'[77] Winterson also revels in the accompanying irresponsibility that the Internet allows. On one level, this is politically liberating; as Slavoj Žižek puts it, cyberspace 'realizes in our everyday practical experience the "deconstruction" of old metaphysical binaries ("real Self" versus "artificial mask," etc.),' which frees us from the role of 'patriarchal Law.'[78] At the same time, however, both Gibson and, albeit to a lesser extent, Winterson use this freedom to flirt with those very worlds that have traditionally imprisoned women: those of illicit sex and the newer one of Internet/cybernetic 'stalking': 'Here, in these long lines of laptop DNA. Here we take your chromosomes, twenty-three pairs, and alter your height, eyes, teeth, sex. This is an invented world. You can be free just for one night' (*PB*, 4). Real life, Winterson's narrator suggests, is a constraint upon the flesh, and the choices hung before us in *The PowerBook* swing repeatedly between freedom and imprisonment, begging questions such as 'Do our bodies free us or en[C]ase us?' 'Are they an expression of who we are or a disguise that prevents others from perceiving who we are?'

Fred Botting identifies, in *Neuromancer*, an attempt to master 'mater' through the status of the matrix as a kind of originary space of desire. In order to allow for this, however, the subject must both 'subject himself' and 'play (with) himself' in the larger virtual game: 'An oedipal fantasy exceeds itself through the mastery provided by technology, a virtual erasure of the gap by which fantasy remains fantasy, separated from its object. At last, man can return home, taking fantasy beyond fantasy in a palpable fulfilment of desire for a mother simulated as matrix.'[79] Furthermore, this maternal connection is enlarged upon by Botting reading the means of access as a technological omphalos: 'One enters the matrix by plugging a jack into a socket in the head . . . [Thus t]he socket forms an artificial navel, as it were . . .'[80] Nevertheless, I perceive far more of a corporeal grounding in Winterson's work than in Gibson's, and one that derives from differing fantasies of the mother.

Botting's view of maternal fantasy derives in part from Žižek, whose rather cynical reading of virtual desire as a form of skewed narcissism certainly rings true in *Neuromancer*: 'if I never really want to encounter the Other, why bother at all with a Real Other? Isn't a machine which manipulates and fabricates substanceless signals of the Other good enough?'[81] In *The PowerBook*, we find the same type of maternal melancholia detectable in Winterson's oeuvre as a whole: 'My search for you, your search for me, is a search after something that cannot be found' (*PB*, 78). Instead, we return to magic mirrors, those decoy spaces that reflect our own fantasy images back upon ourselves and take the forms we give them:

> Sex between women is mirror geography. The subtlety of its secret—utterly the same, utterly different. You are a looking-glass world. You are the hidden place that opens to me on the other side of the glass. I touch your smooth surface and then my fingers sink through to the other side. You are what the mirror reflects and invents. I see myself, I see you, two, one, none. I don't know. Maybe I don't need to know. Kiss me. (*PB*, 174)

Here, though the central metaphor of this passage is a glass screen, it is not simply a projected play of light, such as that from which Gibson's character Riviera constructs his 'dreaming real' showpiece, 'The Doll.' Ultimately, the surface in Winterson's text is permeable, and at that moment of permeability, touch becomes fleshly ('my fingers sink through') and the woman 'breathes.' To live, however, is also to die, and in Chapter 6 we consider the role of the uncanny as the 'ghost in the machine' of and in the literary fantastic.

Notes

1. Marin, Louis, 'The Frontiers of Utopia,' in *Utopias and the Millennium*, Krishan Kumar and Stephen Bann, eds. (London: Reaktion Books, 1993), 7–16 (p. 13).

2. Paul Turner, 'Introduction,' in Thomas More, *Utopia* (1516; Harmondsworth: Penguin, 1965), 7–23 (p. 16). Further quotations from this book will be referenced within the main body of the text, accompanied by the abbreviation *U*.

3. For an application of this etymological shift, see Angelika Bammer's reading of *The Book of the City of Ladies*, in *Partial Visions: Feminism and Utopianism in the 1970s* (New York: Routledge, 1991), 10–11.

4. Bammer, *Partial Visions*, 13; my emphasis.

5. Northrop Frye, 'Variety of Literary Utopias,' in *Utopias and Utopian Thought*, F. E. Manuel, ed. (Boston: Beacon Press, 1967), 25–50 (p. 26). Cited in Bammer, *Partial Visions*, 11–12.

6. Jonathan Swift, *Gulliver's Travels* (1726; Harmondsworth: Penguin, 2001). Further quotations from this novel will be referenced within the main body of the text, accompanied by the abbreviation *GT*.

7. So Lilliput appears to lie southwest of Sumatra, Brobdingnag due west of California, Laputa and associated territory due east of Japan in the Pacific Ocean, and Houyhnhnms Land (less precisely charted) somewhere off the south coast of Australia. Gulliver claims to set sail from Bristol on May 4, 1699, flees Lilliput on September 24, 1701, and returns home to Kent on April 13, 1702. He sets sail again on June 20, 1702, arrives in Brobdingnag on June 17, 1703, is cast adrift off the coast of Brobdingnag in September 1705, and arrives back in England nine months later, on June 3, 1706. He then sets sail for the East Indies on August 5, 1706, and arrives en route at Madras on April 11, 1707. After a three-week rest, Gulliver and his crew set sail again to trade with neighbouring islands, only to encounter a storm that sets them off course. A fortnight later, he alights at an unnamed island, from which he first spots the floating island of Laputa. He leaves Laputa for the metropolitan capital of Balnibarbi, named Lagado, on February 16, 1709. After a further brief sojourn on the island of Glubbdubdrib, he arrives at Luggnagg on April 21, leaves for Japan on May 12, and arrives in Japan on May 27, 1709. He then acquires transport to take him to Nagasac in order to set sail for Europe. He leaves on June 9, 1709, and returns to Amsterdam on April 16, returning to England on May 10, 1710, which, as he states, is 'Five Years and Six Months complete' (*GT*, 201) since he left. After five months, Gulliver sets sail again, this time for the land of the Houyhnyms, sailing out of Portsmouth on August 2, 1710. After an unfortunate encounter with pirates, he sets ashore on May 9, 1711. He leaves for home again on February 15, 1714 (Robert Demaria Jr. reminds us that the introduction of the Julian calendar on March 25 of that year, changing the new year to 1715 means that Gulliver's arrival in Lisbon on November 5, 1715, is nine, not twenty-one months later [*GT*, 296n]), setting sail for England on November 24, arriving on December 5, 1715.

8. Robert Demaria Jr., 296n. See also Arthur Case, *Four Essays on Gulliver's Travels* (Princeton University Press, 1945).

9. Furst, Lilian R., *All Is True: The Claims and Strategies of Realist Fiction* (Durham: Duke University Press, 1995), 2; original emphasis.

10. Paul Turner draws our attention to the fact that the publisher of More's subsequent *Latin Epigrams* (1518) mentions, in the Introduction, '"a certain fathead" who said he did not see why More should be so much admired for his *Utopia*, since all he did was write down what somebody else had told him' (*U*, 9–10).

11. Angus Fletcher, *Allegory: The Theory of a Symbolic Mode* (Ithaca: Cornell University Press, 1964), 172–173.

12. Robert Demaria Jr. claims that Swift took several of the ideas for this scene from extracts he read in *Philosophical Transactions*, the journal of the Royal Society (*GT*, 287n).

13. Bammer, *Partial Visions*, 10.

14. Bammer, *Partial Visions*, 11.

15. Lucie Armitt, *Theorising the Fantastic* (London: Arnold, 1996), 29.

16. By 1915, only eleven of the individual American states had granted women the vote. Between 1915 and 1920, when the Nineteenth Amendment was finally passed, pressure continued to mount on the federal government. Charlotte Perkins Gilman, herself a suffrage campaigner, both capitalises on this sense of changing times in *Herland* and adds further fuel to the fire in publishing it.

17. Charlotte Perkins Gilman, *Herland* (1915; London: The Women's Press, 1979), 5. Further quotations from this novel will be referenced within the main body of the text, accompanied by the abbreviation *H*.

18. Bammer, *Partial Visions*, 2–3 and 42; my emphasis.

19. This is one of three such ages Mandel identifies, the other two being the 'Machine production of steam-driven motors since 1848 . . . [and the] machine production of electronic and nuclear-powered apparatuses since the 40s of the 20th century . . .' Ernest Mandel, *Late Capitalism* (London, 1978), 118. Cited in *Frederic Jameson, Postmodernism: Or, the Cultural Logic of Late Capitalism* (London: Verso, 1991), 35.

20. Sigmund Freud, 'On Narcissism: An Introduction,' in *The Standard Edition of the Complete Psychological Works of Sigmund Freud, Vol. 14, On the History of the Psycho-Analytic Movement, Papers on Metapsychology, and Other Works*, James Strachey, ed., in collaboration with Anna Freud (London: The Hogarth Press, 1957), 67–102 (pp. 88–89).

21. Freud, 'On Narcissism,' 91.

22. H. G. Wells, *The First Men in the Moon* (1901; London: J.M. Dent, 1993), 3. Further quotations from this novel will be referenced within the main body of the text, accompanied by the abbreviation *FMM*.

23. A. L. Morton, *The English Utopia* (London, 1952), 89. Cited in Louis James, 'From Robinson to Robina, and Beyond: *Robinson Crusoe* as a Utopian Concept,' in *Utopias and the Millennium*, Krishan Kumar and Stephen Bann, eds. (London: Reaktion Books, 1993), 33–45 (p. 33).

24. Daniel Defoe, *Robinson Crusoe* (1719; Harmondsworth: Penguin, 1985), 30.

25. H. G. Wells, *The Time Machine* (1895; London: J.M. Dent, 1995), 18. Further quotations from this novel will be referenced within the main body of the text, accompanied by the abbreviation *TM*.

26. Nick Bingham, 'In the Belly of the Monster: Frankenstein, Food, Factishes and Fiction,' in *Lost in Space: Geographies of Science Fiction*, Rob Kitchin and James Kneale, eds. (London: Continuum, 2002), 180–192 (p. 183).

27. Bingham, 'Belly of the Monster,' 191.

28. Bingham, 'Belly of the Monster,' 185.

29. Nicola Bown, *Fairies in Nineteenth-Century Art and Literature* (Cambridge: Cambridge University Press, 2001), 1.

30. Bown, *Fairies*, 1.

31. 'The Art of England' in *The Complete Works of John Ruskin* (Library Edition), E. T. Cook and Alexander Wedderburn, eds. 39 vols. (London: George Allen, 1903–12, vol. XXXIII), 327–349 (pp. 346–347). Cited in Bown, 40.

32. Kathryn Hume, *Fantasy and Mimesis: Responses to Reality in Western Literature* (New York: Methuen, 1984), 63.

33. According to legend, Warwick Castle has been haunted since the seventeenth century, when Sir Fulke Greville 'spent a sizeable part of his income . . . turning the semi-derelict [fourteenth-century] castle into a stately residence.' However, following Greville's murder by one of his servants in London, Greville is believed to have returned to the castle in spirit form and haunts what is now known as the Ghost Tower. http://www.warwick-castle .co.uk/castle/ghost_tower.asp

34. Mark Twain, *A Connecticut Yankee at King Arthur's Court* (1889; Harmondsworth: Penguin, 1971), 33. Further quotations from this novel will be referenced within the main body of the text, accompanied by the abbreviation *CY*.

35. Janet Cowen, 'Old Sir Thomas Malory's Enchanting Book': A Connecticut Yankee reads Le Morte d'Arthur,' in *Arthurian Studies in Honour of P. J. C. Field*, Bonnie Wheeler, ed. (Woodbridge: Boydell and Brewer, 2004), 311–324 (pp. 313–314).

36. Yann Martel, *Life of Pi* (Edinburgh: Canongate, 2002), 34. Further quotations from this novel will be referenced within the main body of the text, accompanied by the word *Pi*.

37. Julia Kristeva, *Powers of Horror: An Essay in Abjection* (New York: Columbia University Press, 1982), 38.

38. Kristeva, *Powers of Horror*, 39.

39. Marin, 'The Frontiers of Utopia,' 14–15.

40. Marin, 'The Frontiers of Utopia,' 14.

41. Marin, 'The Frontiers of Utopia,' 10; original emphasis.

42. Fletcher, *Allegory*, 2.

43. Fletcher, *Allegory*, 7.

44. J. R. R. Tolkien, 'On Fairy-Stories,' in *Tree and Leaf* (London: HarperCollins, 2001), 1–81 (p. 50).

45. Fletcher, *Allegory*, 320.

46. George Orwell, *Animal Farm* (1945; Harmondsworth: Penguin, 1951), 17. Further quotations from this novel will be referenced within the main body of the text, accompanied by the abbreviation *AF*.

47. Bammer, *Partial Visions*, 18.

48. Fletcher, *Allegory*, 124.

49. Irving Massey, *The Gaping Pig: Literature and Metamorphosis* (Berkeley, CA: University of California Press, 1976), 11–12.

50. R. S. Sharma, 'Anthropomorphism in the Language of Poetry,' in *Language and Style*, vol. 20, part 3 (1987), 257–267 (pp. 259 and 257 respectively).

51. Fletcher, *Allegory*, 23.

52. Hume, *Fantasy and Mimesis*, 161.

53. Fletcher, *Allegory*, 22.

54. J. R. R. Tolkien, *The Lord of the Rings, Volume III: The Return of the King* (1955; London: HarperCollins, 1999), 348. Further quotations from this novel will be referenced within the main body of the text, accompanied by the abbreviation *RK*.

55. Fletcher, *Allegory*, 207.

56. Hamlin Hill, 'Mark Twain: Texts and Technology' in *Cultural Artefacts and the Production of Meaning: The Page, the Image and the Body*, Margaret Ezell and Katherine O'Brien O'Keeffe, eds. (Ann Arbor, MI: University of Michigan Press, 1994), 71–83 (pp. 74–75).

57. Hill, 'Mark Twain,' 75.

58. Hill, 'Mark Twain,' 81.

59. J. K. Rowling, *Volume V, Harry Potter and the Order of the Phoenix* (London: Bloomsbury, 2003), 122. Further quotations from this novel will be referenced within the main body of the text, accompanied by the abbreviation *HPOP*.

60. J. K. Rowling, *Volume II, Harry Potter and the Chamber of Secrets* (London: Bloomsbury, 1998), 57. Further quotations from this novel will be referenced within the main body of the text, accompanied by the abbreviation *HPCS*.

61. The TARDIS (Time And Relative Dimension In Space) was a 1960s police telephone box (in reality designed to be used by police for emergency calls) in which Dr. Who travelled through time and space. It had its own

'magic,' in that its interior was of large scale yet somehow compressed to fit the dimensions of its smaller outer case.

62. Jeanette Winterson, *The PowerBook* (London: Vintage, 2001), 3. Further quotations from this novel will be referenced within the main body of the text, accompanied by the abbreviation *PB*.

63. Angela Carter, *The Magic Toyshop* (1967; London: Virago, 1981).

64. Sally Petitt, 'Tulips as Nature Intended,' in *The Garden: Journal of the Royal Horticultural Society*, vol. 128, no. 4 (April 2003), 260–265 (p. 260).

65. Jeanette Winterson, *Written on the Body* (London: Jonathan Cape, 1992), 120.

66. Jeanette Winterson, *Sexing the Cherry* (London: Bloomsbury, 1989), 8.

67. Donna J. Haraway, 'A Cyborg Manifesto: Science, Technology, and Socialist-Feminism in the Late Twentieth Century,' in *Simians, Cyborgs and Women: The Reinvention of Nature* (London: Free Association Books, 1991), 149–181 (pp. 151, 150, and 149 respectively).

68. Fletcher, *Allegory*, 40–41.

69. Haraway, 'A Cyborg Manifesto,' 149.

70. Haraway, 'A Cyborg Manifesto,' 150 and 151.

71. For a fuller discussion of Piercy's *Body of Glass* as feminist *sf*, see Lucie Armitt, *Contemporary Women's Fiction and the Fantastic* (London: Macmillan, 2000), Chapter 2.

72. Haraway, 'A Cyborg Manifesto,' 170.

73. William Gibson, *Neuromancer* (London: HarperCollins, 1995), 242. Further quotations from this novel will be referenced within the main body of the text, accompanied by the abbreviation *N*.

74. Peter Stoneley, ' "Never Love a Cowboy": Romance Fiction and Fantasy Families,' in *Writing and Fantasy*, Ceri Sullivan and Barbara White, eds. (London: Longman, 1999), 223–235 (p. 224).

75. Ibid.

76. Sigmund Freud, 'The "Uncanny,' in the *Penguin Freud Library, Vol. 14, Art and Literature*, Albert Dickson, ed. (Harmondsworth: Penguin, 1990), 335–376 (p. 352).

77. Slavoj Žizěk, 'Is it Possible to Traverse the Fantasy in Cyberspace?' in *The Žizěk Reader*, Elizabeth Wright and Edmond Wright, ed. (Oxford: Basil Blackwell, 1999), 107–114 (pp. 112–113).

78. Žizěk, 113.

79. Fred Botting, *Sex, Machines and Navels: Fiction, Fantasy and History in the Future Present* (Manchester: Manchester University Press, 1999), 170.

80. Ibid.

81. Žizěk, 'Fantasy in Cyberspace,' 108.

Chapter Six

One Key Question: Is There Life for Fantasy Beyond Genre?

Introduction

There is no more pertinent or influential question in the current field of fantasy than the question of the role genre plays in it. We have established fantasy, here, as the type of writing that questions what happens beyond the horizon, but in doing so we remain defined by that boundary, even in the act of crossing it. In effect, the boundary marks the point at which worlds begin and end—the Primary World versus the Secondary World, the point at which sleep becomes dream. In realism, we never reach these boundaries, and so are less conscious of their presence. As a result, the realist world gives the illusion of being boundless, but only because we never get the chance to test its limits. Boundaries define what fantasy is, and genre is another form of boundary demarcation. What happens, then, if we dismiss the concept of boundaries altogether: can fantasy still exist? The answer is yes and no. At that point, we lose sight of genre fantasy and open up onto a more challenging type of writing that engages with the fantastic, but in a far more disruptive sense, what I have elsewhere referred to as the 'loose ends . . . narrative difficulties and . . . wilful paradoxes' of fantasy,[1] what Tzvetan Todorov calls the literary fantastic.

When we start to examine Todorov's perspective on the fantastic more closely, we discover he neither outlines nor characterizes what it actually is. Instead, he endows it with a kind of narrative animation: 'The fantastic . . . leads a life full of dangers, and may evaporate at any moment.' Again, 'The fantastic is always a break in the acknowledged order, an irruption of the inadmissible within the changeless everyday legality.'[2] Like Marin's fraying edge, the fantastic is less something in itself (for it dismantles itself in its own expression) and more the impulse enabling textual borders to open up to readerly interjection. As such, it tends to be an area of greater interest for literary critics, because Todorov's fantastic tends to comprise works with a more ambitious narrative structure and is particularly characteristic of two of the greatest recent growth areas in fantasy studies, the Gothic and magic realism.

What the Gothic and magic realism have in common is their shared fascination for ghosts. Elsewhere I have argued that

> Some might read the very narrative structure of magic realism as following a type of ghosting formula which, in its attempt to demonstrate the inadequacies of realism and its attempts to come to terms with the genuinely marvellous within the real, constructs a palimpsest which interrogates the mimetic as it coincides with it and tracks its progress.[3]

Magic realism, then, haunts 'the real,' tracing a largely mimetic outline, the coherence of which dissolves in the face of unexpectedly disruptive moments of (usually) supernatural content. In the process, the 'normativity' of the society under scrutiny becomes challenged. Such narrative disruption, with its explosive impact, becomes a particularly powerful means of communicating volatile political unrest. For all its progressive political aims, however, magic realism relies for its effect on a much older narrative form, the Victorian ghost story, for in order for the spectral text to evoke a *frisson* it must draw upon the uncanny, that element of writing upon which we base the Gothic.

The attraction Todorov's reading of the fantastic has for the darker side of fantasy lies in his identification of readerly hesitancy as its key characteristic. In this type of writing, the reader is required to continually adjudicate between two equally possible interpretations of the fictional material, one psychological and one supernatural. The space of the fantastic inhabits the duration of that hesitancy, for once the reader plumps for one interpretation over another, Todorov's sense of the fantastic is lost and genre takes over. Thus the reader becomes implicated within the fantastic text, or, to put it more powerfully, we are almost required to *haunt* its parameters. In this chapter, therefore, we turn to some characteristic examples of the ghost story to consider the role played within them by the fantastic and the impact this has upon reader hesitancy.

Ghosts and Their Readers

We need to remember, though it is all too easy to forget, that when Mary Shelley wrote *Frankenstein*, she considered it a ghost story. As such, she believed it must 'speak to the mysterious fears of our nature and awaken thrilling horror . . . make the reader dread to look round, to curdle the blood, and quicken the beatings of the heart.'[4] The reason we no longer read *Frankenstein* as a ghost story, though we may certainly identify it as a Gothic narrative, is because we, who come to the ghost story almost one hundred years since Freud claimed no intelligent person still believed in the supernatural[5], find it difficult to derive such horror from supernatural tales alone. Instead, our ghouls lie rather closer to home in the form of child murderers, psychopaths, diseases such as cancer or AIDS, the prospect of biological warfare, or dying a lonely death.

To some extent, this may also explain why the Gothic has taken over from the ghost story in terms of critical attention, and also why the contemporary Gothic is so much more fluidly defined than it once was. During the period of Romanticism, for a text to be Gothic it was required to have vast medieval architectural structures such as cathedrals and castles, usually in combination with the sublime. Hence, in Ann Radcliffe's *The Mysteries of Udolpho* (1794), the early chapters comprise an extended journey through the Pyrenees, the primary function of which is to build an atmosphere in which nature, in all its awesome magnitude, might somehow consume or overcome frail humanity: 'Over these crags rose others of stupendous height, and fantastic shape . . . Around, on every side, far as the eye could penetrate, were seen only forms of grandeur—the long perspective of mountain-tops, tinged with ethereal blue, or white with snow; vallies of ice, and forests of gloomy fir.'[6] As the nineteenth century progresses, the Gothic becomes increasingly urbanised and domesticated. In her 1831 introduction to *Franken-stein*, when Shelley describes the bedchamber wherein her plot was conceived, she paints, in her mind's eye, a vision of a chamber that retains elements of the sublime: 'I see them still: the very room, the dark parquet, the closed shutters with the moonlight struggling through, and the sense I had that the glassy lake and white high Alps were beyond' (*F*, 59). By the end of the nineteenth century, Robert Louis Stevenson's monster will have a very different 'home,'

> The door [of] which was equipped with neither bell nor knocker, [being] blistered and distained. Tramps slouched into the recess and struck matches on the panels; children kept shop upon the steps; the schoolboy had tried his knife on the mouldings; and for close on a generation no one had appeared to drive away these random visitors or to repair their ravages.[7]

This gradual process of domestication, along with the transformation of an agoraphobic landscape into a claustrophobic one, is what enabled Freud to establish the uncanny as 'a sub-species of *heimlich*' (the homely/familiar),[8] in that it takes its potency from the proximity of a reassuringly familiar and private space and just 'twists' it very slightly to evoke the chill of secrecy and something concealed. What also happened during the course of this transitional nineteenth century was that the reader was called upon to establish a different relationship to that content. From initially being handed the role of awestruck spectator, once the Gothic moves indoors the reader became a participant sensing the implications inherent in the act of reading. By extension, the role played by reading and writing *within* the construction of the uncanny becomes a prominent narrative theme in itself. Rather than identifying the supernatural with an atavistic sense of the past, writers started to address the manner in which the supernatural was constructed within our present and future imaginations. As Todorov puts it, 'The supernatural is born of language . . . not only do the devil and vampires exist only in words, but language alone enables us to conceive what is [otherwise] always absent.'[9]

Charles Dickens, *A Christmas Carol*

Though Dickens's *A Christmas Carol* (1843) is one of the most famous and popular of all ghost stories, it is actually closer in structure to the medieval dream vision already discussed in Chapter 3 than it is to Todorov's conception of the fantastic, though it certainly retains enough of those trappings to operate as an uncanny tale. Ebeneezer Scrooge is a miser whose heartless treatment of others leads to his social isolation. As Scrooge returns to his lodgings, just before Christmas, he is confronted by the ghost of his dead business partner, Jacob Marley, who warns him that he will be visited by three additional spirits: the Ghosts of Christmas Past, Present, and Yet to Come. In summary, through a combination of supernatural terror and fearful shame, Scrooge gradually repents his ways. As such, *A Christmas Carol* has elements of the allegorical quest in it, the ghosts taking on the roles we would expect angels to fulfill in a Christian allegory.

Nevertheless, though the sinister aspects of the narrative are undeniably compromised, certain trappings of the ghost story remain, one of which is its hearsay structure. As we will see commonly, the narrative voice is in the first person throughout and, in its use of the past tense, suggests a retrospective view on the plot, hence, by extension, implying the presence of an audience beyond the reader. What is never made fully clear is to whom the storytelling voice belongs. On one level, we might attribute it to the character of the reformed Scrooge, telling the cautionary tales of his own past. However, there is no stage in the narrative at which he reveals himself as Scrooge in this storytelling role, and at the end of the text, when this narrator continues to refer to Scrooge in the third person and makes no attempt to convey a sense of greater intimacy with him, this possibility appears less likely. The only other feasible presence, therefore, is that of the implied author casting himself in the role of oral storyteller—for the face-to-face implications of presence facilitate the *frisson* of the uncanny more easily.

Todorov's own view of the fantastic as writing that offers a suspended sense of hesitancy propels such narratives out of the kind of spatial vocabulary we explored in Chapter 4, and into a framework in which time dominates:

The classic definition of the present, for example, describes it as a pure limit between the past and the future . . . the marvellous corresponds to an unknown phenomenon, never seen as yet, still to come—hence to a future; in the uncanny, on the other hand, we refer the inexplicable to known facts, to a previous experience, and thereby to the past.[10]

The presence, within any ghost story, of a teller for the tale enables all three phases of time to conjoin. Hesitancy is ravelled up in the audience's relationship to the tale (What can it mean? Is it this? Is it that?), while the unknown lies still before us, told in the guise of that which *cannot* happen—but already has. Dickens's opening sentence works similarly: 'Marley was dead: to begin with.'[11] The overt trick of the sentence draws attention to the storyteller's art. Does the phrase 'to begin with' simply signal a variant on 'Once upon a time,' or does it mean that Marley was dead, but then entered a different state—that in which he rises from the dead to haunt the living? Scrooge's own relationship to the living and the dead is similarly unclear. He inhabits a kind of border territory, neither cutting out a real life for himself nor fully seeming to inhabit living flesh: 'The cold within him froze his old features . . . A frosty rime was on his head, and on his eyebrows, and his wiry chin. He carried his own low temperature always about with him . . .' (CC, 11). As in Stevenson's *The Strange Case of Dr. Jekyll and Mr. Hyde* (1886), here the infamous smog of nineteenth-century London takes on the connotations of a pathetic fallacy. Thus, where the otherwise cheery fire in Jekyll's grate is to some extent smothered, 'for even in the houses the fog began to lie thickly,'[12] so one might expect that, in Scrooge's rather chillier counting-house, 'The fog came pouring in at every chink and keyhole, and was so dense without, that . . . the houses opposite were mere phantoms' (CC, 12).

This sensation of domestic privacy being infiltrated by the supernatural is an important aspect of the ghost story, and it is after Scrooge returns home that his problems really start. Having entered his house, he mounts the stairs and enters his bedchamber. By that time, he has already perceived the shape of the doorknocker having taken on the form of Jacob Marley's head and imagines, as he ascends, 'a locomotive hearse going on before him in the gloom'

(CC, 25). This *frisson* is sufficient to unsettle Scrooge to the extent that he feels the need to double-lock himself in his rooms. It is not, however, entirely sufficient to unsettle the reader, who can still put all this down to autosuggestion. What does unsettle us, however, is when Scrooge, seated before his fire, glances up at a disused communication bell, only to see it begin to swing and ring out. Furthermore, as it does so we 'hear' a sound that genuinely holds fear for us:

> [A] clanking noise, deep down below; as if some person were dragging a heavy chain over the casks in the wine-merchant's cellar . . .
> The cellar-door flew open with a booming sound, and then [Scrooge] heard the noise much louder, on the floors below; then coming up the stairs; then coming straight towards his door. (CC, 27)

Of course this is clichéd spectre portrayal, an aspect that partially compromises the chill conveyed. Nevertheless, the reason we, in the twenty-first century, still experience this passage as uncanny, where we do not fear the apparitions on the doorknocker and stairs, is that this sound does not need to have a supernatural explanation to be terrifying. Many of us feel most threatened when in our own homes at night—particularly if alone and in bed—and Scrooge is being targeted by a particularly determined predator who has managed to penetrate the walls of the house. Perhaps this explanation— which belongs to the type of fear evoked by the thriller or terror narrative rather than the ghost story—also suggests why, once the phantom is confronted, it ceases to frighten in and of itself. Though Scrooge is dismayed by the sight of his old partner's transparent form and bandaged jaw, he finds sufficient courage, when faced by the spectre, to affirm, 'There's more of gravy [i.e. indigestion] than of the grave about you, whatever you are!' (CC, 29).

Charles Dickens, 'The Signalman'

Although the ghost story is predominantly a domesticated genre, in Dickens's later and more intriguing ghost story 'No. 1 Branch Line: The Signalman' (1866), he opts for an outdoors setting—in the open air beside a railway line—even if the extent to which this location is truly 'open' is reduced through becoming hemmed in by a set of forbidding exterior boundaries:

> His post was solitary and dismal . . . On either side, a dripping-wet wall of jagged stone, excluding all view but a strip of sky; the perspective one way only a crooked prolongation of this great dungeon; the shorter perspective in the other direction terminating in a gloomy red light, and the gloomier entrance to a black tunnel, in whose massive architecture there was a barbarous, depressing, and forbidding air. So little sunlight ever found its way to this spot, that it had an earthy, deadly smell; and so much cold wind rushed through it, that it struck chill to me, as if I had left the natural world.[13]

Here there is a paradoxical combination of a beckoning horizon and the prohibition of unseen obstacles, the sense of endless recession being heightened by the presence of the railway tracks, though compromised by seeming to end with the blackened 'mouth' of the tunnel. On the one occasion on which we read of the Signalman entering the tunnel, far from experiencing it as a way of extending his vista, he rapidly retreats back to known territory: 'I ran out again faster than I had run in (for I had a mortal abhorrence of the place upon me)' (S, 151).

In other ways, nevertheless, the typical dynamics of ghost story telling are adhered to quite closely. Once again, we have a first-person narrator who tells it—not about himself but about another person. His encounter is with a complete stranger, thus ensuring that the central character is, as far as he can be, as 'strange' to us as he is to the narrator. We encounter him as a nocturnal presence, his shift patterns taking place at night. Ghost stories are like time travel narratives, in that their major identification is with time, and in both of these stories by Dickens, clock time dominates. Marley's ghost tells Scrooge to 'Expect the first [Spirit] to-morrow, when the bell tolls one . . . Expect the second on the next night at the same hour. The third upon the next night when the last stroke of twelve has ceased to vibrate' (CC, 35–36). In 'The Signalman,' the shift patterns of the eponymous protagonist combine with the railway timetable to govern both the trains and his own arrival and departure (not to mention those of the curious visitor who tells us the tale). In these terms, it is ironic that the Signalman's death, timed to coincide with the return of the visitor after ten o'clock the following evening, leaves our punctual storyteller with a sense of having brought lateness to the tale: too late to help the signalman, who in death also becomes 'late.'

The real issue of this story seems to revolve around the aspect of contagion such hauntings involve. Where the narrator of *A Christmas Carol* reminds us that 'while there is infection in disease and sorrow, there is nothing in the world so irresistibly contagious as laughter and good-humour' (CC, 91), in 'The Signalman' there is no such festive alleviation. The Signalman, sensing 'death overhanging somewhere on the Line' (S, 155), finds himself the embodiment of that danger. The narrator, listening to the Signalman's fears, wonders if he has 'infection in his mind' (S, 146). Furthermore, once the narrator hears the Signalman's story, he also comes to feel haunted as well as impotent to prevent death. His primary motivation on returning is to 'heal' the Signalman by taking him to 'the wisest medical practitioner we could hear of in those parts' (S, 157), a desire that suggests haunting may well have a psychological rather than a supernatural explanation. Nor does the end of the story resolve our doubts, for the Signalman may have been driven to commit suicide. Is it, then, that disturbed people are haunted, or that haunting causes disturbance? This is perhaps the greatest question the ghost story asks.

Henry James, *The Turn of the Screw*

Henry James's *The Turn of the Screw* (1898) is one of the most puzzling and frustrating of ghostly tales. Again, we have the presence of a frame narrative and the telling of the main story by another character and in retrospect. It is again Christmas Eve, a traditional time for such stories and one having ancient links to legend and folklore. Lewis Spence, for instance, refers to a traditional ritual in the Scottish Shetland Isles when, on Christmas Eve, 'all the doors [are] opened and a pantomime [is] indulged in of 'chasing and driving and dispersing unseen creatures . . . Unless a child in Shetland was "sained" [christened] at Yuletide it was liable to be carried off by the trows [the fairies of the isles of Orkney and Shetland].'[14] James's story proper emerges out of another, prefatory story about a boy and his mother, but is relayed by a third party in the room, not our storyteller. That this is as much a story *about* stories is clear from the title: 'If the child gives the effect another turn of the screw, what do you say to two children—?' 'We say of course,' somebody exclaimed, 'that two children give two turns! Also that we want to hear about them.'[15]

The emphasis placed upon the art of storytelling at the start of James's text draws attention to the space set up within it for 'truths' to be questioned. The story itself has a picture-book quality to it, and every attempt is made to draw attention to the artifice of the tale; even Douglas, its teller, grooms himself beforehand 'with quiet art' (*TS*, 145). Once the teller starts, we learn that, although it is to be narrated orally, he will have to retrieve a written text from a locked drawer, and in order to do this he will have to 'send to town . . . write to [his] man and enclose the key; he could send down the packet as he finds it' (*TS*, 146). The manuscript version 'Is in old faded ink and in the most beautiful hand . . . A woman's. She has been dead these twenty years. She sent me the pages in question before she died' (*TS*, 146). Furthermore, the version we are reading is not the version Douglas tells, but a further written version, 'made much later' (*TS*, 148) by our frame narrator. By the time we hear this version, Douglas is dead and the manuscript has passed into our narrator's hands; nevertheless he chooses to read from a copy he writes out himself. This is pure Gothic formula, with secrets ravelled up in secrets to evoke a labyrinthine quest for a truth that recedes as quickly as it is chased.

The Turn of the Screw is certainly a strange and unsettling tale, but not necessarily in terms of what is actually said in the telling. That we will not be told everything is made clear from the start: '[S]he was in love. That is she had been. That came out—she couldn't tell her story without its coming out. I saw it, and she saw I saw it; but neither of us spoke of it' (*TS*, 147). This leads us to expect the presence of a romance in the tale, but only briefly, for almost immediately we are rebuked, along with the other characters:

'Who was it she was in love with?'

'The story will tell,' I took upon myself to reply.

'Oh I can't wait for the story!'

'The story *won't* tell,' said Douglas; 'not in any literal vulgar way.' (*TS*, 147)

To some extent, as we have seen in the context of Tolkien, genre fantasy texts can be used as blank canvases across which we inscribe the tales of our own culture, and *The Turn of the Screw* reveals that narratives of the fantastic can work similarly. In my opinion, a twenty-first-century reader has little doubt in labelling James's story a tale of pedophilia, articulated in a culture with no clear definition of the term. I have made brief mention of the preliminary tale that gives birth to the main narrative. To go into what little detail we are given of it, this pre-text concerns 'an appearance, of a dreadful kind, to a little boy sleeping in the room with his mother' (*TS*, 145). A psychoanalytic interpretation of this frame narrative might well fasten on the words 'dreadful' and 'appearance' here and, in so doing, remind us of Freud's claim that there is no more uncanny site (sight?) than that of the mother's genitals:

> This *unheimlich* place . . . is the place where each one of us lived once upon a time and in the beginning. There is a joking saying that 'Love is home-sickness'; and whenever a man dreams of a place or a country and says to himself, while he is still dreaming: 'this place is familiar to me, I have been here before,' we may interpret this place as being his mother's genitals or her body.[16]

In doing so, this preamble breaches a taboo and a silence in one: it articulates, despite itself, the presence of sexual intimacy between an adult and a child, albeit that here it seems to have an accidental motivation born from an otherwise innocent sense of nocturnal intimacy. Once those boundaries are breached, there is no going back, when the mother awakes, her inability to erase the image takes the form of her being similarly confronted by 'the same sight that had shocked him' (*TS*, 145).

Once we embark on reading the embedded main story of *The Turn of the Screw*, we find this initial, and apparently only preliminary, tale has a more significant role to play. Through the presence of that tale, we are left questioning where the mother of the children in this case is, for she has been erased. We are told that their guardian is their uncle, and that he inherited the children on the death of his parents, not theirs. Why they were living previously with their grandparents is not explained. All we are told is that the tale 'cannot tell' in that it concerns something unspeakable right from the start:

> 'Nothing at all that I know touches it.'
> 'For sheer terror?' I remember asking.
> He seemed to say it wasn't as simple as that; to be really at a loss how to qualify it . . . 'For dreadful—dreadfulness!'
> 'Oh how delicious!' cried one of the women.
> He took no notice of her; he looked at me, but as if, instead of me, he saw what he spoke of. 'For general uncanny ugliness and horror and pain.' (*TS*, 146)

This returns us to a sense of ghost stories afflicting us with a sense of contagion. As cultures we are haunted by certain ghosts that speak as much of who we are as of what we shun. The governess is haunted by fears of the nature of the relationship between the monster/ghost Quint and her childhood charges:

> ' . . . [Y]ou tell me they were "great friends."'
> 'Oh it wasn't *him*! . . . It was Quint's own fancy. To play with him, I mean—to spoil him . . . Quint was much too free.'
> This gave me . . . a sudden sickness of disgust. 'Too free with *my* boy?'
> 'Too free with every one!' (*TS*, 177)

We cannot but notice the linguistic peculiarities of the name Quint, which, in its evocation of the word squint, immediately suggests something unnaturally awry, or skewed. According to Kathryn Hume, in order for ghost stories to retain their affective properties for a readership not easily disposed to superstition, that readership must be prepared to allow for a 'contraven[tion of] normal reality.' Thus far I agree, but not with how she continues: '*The Turn of the Screw* would be greatly impoverished if we could not allow ourselves to entertain the possibility that ghosts exist.'[17] 'Contravention of normal reality' need not mean the supernatural; it may merely mean the unnatural. In other words, what the Victorians envision metaphorically as a ghost we may well wish to evoke more metonymically as a horror. In James's story, what matters is less our belief in ghosts and more our willingness to read this 'ghost' as an ill-defined sense of something or somebody sinister preying upon children. It is this, contributed to by the strange relationship between speaking and not 'telling,' that enables this story to retain its haunting—indeed chilling—potential.

But in relation to Todorov's theory of hesitancy, it is less the role played by Quint and his accomplice Jessel that disturbs us—for they are consistently outward projections of monstrosity—and more the role of the governess herself. For, as we try to understand her, what we become increasingly unable to do is distinguish her from the horrifying story she tells. This begins with her inability to protect the children from the evil threat that surrounds them. Increasingly, a kind of rivalry develops between her and the two predators, the governess fearing the children will choose 'them' above her: '[The children] want to get to them . . . For the love of all the evil that, in those dreadful days, the pair put into them' (TS, 207). It is almost as if Quint and Jessel step into the spaces left by the missing parents, who might return (much like the trows) at any moment to reclaim them. Only by determinedly setting up the adult rivals as a type of diseased contamination capable of passing on those traits to the children can the governess veil her own dangerous potential from the reader. That this is a fear of contagion emanating, in her mind, from the parents seems clear from the fact that the governess believes at least one of the children to be tainted even before we encounter their third-party projections in the form of Quint and Jessel.

As the boy, Miles, returns from school for the holiday, he brings a letter explaining that he has been expelled. Reading it aloud to the illiterate Mrs. Grose, both she and we are wholly dependent on the version—and interpretation—of events the governess offers: 'They go into no particulars. They simply express their regret that it should be impossible to keep him. That can have but one meaning . . . That he is an injury to the others' (TS, 158). As her paranoia, jealous rivalry, and determination to control what the children see, do, and even think mounts, her preeminence as first-person narrator mirrors, to the reader, the absolute power she has over the children in the tale. As we struggle to piece together what is hallucination and what is truth, we find that we, too, are looking in the wrong place for answers. Only as she reveals herself in the act of child murder do we see that she is the evil by which they are possessed, even, in Miles's case, to the death:

> 'What does he [Quint/the father] matter now, my own?— what will he *ever* matter? *I* have you' . . . With the stroke of the loss I was so proud of he uttered the cry of a creature hurled over an abyss, and the grasp with which I recovered him might have been that of catching him in the fall. I caught him, yes, I held him—*it may be imagined with what a passion*; but at the end of a minute I began to feel what it truly was that I held. We were alone with the quiet day and his little heart, dispossessed, had stopped. (*TS*, 261–262; my emphasis)

Beyond the shock of the murder of a child, what this tale leaves us with is the realisation that the young woman who tells the tale to Douglas seems to be the governess herself. Furthermore, Douglas has already told us that she is 'my sister's governess' (*TS*, 146). If so, the child-murderer lives to take on more charges, an ending that far from resolves the tale.

Edith Wharton, 'The Eyes'

As in James's text, the role of the ghost in Wharton's stories seems to stand in for sexual deviance: the unnatural, the unspeakable, the horror of what one does not wish to believe possible (in her case, male homosexual desire, which she repeatedly writes about as a predatory threat to female heterosexual security). Also shared is the same use of embedded oral narration and a kind of competitive attitude towards the telling. Her story 'The Eyes' (1910) opens with a friendly male gathering in a host's library. Each man present tells a story, of which our frame narrator observes, 'on the whole, we had every reason to be proud of our seven "exhibits."'[18] Other wording used introduces the language of business: 'we proceeded to take stock of our group and tax each member for a contribution' ('Eyes,'

28). Storytelling thus becomes a form of outbidding—as it is in *The Turn of the Screw*, not to mention *Frankenstein*.[19] We have seen James's storyteller summing up the bidding as the distinction between a ghost story involving one child or two. In Wharton's case, the competition runs similarly, the host, Culwin, allowing himself to be persuaded, though also retreating behind a fake piece of self-deprecation: 'Oh, of course they're not show ghosts—a collector wouldn't think anything of them . . . Don't let me raise your hopes . . . their one merit is their numerical strength: the exceptional fact of their being *two*' ('Eyes,' 31).

Culwin's own role within this heavily masculine atmosphere takes on an almost coquettish characteristic. We are told that his presence at parties typically took the form of 'slipping out of his seat now and then for a brief dip into the convivialities at the back of the house' ('Eyes,' 28) and that his 'sociability was a night-blooming flower' ('Eyes,' 30). A man with a past ('among his contemporaries there lingered a vague tradition of his having, at a remote period, *and in a romantic clime*, been wounded in a duel' ['Eyes,' 28; my emphasis]), the tale Culwin goes on to tell turns into one of homo-erotic desire. As the narrative unfolds, he talks of two relationships; the first is with a young woman called Alice Nowell, whom he claims to have found 'neither beautiful nor intelligent' ('Eyes,' 32) and whom he abandons purportedly out of fear of the haunting effect of the 'eyes.' Alice Nowell is his cousin, though once he leaves for Rome she sends him another cousin, this time a man, Gilbert Noyes, 'appealing to me to befriend him' ('Eyes,' 37). This man Culwin finds 'beautiful to see,' and continues, 'the more I saw of him the better I liked him' ('Eyes,' 38). Alice's action, along with her docile acceptance of her abandonment, suggests that she sees in Culwin the truth of his sexual orientation.

Wharton's treatment of male homosexuality has a Gothic element to it, typified by a parasitic power imbalance that Carol J. Singley calls 'a vampirish tendency . . . to prey on the younger [man].'[20] As Culwin's tale progresses, he positions himself as not just writer but also critic of his tale, analysing its 'meaning' in the very act of telling. The two otherwise disembodied eyes by which he is haunted are a source of fascination to him. On their first appearance, he describes them as

> . . . a man's eyes—but what a man! My first thought was
> that he must be frightfully old. The orbits were sunk, and
> the thick red-lined lids hung over the eyeballs like blinds of
> which the cords are broken. One lid drooped a little lower
> than the other, with the effect of a crooked leer . . . ('Eyes,'
> 34)

The second time he sees them, the effect is stronger:

> I saw now what I hadn't seen before: that they were eyes
> which had grown hideous gradually, which had built up
> their baseness coralwise, bit by bit, out of a series of small
> turpitudes slowly accumulated through the industrious
> years . . . and as their stare moved with my movements,
> there came over me a sense of their tacit complicity, of a
> deep hidden understanding between us . . . Not that I
> understood them; but that they made it so clear that some-
> day I should . . . ('Eyes,' 41)

Though their identity is visual, the eyes' proclivities are orally
driven: 'They reminded me of vampires with a taste for young flesh'
('Eyes,' 41). In that sense, of course, what Culwin sees looking back
at him are his own eyes and appetites. And this is where, I think, the
focus of the story is more interesting than its simple 'moral' message
implies. These eyes are not there to chide Culwin for his poor treatment of Alice and Gilbert, they are there to goad him on to feed off
his pleasure. They offer a mirror to his own ego, an outward manifestation of his own carnal appetites projected also into the future.
The language of death requires that a character be sacrificed to
them: Gilbert or him. And yet, once Gilbert—or at least the attraction he holds for Culwin—has been sacrificed ('I saw him once . . .
He was fat and hadn't shaved. I was told he drank. He didn't recognize me' ['Eyes,' 44]), Culwin himself appears to shrivel in stature,
shrinking back into his chair 'like a heap of his own empty clothes'
('Eyes,' 42). Gradually, we see that Frenham, the man who goaded
him into the telling in the first place, is motivated by more than
pure competition. They are, we suspect, his eyes, and both outside
and inside the story he is the phantom of Culwin's past, the man
whom Culwin beat (hence killed) in the duel. As Frenham's face is
viewed through the mirror, what we find is that these two sets of

eyes meet once more: 'for an appreciable space of time he and the image in the glass confronted each other with a glare of slowly gathering hate' ('Eyes,' 45). We recall Culwin's boast that he has seen not one but two ghosts. Where we initially took this to mean each of the two eyes, now we see the dual/duel significance of that ghost. Frenham has successfully lured Culwin into articulating his own destruction, and his death will presumably follow (as that is what commonly follows a visitation from the apparition in human form in Wharton's stories).

To conclude, these four stories span what is perhaps the greatest era of the ghost narrative, the Victorian and early-twentieth-century period. This continued into the 1920s, catering to the collective cultural melancholia following the mass genocide of so many young men in World War I. As the century progressed and the machine age took over, however, increasing secularization combined with the new technologies, ghost writing tending to mutate into the newer narrative modes of cyberpunk (see Chapter 5) or, as suggested above, the more politicized magic realism. What we might now call the New Gothic has become so expansive, it claims to be able to encompass works as diverse as *Neuromancer* and Lord of the Rings.[21] And, though such elastic understandings of the Gothic can prove frustrating, or even faddish, perhaps this is the way forward for fantasy too. Genre is a great structural underpinning for the development of ideas, but as a narrative framework it quickly runs its course. Newer areas of fantasy should identify themselves less in terms of genre and more in terms of ideas and motifs—dare I say more Todorov than Tolkien? In Chapter 7, we examine some of the key works of criticism that have shaped and are shaping this more positive reading of fantasy in the past, present, and into the future.

Notes

1. Lucie Armitt, *Theorising the Fantastic* (London: Arnold, 1996), 30.

2. Tzvetan Todorov, *The Fantastic: A Structural Approach to a Literary Genre*, Richard Howard, trans. (Ithaca: Cornell University Press, 1975), 41 and 48.

3. Lucie Armitt, 'The Magical Realism of the Contemporary Gothic,' in *A Companion to the Gothic*, David Punter, ed. (Oxford: Blackwell, 2000), 305–316 (p. 307).

4. Mary Shelley, *Frankenstein, or, The Modern Prometheus* (1818; Harmondsworth: Penguin, 1985), 57–58.

5. 'All supposedly educated people have ceased to believe officially that the dead can become visible as spirits,' Sigmund Freud, 'The "Uncanny,"' in the *Penguin Freud Library, Vol.14, Art and Literature*, Albert Dickson, ed. (Harmondsworth: Penguin, 1990), 335–376 (p. 365).

6. Ann Radcliffe, *The Mysteries of Udolpho* (1794; Oxford: Oxford University Press, 1980), 42–43.

7. Robert Louis Stevenson, *The Strange Case of D.r Jekyll and Mr. Hyde* (1886; Harmondsworth: Penguin, 1979), 30.

8. Freud, 'The "Uncanny,"' 347.

9. Todorov, *The Fantastic*, 82.

10. Ibid., 42.

11. Charles Dickens, *A Christmas Carol* (1843; Harmondsworth: Penguin, 1984), 9. Further quotations from this story will be referenced within the main body of the text, accompanied by the abbreviation CC.

12. Stevenson, *Jekyll and Hyde*, 51.

13. Charles Dickens, 'No. 1 Branch Line: The Signalman,' in *The Supernatural Short Stories of Charles Dickens*, Michael Hayes, ed. (1866; London: John Calder, 1978), 144–159 (pp. 145–146). Further quotations from this story will be referenced within the main body of the text, accompanied by the abbreviation S.

14. Lewis Spence, *The Fairy Tradition in Britain* (London: Rider and Company, 1948), 312.

15. Henry James, 'The Turn of the Screw,' in *The Aspern Papers and The Turn of the Screw* (1898; Harmondsworth: Penguin, 1986), 143–262 (p. 145). Further quotations from this story will be referenced within the main body of the text, accompanied by the abbreviation *TS*.

16. Freud, 'The "Uncanny,"' 368.

17. Kathryn Hume, *Fantasy and Mimesis: Responses to Reality in Western Literature* (New York: Methuen, 1984), 77.

18. Edith Wharton, 'The Eyes,' in *The Ghost Stories of Edith Wharton* (1910; London: Virago, 1996), 27–45 (p. 28). Further quotations from this story will be referenced within the main body of the text, accompanied by the word 'Eyes.'

19. The wider social context for the conception of *Frankenstein* is well known Mary and Percy Bysshe Shelley were in Switzerland with a group of intellectual friends, including Lord Byron. One evening Byron challenged all present to write a ghost story. *Frankenstein* was Mary Shelley's resulting effort. Since the story was the most successful offering of the assembled gathering, arguably she won the bet.

20. Carol J. Singley, 'Gothic Borrowings,' in *Edith Wharton: New Critical Essays*, Alfred Bendixen and Annette Zilversmit, eds. (New York: Garland Press, 1992). Cited in Richard A. Kaye, ' "Unearthly Visitants": Wharton's Ghost Tales, Gothic Form and the Literature of Homosexual Panic,' *Edith Wharton Review*, vol. 11, no. 1 (Spring 1994), 10–18 (p. 12).

21. At the sixth biannual conference of the Gothic Association Conference, 'Gothic Ex/Changes,' Liverpool Hope University College, Liverpool, UK, July 17–20, 2003, I was struck by the fact that not one but two of the plenary speakers chose Tolkien's Lord of the Rings trilogy as their key Gothic text. Truly, fantasy offers us a blank canvas across which we write what it is we wish to see . . .

Chapter Seven

Fantasy Criticism

Introduction

One of the difficulties facing any critic of fantasy and the literary fantastic is the challenge of how one can possibly be worthy of the material about which one is writing. By its very nature, fantasy writing takes risks, stretches imagination to its breaking point, and effects hyperbole at every turn of the page. In contrast, all too often the criticism written on fantasy has fallen short, categorising, classifying, compartmentalising literature into division and subdivision, and arguing over whether the boxes into which these texts are crammed should be labelled 'marvellous' or 'fabulous,' 'sword and sorcery' or 'space opera,' 'myth' or 'faerie.' This is not criticism, it is travesty, and the works outlined in brief in this chapter are included for the positive role they have played in negating that death wish.

This tendency to overplay the importance of classification over evaluation might be blamed on the legacy of Vladimir Propp who, in his book *Morphology of the Folktale* (1928), set out to classify fairy tales on the basis of an identifiable list of core narrative functions, his project being to catalogue precisely what it was about this abstruse collection of tales that led us, as readers, to perceive them to be linked. However, Propp's aim was different from that of literary criticism; he set out to identify a shared structural principle common to a body of work, for which he employed linguistic rather than literary critical paradigms. It was a type of anthropology of the written word, not an evaluation of the literary techniques of individual stories, and he left it to those who succeeded him to apply literary critical readings to further his data.

Of course, not all Propp's successors have sold fantasy short, and two of the most interesting studies of fantasy to emerge during the last twenty-five years are Christine Brooke-Rose's *A Rhetoric of the Unreal* and Rosemary Jackson's *Fantasy: The Literature of Subversion*, both first published in 1981. Brooke-Rose's study is particularly valuable for its readiness to transcend genre in her consideration of what she calls, in her subtitle, *Narrative and Structure, Especially of the Fantastic*. For her, one cannot consider fantasy aside from the 'real world' out of which that fantasy is written; hence, at times when people feel alienated by their environment, they are more likely to embrace the alternative fictional worldviews allowed for in fantasy. Similarly, fantasy comes to the fore when other literary modes become well worn, and so one cannot consider fantasy outside other literary factors. It is Brooke-Rose's refreshingly inclusive approach that enables her to look at other literary means via which the preeminence of realism is challenged, including some of the more avant-garde writers of literary modernism. In the work of Joyce and Robbe Grillet, then, Brooke-Rose identifies the same kind of narrative trickery with time and tense that one might more commonly expect to find in science fiction, and in her opening discussion of common perceptions of 'the real,' reminds us that philosophers through the ages, from Plato to Derrida, share precisely the same sense of our cognition of the real remaining at a stage of removal from it.

For Jackson, it is the ideological impact of fantasy that really counts. She takes a particularly (though not exclusively) Anglo-European focus, grounding psychoanalysis within a social context and paying special attention to the darker or more grotesque areas of fantasy. So, where Brooke-Rose places a significant amount of emphasis on continental philosophy, Jackson is particularly interesting for her willingness to include readings of writers such as de Sade, arguing that his work represents the ultimate drive towards entropy, which subsequent writers from Lautréamont to Kafka can only emulate. Like Brooke-Rose, Jackson refuses to be overly constrained by questions of genre, equally willingly examining the role played by the Gothic in the otherwise realist writings of Elizabeth Gaskell and Charlotte Brontë as she is the more conventionally fantastic James Hogg or Bram Stoker. Ultimately, Jackson's claim is that fantasy propels itself towards a paradox, namely the necessity of articulating that which cannot be said and, in the process, is most effective in its ability to breach those social taboos shored up by collective silence. These three studies, Propp's, Brooke-Rose's, and Jackson's are certainly landmarks in terms of our evaluation of fantasy writing, but in the rest of this chapter I want to more fully consider the impact on fantasy of a small but revolutionary selection of texts that challenge the very parameters through which fantasy itself is expressed. In my opinion, this began in earnest with Tzvetan Todorov.

Interrogating the Boundaries of Fantasy: Todorov, Marin, and Tolkien

Tzvetan Todorov's book *The Fantastic: A Structural Approach to a Literary Genre* (1975),[1] discussed in brief in Chapter 6, is *the* classic text on the literary fantastic. Its primary aim is to differentiate between genre fantasy and those less accommodating, more disruptive texts that actively interrogate the classic genre/reader interface, the most obvious instances of which are the ghost story (because of its refusal to 'resolve' comprehension) and, perhaps, the more recent magic realism, which uses similarly supernatural material for political ends. Todorov is, as his subtitle for the book suggests, a structuralist, an identification that can result in an overidentification with labels and what we might call grids: the need to classify literature in terms of a kind of scientific spreadsheet or statistical model. However, rather than becoming unnecessarily bogged down in these substrata, Todorov works first within those limits, then interrogates them to explore which of those boundaries can be forced. For this he takes a two-stage approach, initially identifying the importance of genre before going on to challenge genre as a limitation, through the deployment of the fantastic.

Having moved beyond the basic boundary between mimesis and non-mimesis, he then sets up two subdivisions: the uncanny and the marvellous. Once Todorov's reading of the uncanny is established, he subdivides the marvellous into four further categories: hyperbolic marvellous, exotic marvellous, instrumental marvellous, and scientific marvellous, distancing all four from what he calls 'the marvelous in the pure state.'[2] Rather than becoming overly focused on these compartments, however, Todorov tackles the boundary marker between the uncanny and the marvellous and examines what happens when genre demarcations start to dissolve. As we saw in Chapter 6, it is at this point that we can no longer look on as spectators, but become involved as readers in the interrogation of possibilities.

For Todorov, the literary fantastic involves a sense of prevarication that occupies only the duration of this moment of hesitancy; the instant we decide upon a single reading—supernatural over psychological, or vice versa—we leave the fantastic for 'genre fantasy' and place the text in a box. Thus, precisely because the fantastic comes to the fore at the point of interaction, it results in the reader being always, to a greater or lesser extent, 'on edge': reading becomes always provisional and thus always in process—as opposed to classification theories, which always treat texts as somehow 'finished.' Rather than employing a spatial dynamic, therefore, Todorov's sense of the fantastic takes up no space at all. Instead, it demarcates the place of the frontier, a 'between worlds' location—hence its close affinity with Louis Marin's reading of the endlessly receding horizon.

The importance of Marin's essay to this book must by now have become clear. In 'The Frontiers of Utopia' (1993), Marin takes the image of the horizon and places it under etymological scrutiny, before examining the paradoxical relationship between the boundary it marks and the signifying space(s) it drags in its wake as it moves ever onwards, unreachable and thus infinite in its power. As so often in utopian writing, Marin's vision of the horizon has a political application. It is, he says, 'the place where two kings meet to make peace after having been at war with each other for many years, *a neutral place* . . .'[3] In that vision, Marin effects another paradox, endowing this space of neutrality with a utopian significance: it is literally 'no-place.'[4] Going on to a discussion of More's *Utopia*, Marin ponders the question, raised by More's own peri-text, of why the location of the island Utopia is unknown: 'should [it] not already be on the existing maps?' In pondering this rhetorical question, Marin considers that, in the absence of that inscription of a map upon a page, the island itself forms the very horizon point of the known; 'constantly, unceasingly displaced, about to be inscribed at the very moment when it is about to be erased amidst all the real islands that travellers register when they find them, among all the potential islands which other travellers will discover.'[5] What particularly appeals about Marin's work is his ability to mix the same combination of philosophical ambition and creative intoxication that one finds in the best fantasy literature. A similar ability is apparent in a short essay by J. R. R. Tolkien, 'Leaf by Niggle' (1938–39),[6] in which he addresses the parameters of the fantasy text.

I have called 'Leaf by Niggle' an essay, even though it is written in the form of a story, because its allegorical style only works as a reflection on the same kind of space-boundary debate that we see Marin adopt in approaching the utopia. The relationship between frontiers, space, and time is not, of course, only pertinent to fantasy texts. As Susan Stewart observes, it is the key dynamic of all narrative:

> The picture frame and the printed page form ready-made closed fields. They invite simultaneity by their primary spatial quality and rearrangement by their absolute boundaries. As what is enclosed in the picture frame or the page increasingly flaunts its arranged quality, its artifice and contrivance, the message 'This is a fiction' becomes increasingly clear.[7]

Nevertheless, in fantasy writing these dynamics are also mirrored in the content-related themes of a text, and this is the message of Tolkien's allegory. The title of the piece, 'Leaf by Niggle,' refers to a painting that Niggle, the central character, has created and by which he is obsessed. His focus in this picture adapts itself to a miniature scale ('He used to spend a long time on a single leaf, trying to catch its shape, and its sheen, and the glistening of dewdrops on its edges'),[8] but becomes magnified through multiplication to such an extent that Niggle is unable to maintain any relation to appropriate boundaries. As well as the spatial constraints against which Niggle struggles, an additional temporal frontier is introduced: Niggle must undertake a journey, an event that, when it comes, will enforce closure upon the work of art.

So we come to perceive the journey as extended horizon (taking him into the unknown), which conflicts with Niggle's determination to endlessly push back the frontiers of his artistry. In itself the painting, rather like the journey, also brings together the conflicting demands of space and boundaries (infinity versus completion, the painting versus the frame, the journey that beckons, to destination unknown). One day Niggle's painting is interrupted by his neighbour, Parish, who wishes him to run an errand on behalf of his ill wife. That results in a wet bicycle ride and a high fever, keeping Niggle in bed 'for a week or so.'[9] Before Niggle has a chance to resume his painting, he is taken away to a sanitorium (the journey he was expecting, it turns out) and his painted canvas is used by the Inspector of Houses to mend his leaking roof. The precise amount of time spent in the sanitorium is unclear, though the narrator uses the phrase 'during the first century or so (I am merely giving his impressions)'[10] to demonstrate once again the tension between the constraining nature of space and Niggle's inability to match it up with time.

Incarcerated by space and time, Niggle is forced to redress the balance between the two. On his release, he discovers this is not a limitation but an opening onto new frontiers: 'he had expected to walk out into a large town . . . but he did not. He was on the top of a hill.'[11] Taking the train to another unspecified destination, he alights when it stops next to his own bicycle and follows the path. Gradually, he finds that 'the path on which he had started had disappeared, and the bicycle was rolling over a marvellous turf. It was green and close; and yet he could see every blade distinctly. He seemed to remember having seen or dreamed of that sweep of grass somewhere or other.'[12] What Niggle discovers is that he has entered the world of his own painting. So he finds himself confronted by his own tree, its foliage living just as he had created it, and in the distance lies the forest he painted as part of the backdrop. What had been two-dimensional now becomes sensory: 'he could approach it, even enter it, without it losing that particular charm.'[13] Ultimately, space, which was formerly constrained by limitation, becomes able to transcend its own boundaries: 'as you walked, new distances opened out; so that you now had double, treble, and quadruple distances, doubly, trebly and quadruply enchanting. You could go on and on . . .'[14]

On one level, this is an essay that, in general terms, explores the boundaries between art and life. More specifically, however, Tolkien demonstrates that unlike realism, in which at least some of the boundaries are predetermined by the world in which we live, those of fantasy may require renegotiation. Once we are open to that renegotiation, fantasy allows us to open up onto (im)possibility. Niggle's quest is not over as he returns to his own picture. After he has extended his sense of the frame sufficiently to make space and time for Parish, one further challenge awaits. Both Niggle and Parish are taken to what is referred to as 'the Edge.' In the process, we return to Marin's signifying locus of neutrality: '[The Edge] was not visible, of course: there was no line, or fence, or wall; but they knew that they had come to the margin . . .'[15] Parish, who, as his name suggests, sits far more easily within limits than the agitating 'Niggle,' decides to stay. Niggle, however, moves on, and as he takes that point of the horizon with him, the narrator observes, 'I cannot guess what became of him . . .'[16]

Determining Spaces: Tolkien, Bettelheim, and Zipes

Where 'Leaf by Niggle' addresses fantasy structure, another essay by Tolkien, 'On Fairy-Stories' (1939), concentrates on content. Beginning, like Marin, with etymology, Tolkien initially draws attention to the disparity between our cultural understanding of the term *fairy* and that of *fairy tale* or *fairy story*. This has become a well-worn road for fantasy criticism since, though what becomes apparent here is that what Tolkien calls 'faerie' we have called 'fantasy':

> *Faërie* contains many things besides elves and fays, and besides dwarfs, witches, trolls, giants, or dragons: it holds the seas, the sun, the moon, the sky; and the earth, and all things that are in it: tree and bird, water and stone, wine and bread, and ourselves, mortal men, when we are enchanted . . . [17]

'On Fairy-Stories' is really Tolkien's personal manifesto, and as such, it gives him free rein to articulate his rather rigid views about 'what's in and what's out' as far as faerie/fantasy is concerned. In the process, he takes a swipe at a number of the works discussed in this book. *A Connecticut Yankee in King Arthur's Court*, for instance, would be 'out' for Tolkien because, although magic forms part of Tolkien's vision for fantasy,

> . . . it is magic of a peculiar mood and power, at the furthest pole from the vulgar devices of the laborious, scientific magician . . . if there is any satire present in the tale, one thing must not be made fun of, the magic itself. That must . . . be taken seriously, neither laughed at nor explained away.[18]

In Chapter 5, we have already noted Tolkien's suspicions about Wells's 'preposterous and incredible' Time Machine.[19] Toward the end of 'On Fairy Stories,' we discover this is also his view of science fiction as a whole, accusing its practitioners of desiring to transform the world into 'one big glass-roofed railway-station.'[20] Again, and as we saw in Chapter 3, Tolkien equally dislikes texts employing dream structures as the mechanism for moving characters between Primary and Secondary Worlds, equally excluding what he calls 'Beast-fable,' even if he grants that 'The stories of Beatrix Potter lie near the borders of Faerie, but outside it, I think, for the most part.'[21]

It is in this essay that Tolkien sets out his basic fantasy formula of the Primary and Secondary Worlds and directly addresses the contentious subject of escapism. This is a term causing great problems for fantasy critics, for in itself it implies fantasy to be a 'lesser' art form. Tolkien, however, has no such reservations, seeing in it a rejection of the inferior world malformed by humanity in contrast to the writer who aspires towards a new world vision, for in that aspiration she/he endows creativity with the status of religious devotion: 'Fantasy remains a human right: we make in our measure and in our derivative mode, because we are made: and not only made, but made in the image and likeness of a Maker.'[22]

In the work of Bruno Bettelheim and Jack Zipes, we have two critics who turn to the fairy story as a form defined within spatial (generic) parameters, but who address its importance specifically to child readers; Bettelheim adopts a psychoanalytic approach, Zipes a sociohistorical one. Zipes's interest lies in the historical development of the fairy tale form, and in *Fairy Tales and the Art of*

Subversion (1983)[23] he examines, in some detail, the influence of Charles Perrault, the Brothers Grimm, and Hans Christian Andersen respectively on the shaping and reception of the genre. For Zipes, the political importance of the fairy tale lies in the manner in which it brings children into contact with ideology early on and provokes them into questioning aspects of life that might otherwise appear as givens. The specific role of fantasy in this process is that it enables alternative visions to be provided that necessarily cast light (positive or negative) on the only world children would otherwise know: everyday reality.

Bettelheim's work on the fairy tale is one of the most cited of all pieces of fantasy criticism. His book *The Uses of Enchantment* (1976) examines the reasons why child readers return repeatedly to fairy tales, arguing that what they find within them is a form of narrative therapy: '[They] start where the child really is in his psychological and emotional well being.'[24] His journey takes us through a wide range of fairy tales from a variety of cultures, from 'The Fisherman and the Jinny' in the *Thousand and One Nights* (better known to Western readers as the story of 'The Genie in the Bottle'), to 'The Queen Bee' by the Brothers Grimm (a little-known story involving three brothers, the youngest of whom befriends and protects the animals his older two brothers mistreat and is rewarded with their help as a result), to 'Goldilocks and the Three Bears' (believed to be of Scottish origin). In all, Bettelheim identifies the reader/text interface as a means of teaching children how to negotiate the world.

The strength of Bettelheim's analysis lies in the central role he gives the reader in the construction (as opposed to the consumption) of fantasy. Only by bringing anxiety to the text can it mingle with the narrative content to effect eventual resolution. However, as I argue elsewhere, I have two reservations about Bettelheim's approach to reading fairy tales. The first is literary: although Bettelheim allows for an active reader/text relationship in the importance he attributes to the (child) reader of fantasy, he perceives the nature of that reading once 'in' the text to be one in which the child looks for simple models: 'When all the child's wishful thinking gets embodied in a good fairy; all his destructive wishes in an evil witch; all his fears in a voracious wolf . . . then the child can finally begin to sort out his contradictory tendencies.'[25] What, then, of reading 'creatively' against the grain? Are we never to encourage children to question the ideology implicit in a text? Fantasy narratives deal in the unknowable and, as such, offer up a continual challenge to break moulds—including those that shape our own thinking. Employing fantasy as a means of nullifying a child's consciousness strikes me as no very admirable model for active readership, and this is where Zipes has the advantage over Bettelheim, for he recognises the empowering potential for children in such abrasive readings: 'Consequently, the reader . . . consider[s] the negative aspects of anachronistic forms and perhaps transcends them . . . break[ing], shift[ing], debunk[ing], or rearrang[ing] the traditional motifs to liberate the reader from the contrived and programmed mode of literary reception.'[26]

The second concern I have is ideological: Bettelheim introduces a family dynamic for reading in his text, within which something he sets up as a positive learning experience for the child metamorphoses into something more sinister. Bettelheim establishes a hierarchy of reading in which the adult 'knows' but cannot tell, and the child 'sees' but cannot share. Hence, irrespective of what fairy tales might be argued to offer the child, Bettelheim shows them to be a means whereby the adult learns to 'read' the child's reading. The child is, we are told, simultaneously innocent and unconsciously knowing, but reads in good faith. What that child will find, as she 'strays from the well-worn path,' is material she does not fully know how to process:

> Fairy tales contain some dreamlike features, but these are akin to what happens in the dreams of adolescents or adults, not of children . . .
>
> Children's dreams are very simple: wishes are fulfilled and anxieties are given tangible form . . . A child's dreams contain unconscious content that remains practically unshaped by his ego . . . For this reason, children cannot and should not analyze their dreams.[27]

As Bettelheim specifically warns the adult not to share the 'true meaning' of this content with the child, the adult becomes the 'hidden' wolf in the tale: 'luring the child into a truly unheimlich sense of false security and misplaced trust.'[28] This strikes me as establish-

ing a damaging fantasy at the heart of the family unit, using literature as a decoy for deception.

Fantasy as (Dream-)Screen: Psychoanalytic Approaches

Bettelheim is, of course, only one of many critics of fantasy who
have found psychoanalysis and what it has to say about desire and
family relationships foundational to an understanding of 'other
worlds.' In their landmark essay, 'Fantasy and the Origins of
Sexuality' (1968), Jean Laplanche and Jean-Bertrand Pontalis situ-
ate fantasy as the wellspring from which psychoanalysis drinks.
Though they do not directly apply this work to fiction, as such, their
vocabulary shares what we have seen to be the cartographic concerns of such writing. So they refer to 'new avenues open[ing] out'
as psychoanalysis paves the way for a fuller understanding of the
desiring subject (the source of all utopianism, of course). From here
they shift to a reflection upon what they call 'the world of fantasy
. . . located exclusively within the domain of opposition between
subjective and objective, between an inner world, where satisfaction is obtained through illusion, and an external world which gradually . . . asserts the supremacy of the reality principle.'[29] In this
distinction between external and inner worlds, we find a mirror to
Tolkien's Primary and Secondary Worlds, in which the 'reality principle' governs the Primary World, 'illusion' inhabiting the Secondary one.

Laplanche and Pontalis are interested in tracing what we might
call a fable of the family, based on 'the myth of the origin of sexuality.'[30] They offer an extended critique of Freud's work on sexuality, based on his uneven use of the term *fantasy*. In effect, what they
take issue with is Freud's refusal to differentiate between what we
have called 'phantasy' (in their terms 'the ultimate unconscious
desire, the "capitalist" of the dream'), and 'fantasy' (in their terms,
'the secondary elaboration . . . the story of the dream once we are
awake').[31] In this definition, we see that this secondary elaboration
has indeed become a form of fantasy writing—a text, consciously
ordered like a narrative, complete with full plot structure.
Nevertheless, as Laplanche and Pontalis further develop this idea,

their vocabulary moves away from that of story, through drama (the play), and on to a more cinematic image in the light patterns of a kaleidoscope:

> The daydream is a shadow play, utilizing its kaleidoscopic material drawn from all quarters of human experience . . . whose dramatis personae, the court cards, receive their notation from a family legend [king, queen, jack/father, mother, son] which is mutilated, disordered and misunderstood. Its structure is the primal fantasy . . . but also the daydream—if we accept that analysis discovers typical and repetitive scenarios beneath the varying clusters of fable.[32]

A significant amount of the work that examines desire in relation to dreams manifests itself as film theory, in part because the cinema screen functions as a kind of surface across which the dark secrets of our unconscious can be played out before us. Seated in the dark, we have a sort of semidetached relationship to that material: it speaks of us, but does not emanate from us; like a confessional, it allows us to replay unspeakable desires, and yet leave the cinema 'absolved.'

More recently, however, fantasy engages with a different scale of screen projection through the wholesale development of virtual technology. The work of Slavoj Žižek particularly comes into its own here, especially in relation to the manner in which we conceptualise the fantasising subject within cyberspace. In all fantasy texts, there is one whose vision is privileged, and the identity politics of this subject is Žižek's main concern. In his essay 'Fantasy as a Political Category: A Lacanian Approach' (1996), for instance, Žižek examines the slippage between our outward projections of fantasy and the bearing they have upon 'the real.' On one level, he addresses the notion of fantasy as 'day-dream,' a 'scenario that obfuscates the true horror of a situation . . .'[33] The example he gives for this is the safety demonstration given at the start of any journey by aeroplane and that, as he points out, always seems to take the form of an emergency landing on water. The slippage exists in the space between the 'performance' of the demonstration itself, which takes on a kind of innate reassurance as ritual, and the horror it simultaneously conceals in that very act of apparent exposure. For

Žižek, the watery surface then performs a kind of screen function outlining the manner in which the veneer of realism only ever partially erases the power of mythmaking. Hence, in the very act of 'pouring cold water' on one's fears, fantasy surfaces in a kind of sea-monster form: 'Are not the images of the ultimate horrible Thing, from the deep-sea gigantic squid to the ravaging twister, fantasmatic creations *par excellence?*'[34]

In his use of the term *fantasmatic,* we recall our previous discussion of terminology in Chapter 2. Reminding ourselves that f/phantasms exist as 'a result of memory working on itself . . . [forming] the vital link between memory and the creative usage of the imagination,'[35] we can see that, like the contrasting flux of the tides, Žižek's use of this term establishes the preeminence of process over fixity, shifting patterns disrupting a clear space of projection. Hence, while 'thinking forward' (through imagination), the past interrupts, fear and utopia meet, reshape, but never resolve—much like patches of spilt oil on water. By extension, Žižek reminds us that there is a clear sense in which we do not 'own' our fantasies but, in some way, they possess us: '[F]antasy does not simply realize a desire in a hallucinatory way, but rather constitutes our desire, provides its co-ordinates—i.e., literally "teaches us how to desire"'[36]

In the essay 'Is It Possible to Traverse the Fantasy in Cyberspace?' (1999),[37] Žižek examines the construction of the fantasising subject in relation to virtual technologies. He takes as his main frame of reference the 'fad' child's toy, the *tamagochi,* a digital pet. Two aspects of the *tamagochi* interest Žižek: the lack of any metonymic resemblance between the plaything and what it purportedly represents (real animals), combined with its reversal of the norms of play structures. Whereby we think of games as something we devise and control, this object emits demands to which the child is 'programmed' to respond. One aspect of Žižek's essay strikes me as an intriguing counterresponse to Freud's incomprehending view of play as set out in his essay on 'The "Uncanny"' (1919). In his discussion of the *unheimlich* effect produced when an apparently inanimate object comes to life, he wishes to exclude children's toys from this list, claiming that because children 'are especially fond of treating their dolls like live people,' one can equally assume they 'have no fear of their dolls coming to life, they may even desire it.'[38] In fact, what

Freud fails to take account of here is precisely what Žižek attempts to explain: how the slippage between what we think we desire and the manner by which we are mastered by that desire (pleasurably or otherwise) is commonly overlooked. Any child would, of course, be as terrified as any adult, should her toys actually come to life.

This takes us to cyberspace and the role fantasy plays in the construction of the desiring virtual subject. Immediately, though Žižek acknowledges the liberations cyberspace affords, he also draws attention, once again, to the manner in which the subject is virtually 'mastered': 'In cyberspace, I am *compelled* to renounce any fixed symbolic identity, the legal/political fiction of a unique Self guaranteed by my place in the socio-symbolic structure . . .'[39] He sees, in that subject engaged with the virtual self, a kind of doppelgänger effect—a ghost in the machine, if you will: '[F]irst, there is the gap between the "subject of enunciation" (the anonymous X who does it, who speaks) and the "subject of the enunciated/of the statement" (the symbolic identity that I assume in cyberspace, which can be, and in a sense always is, "invented"—the signifier that marks my identity in cyberspace is never directly "myself") . . .'[40] Repeatedly in Žižek's work, we find a kind of Gothic intensity to his thinking. So technology becomes a 'labyrinth' in which 'messages circulate freely without fixed destination, while the Whole of it—this immense circularity of "murmurs"—remains for ever beyond the scope of my comprehension.'[41] This Gothic paradigm takes us on to face other monsters.

New Bodies/New Knowledge: Massey, Haraway, and Botting

Since classical antiquity, fantasy has always concerned itself with metamorphoses, be they metonymic or metaphoric. In Irving Massey's *The Gaping Pig* (1976), he begins by examining the relationship metamorphosis holds to language in a manner directly parallel to the model we employed in Chapter 1 for locating fantasy 'beyond the horizon': '[Metamorphosis] is set up on the other side of language . . .'[42] By this Massey means that metamorphoses embody, in visual form, the kind of figurative conceits only metaphor can otherwise give us. As such they 'body' fantasy, evading the linguistic mediation point so intrinsic to the mimetic foundations of realism. Though *metamorphosis* is not synonymous with *fantasy*, it is dependent upon it. As Massey observes, 'Metamorphosis lies in the province of dream.'[43]

Some of the most inspiring works of criticism examine fantasy as part of a larger cultural/political preoccupation. Donna J. Haraway, for instance, whose work is briefly discussed in Chapter 5, works within a similarly metamorphic model to Massey, focusing on the figure of the cyborg: 'Cyborgs are post–Second World War hybrid entities made of, first, ourselves and other organic creatures in our unchosen 'high-technological' guise as information systems, texts, and ergonomically controlled labouring, desiring and reproducing systems.'[44] As we see, where Massey interprets metamorphosis as the means by which fantasy becomes embodied, for Haraway biology becomes redefined through technology. In effect, her 'A Cyborg Manifesto: Science, Technology and Socialist-Feminism in the Late Twentieth Century' (1985) offers a radical way of rethinking monstrosity. Claiming 'we are all chimeras,'[45] Haraway harnesses together myth and biological science in her choice of terminology. According to myth, a chimera is 'a fire-breathing monster with the head of a lion, body of a goat, and tail of a serpent.' According to biology, it is 'a cultivated plant, consisting of at least two genetically different kinds of tissue as a result of mutation.'[46] One might, in fact, argue that where psychoanalysis roots fantasy within family trauma, postmodernism roots it in anatomical trauma. We seem to move away from fantasy as a group dynamic to one in which each individual 'monster' only has existence as a technological anomaly. However, Haraway argues, the opposite is true.

In the network set up between intelligence machines, Haraway finds a metaphor for community, and a politicised one at that:

> From one perspective, a cyborg world is about the final imposition of a grid of control on the planet, about the final abstraction embodied in a Star Wars apocalypse waged in the name of defence, about the final appropriation of women's bodies in a masculine orgy of war . . . From another perspective, a cyborg world might be about lived social and bodily realities in which people are not afraid of their joint kinship with animals and machines . . . [47]

In this vision of a science-fiction struggle for good over evil, we see a technological version of Tolkien's epic fantasy. For Haraway, however, it is women, not hobbits, who have the most to gain from the freedom cybernetics offers: 'Up till now (once upon a time), female embodiment seemed to be given, organic, necessary; and female embodiment seemed to mean skill in mothering and its metaphoric extensions.'[48] In these 'metaphoric extensions,' we are back to metamorphoses, for what technology offers 'us' (we who are women) is, Haraway claims, 'regeneration' over 'reproduction' and, with it, entry into a 'utopian dream.'[49] In other words, Haraway establishes an alternative myth of womanhood—one which, in eschewing biology, leaves motherhood behind as well. In the process, she takes women forward into an unknowable future, but with the difficulty, surely, of cutting us off from the power of our past.

More integrated, from this point of view, is the fabulous vision of technological maternity offered by Fred Botting in *Sex, Machines and Navels: Fiction, Fantasy and History in the Future Present* (1999). In this book, Botting takes the image of the navel and employs it as the umbilical connection pulling together theology, philosophy, politics, and psychoanalysis. Drawing attention to the fact that severance is a key aspect of who we are, the omphalos embodies that moment of scarred entry: 'produced by a tool, a cutting tool that, these days, would hardly be recognised as belonging in the category of technology.'[50] Informed by a mixture of post-Lacanian psychoanalysis and postmodernist theory, Botting makes the revealing observation that, in contemporary fantasy, 'The object of anxiety and desire appears the same.'[51] Rather than addressing fantasy as formula, Botting employs it as philosophy: the drive wiring us up to desire and, through that desire, utopian possibility. But Botting also raises the dangerously false promises utopia may offer this cynical age: 'The utopia that is nothing but an effect of the images absorbing, transforming and effacing subjectivity inhibits the possibility of escaping the delusional foment and returning to a sense of reality.'[52] If all we are given are images on a screen (Botting uses the comparison of a tourist whose eyes remain glued to a camcorder at the expense of 'seeing'), where is the genuinely transformative aspect of the experience?

The second space of cynicism that fantasy frames in Botting's text is the one through which sex is conceived, and here he draws upon Žižek's work: ' "[R]eal" sex [like virtual sex] depends upon a virtual space of fantasy: "the structure of the 'real' sex act . . . is already inherently phantasmatic—the 'real' body of the other serves only as a support for our phantasmatic projections." '[53] In other words, Botting claims, far from virtual sex being utopian, it reveals a 'true horror,' namely that 'sex always-already was virtual.' In essence, therefore, the space of fantasy turns in upon itself, 'void[ing] phantasmatic space.'[54]

Botting is, by his own admission, intrigued by *post*-ness: 'postindustrial society . . . postmodernity . . . post-reality.'[55] Arguably, as I hope this book has shown, though fantasy writing has manifestations in all of these guises, its potency may derive less from *post*- and more from *pre*-. Though, in Chapter 2, I set out a timeline for fantasy writing, its effectiveness from time immemorial demonstrates, on the level of surface ('leaf,' as opposed to 'tree,' if you will) that fantasy is genuinely timeless in a way that realism is not. Irrespective of whether its surface manifestation takes the form of fairy lore, fabulous travelogues, Disney animation, or cyberpunk, fantasy—like the omphalos—preexists human consciousness, in that we cannot think back to a time *before* desire, and yet that preexistence must—to return to Marin—have been the horizon that heralded the birth of fantasy.

Notes

1. Tzvetan Todorov, *The Fantastic: A Structural Approach to a Literary Genre*, Richard Howard, trans. (Ithaca: Cornell University Press, 1975). A fuller discussion of Todorov's work can be found in Lucie Armitt, *Theorising the Fantastic* (London: Arnold, 1996), 30–36.

2. Todorov offers the following further explication of these four subdivisions. The hyperbolic marvellous describes 'phenomena [that] are supernatural only by virtue of their dimensions,' the exotic marvellous describes 'supernatural events [that] are reported without being presented as such,' the instrumental marvellous deals in 'gadgets . . . unrealised . . . but, after all, quite possible' and the scientific marvellous deals in *sf*. Todorov, *The Fantastic*, 53–56 passim.

3. Louis Marin, 'The Frontiers of Utopia,' in *Utopias and the Millennium*, Krishan Kumar and Stephen Bann, eds. (London: Reaktion Books, 1993), 7–16 (p. 10).

4. Ibid. 11.

5. Ibid. 16.

6. J. R. R. Tolkien, 'Leaf by Niggle,' in *Tree and Leaf* (London: HarperCollins, 2001), 91–118.

7. Susan Stewart, *On Longing: Narratives of the Miniature, the Gigantic the Souvenir, the Collection* (Durham, NC: Duke University Press, 1993), 173.

8. Tolkien, 'Leaf by Niggle,' 94.

9. Ibid. 100.

10. Ibid. 103.

11. Ibid. 108.

12. Ibid. 109.

13. Ibid. 110–11.

14. Ibid. 111.

15. Ibid. 114.

16. Ibid. 115.

17. J. R. R. Tolkien, 'On Fairy-Stories,' in *Tree and Leaf* (London: HarperCollins, 2001), 1–81 (p. 9).

18. Ibid. 10–11.

19. Ibid. 13.

20. Ibid. 64.

21. Ibid. 16.

22. Ibid. 56.

23. Jack Zipes, *Fairy Tales and the Art of Subversion: The Classical Genre for Children and the Process of Civilization* (New York: Routlege, 1983).

24. Bruno Bettelheim, *The Uses of Enchantment: The Meaning and Importance of Fairy Tales* (Harmondsworth: Penguin, 1991), 6.

25. Bettelheim, *The Uses of Enchantment*, 66.

26. Zipes, *Fairy Tales*, 180.

27. Bettelheim, *The Uses of Enchantment*, 54.

28. Armitt, *Theorising the Fantastic*, 45.

29. Jean Laplanche and Jean-Bertrand Pontalis, 'Fantasy and the Origins of Sexuality,' in *Formations of Fantasy*, Victor Burgin, James Donald, and Cora Kaplan, eds. (London: Routledge, 1986), 5–34 (p. 6).

30. Ibid. 11.

31. Ibid. 21.

32. Ibid. 22.

33. Žižek, 'Fantasy as a Political Category: A Lacanian Approach' in *The Žižek, Reader*, Elizabeth Wright and Edmond Wright, eds. (Oxford: Basil Blackwell, 1999), 91–100 (p. 91).

34. Žižek, 'Fantasy as a Political Category,' 91–92.

35. Mark Philpott, 'Haunting the Middle Ages,' in *Writing and Fantasy*, Ceri Sullivan and Barbara White, eds. (London: Longman, 1999), 4–61 (p. 53).

36. Žižek, 'Fantasy as a Political Category,' 100n.

37. Žižek, 'Is It Possible to Traverse the Fantasy in Cyberspace?' in *The Žižek Reader*, Elizabeth Wright and Edmond Wright, eds. (Oxford: Basil Blackwell, 1999), 107–114.

38. Sigmund Freud, 'The "Uncanny"' in the *Penguin Freud Library, Vol. 14, Art and Literature*, Albert Dickson, ed. (Harmondsworth: Penguin, 1990), 335–376 (p. 355).

39. Žižek, 'Is It Possible to Traverse the Fantasy in Cyberspace?,' 112–113; my emphasis.

40. Ibid. 113.

41. Ibid. 114.

42. Irving Massey, *The Gaping Pig: Literature and Metamorphosis* (Berkeley, CA: University of California Press, 1976), 1.

43. Massey, *The Gaping Pig*, 26.

44. Donna J. Haraway, 'Introduction,' in *Simians, Cyborgs and Women: The Reinvention of Nature* (London: Free Association Books, 1991), 1–4 (p. 1).

45. Donna J. Haraway, 'A Cyborg Manifesto: Science, Technology, and Socialist-Feminism in the Late Twentieth Century,' in *Simians, Cyborgs and Women: The Reinvention of Nature* (London: Free Association Books, 1991), 149–181 (p. 150).

46. *Collins English Dictionary, Third Edition* (Glasgow: HarperCollins, 1991).

47. Haraway, 'A Cyborg Manifesto,' 154.

48. Ibid. 180.

49. Ibid. 181.

50. Fred Botting, *Sex, Machines and Navels: Fiction, Fantasy and History in the Future Present* (Manchester: Manchester University Press, 1999), 3.

51. Ibid. 1.

52. Ibid. 195.

53. Here Botting draws on Žižek's *The Metastases of Enjoyment* (New York: Verson, 1994), 210. Botting, *Sex, Machines and Navels*, 204.

54. Ibid.

55. Ibid., 1.

Chapter Eight

A Glossary of Terms

Allegory   A narrative communicating simultaneously on two levels, the surface plot and the symbolic meaning. Common forms of allegory include beast fables and religious quests.

Chronotope   A slice of space and time. Chronotopes can operate on a synchronic or a diachronic plane. The synchronic plane connects different spaces/places within one period of time. The diachronic plane connects spaces/places across time.

Cyberspace   A world defined by what lies on the other side of the computer screen and typically populated by beings of artificial intelligence, cyborgs, and space cowboys (see Chapter 5). In fiction it offers another means of rethinking the agency of the human subject.

Cyborg, the   Donna J. Haraway's figure of future possibility. A seamless amalgam of nature and culture, biology and machine, the cyborg is a metaphorical embodiment of the way forward for women, freeing them from the shackles of biological reproduction and propelling them into a virtual network where new relations to employment, the body, and the collective become possible (see Chapters 5 and 7).

Dream Vision (medieval)   A paradoxical form in which the dreamer is believed to enter a world of enhanced perception while asleep, waking to share that vision with others as 'text.'

Fantasia (phantasia)   Usually having a musical application to works of whimsy, it is also the word Coleridge uses as a synonym for *fancy*, which he considered to be a poor substitute for *imagination* (*Biographia Literaria*).

Fantastic, the Literary (Todorov)   The literary fantastic deals in disruptive impulses rather than genre and fastens on the concept of reader 'hesitancy' about whether what we are reading has a psychological or supernatural basis. It is most often found in the ghost story, the Gothic, or magic realism (see Chapter 6).

Fantasy   A body of material defined by genre and identified by its shared fascination with the (im)possibilities lying 'beyond the horizon.' Its scope is far-reaching and can incorporate modes as diverse as faerie, speculative fiction, animal fable, utopia, and cyberpunk.

'Functions' in the Folktale (Vladimir Propp)   Propp identified a set of 150 narrative function pairings common to the entire corpus of the folktale. This formed the basis of his structuralist analysis *Morphology of the Folktale*.

Phantasm (phantasma)   A slippery term with a variety of applications, from the phantom to a distorted or illusory vision.

Phantasy (psychoanalysis)   The storehouse of fears, desires, and daydreams that inspire realist and fantasy fictions equally and that has its ultimate source in the unconscious.

Primary and Secondary Worlds (Tolkien)   In 'On Fairy-Stories' (1938–39), Tolkien differentiates between the Primary World, which articulates the realist basis out of which so much fantasy emerges, and the Secondary World, where we immerse into that fantasy realm proper. The two worlds are recognisably different from each other, and the boundaries of both are clearly set.

Secondary Elaboration (psychoanalytic)   The waking remnant left behind by the encounter with material from the unconscious while night-dreaming. The secondary elaboration involves the conscious construction of a retrospective version of the dream, taking the form of a surface narrative.

The Sublime (Romantic)   Landscapes inspiring a presiding sense of awe in the reader or spectator. The sublime is simultaneously forbidding and alluring, and it is out of the sublime that the Gothic is born.

The Uncanny   Two applications of the uncanny appear in this book. First, deriving from the work of Tzvetan Todorov, it is one of two main branches of the fantastic, the other being the marvellous. Its second (and most evocative) manifestation is as explored by Sigmund Freud in his 1919 essay 'The "Uncanny."' Here it articulates a shift in sensation when something formerly familiar is rendered unfamiliar, evoking a sense of secrecy and the clandestine. This Freudian derivation forms the basis of the contemporary Gothic.

Utopia   According to Louis Marin, works or visions that take their definition from an endlessly receding horizon. Simultaneously boundary and aperture, this line of significance beckons but can never be attained, trailing behind it a 'fraying edge' or semantic space of promise.

Chapter Nine

Selected Reading List

Armitt, Lucie, *Contemporary Women's Fiction and the Fantastic.*
Basingstoke: Macmillan, 2000.

This book examines fiction by a wide range of writers including Isabel
Allende, Margaret Atwood, Angela Carter, Bessie Head, Toni Morrison,
Jeanette Winterson, and others. It is structured as a feminist analysis of
the role played by certain archetypal fantasy monsters in women's fiction, including ghosts, vampires, cyborgs, and fairies.

Armitt, Lucie, *Theorising the Fantastic.* London: Arnold, 1996.

This is a detailed study of the literary fantastic (after Todorov) and the
manner in which three branches of modern literary theory—structural-
ism, psychoanalysis, and postmodernism—have altered our understanding of the field. Six primary texts are discussed in detail, Banks's *The
Bridge*, Carroll's Alice books, Carter's *The Passion of New Eve*, Perkins
Gilman's 'The Yellow Wallpaper,' Doris Lessing's *Briefings for a Descent
into Hell*, and Stevenson's *The Strange Case of Dr. Jekyll and Mr. Hyde*.

Attebery, Brian, *The Fantasy Tradition in American Literature.*
Bloomington: Indiana University Press, 1980.

Attebery examines fantasy as a counterculture to American empirical
modernity, situating it in contrast to two distinct traditions: on the one
hand, the established canon of American literature, including the
adventure tradition as represented by Melville's *Moby Dick*, and on the
other, what he also sees as the more fully established British and
European tradition of fantasy, which he traces through the German
Mächen (fairy-/folktales) and on to Tolkien. Particularly interesting is
his reading of Frank L. Baum's *The Wizard of Oz* and what it says
about turn-of-the-twentieth-century American culture.

Bammer, Angelika, *Partial Visions: Feminism and Utopianism in the 1970s.* New York: Routledge, 1991.

This is an excellent study of the feminist utopia as process rather than stasis. One of its strengths is the cultural range of material discussed, which includes European as well as Anglo-American writers.

Bettelheim, Bruno, *The Uses of Enchantment: The Meaning and Importance of Fairy Tales.* Harmondsworth: Penguin, 1991.

This is the definitive guide to a psychoanalytic reading of the fairy tale from a child's perspective. See Chapter 7 for more details.

Bown, Nicola, *Fairies in Nineteenth-Century Art and Literature.* Cambridge: Cambridge University Press, 2001.

Bown's study looks not at folklore, but at representation. Her interest therefore lies more in how we read Victorian culture in the light of the Victorian attitude towards fairies and fairyland than in the nature of the fairies themselves. Particularly strong is her chapter 'Queen Mab among the Steam Engines,' in which she considers the role the aesthetic representation of fairies plays in the Industrial novel and various sociopolitical essays of the time.

Brooke-Rose, Christine, *A Rhetoric of the Unreal: Studies in Narrative and Structure, Especially of the Fantastic.* Cambridge: Cambridge University Press, 1981.

A full and scholarly treatment of the field of the fantastic, largely dependent for its application on a detailed reading of Todorov and Darko Suvin. Where Todorov evaluates the uncanny elements of fantasy, Brooke-Rose traces science fiction to the marvellous, through Suvin. In her reading of texts, she pays greater attention than most fantasy critics to the writings of high modernists such as James Joyce and Alain Robbe-Grillet. See Chapter 7 for more details.

Duffy, Maureen, *The Erotic World of Faery.* London: Hodder and Staughton, 1972.

This remains a landmark study of faerie from classical antiquity to the twentieth century. Impressively scholarly in its knowledge of a range of literatures and periods, its only weakness is that some of the applications of psychoanalytic theory to texts now read a little clumsily.

Hume, Kathryn, *Fantasy and Mimesis: Responses to Reality in Western Literature.* New York: Methuen, 1984.

This is a solidly academic treatment of fantasy that is particularly strong in its ability to relate modern fantasy to medieval origins. Hume's reliance on diagrammatic models to illustrate some of her narrative readings, is, however, a little off-putting at times.

Jackson, Rosemary, *Fantasy: The Literature of Subversion.* London: Methuen, 1981.

This is a highly respected study of fantasy employing a psychoanalytic approach. Jackson's aim is to examine the means by which fantasy articulates the 'unspoken' in culture and hence plays an intrinsically subversive role in it. This stance may lead her to be overly dismissive of the fairy tale, however, which she reads in its most sentimental of guises. She also fails to fully grasp the significance of Todorov's fantastic as an approach that dismantles genre, reading it purely as a prevarication between modes. See Chapter 7 for more details.

Kitchin, Rob, and James Kneale, eds., *Lost in Space: Geographies of Science Fiction.* London: Continuum, 2002.

This is an interesting and diverse collection of essays in the crossover territory of cultural geography and popular fiction/film. The fiction writers whose work is discussed include Marge Piercy, J. G. Ballard, and Neal Stephenson. Particularly interesting essays include Nick Bingham's essay on GM foods (discussed in Chapter 5 of this book) and Marcus A. Doel and David B. Clarke's 'Invention Without a Future,' in which they discuss cinema technology *as* science fiction.

Kumar, Krishan, and Stephen Bann, eds., *Utopias and the Millennium.* London: Reaktion Books, 1993.

This is an excellent collection of essays, not least because of its inclusion of Louis Marin's 'The Frontiers of Utopia.' Aside from Marin's essay, however, the broad scope of this volume includes work on politics, literature, history, and McDonalds! This book does more than any other I know to broaden what can be a too rigidly understood term: *utopia*.

Massey, Irving, *The Gaping Pig: Literature and Metamorphosis*. Berkeley: University of California Press, 1976.

This book examines a range of literary works from classical antiquity to the twentieth century and is particularly strong in its application of European philosophy to the texts. Extensive readings are offered of, among other narratives, Hoffmann's 'The Sandman,' Shelley's *Frankenstein*, Gogol's 'The Nose,' and Flaubert's *Saint-Julien l'Hospitalier.*

Mathews, Richard, *Fantasy: The Liberation of Imagination*. New York: Routledge, 2002.

This book offers a detailed discussion of the work of five writers— William Morris, J. R. R. Tolkien, T. H. White, Robert E. Howard, and Ursula K. LeGuin—and the literary and aesthetic context for their work. Though there are good early survey chapters offering a solid grounding in the history of fantasy, the book is better for what it has to say about these individual writers and their oeuvres than the field of fantasy as a whole.

Silver, Carole, *Strange and Secret Peoples: Fairies and Victorian Consciousness*. New York: Oxford University Press, 1999.

This is a very scholarly approach to the subject of fairylore and its manifestation in Victorian literature and art. Silver takes far more cognisance of the 'dark' side of fairylore than Bown (see above), and her book is truer to the origins of faerie in doing so. An impressive range of material is covered, from popular tales to Gaskell, Eliot, and Dickens. This is an important read for any scholar or student of fantasy.

Sullivan, Ceri, and Barbara White, eds., *Writing and Fantasy*. London: Longman, 1999.

This is an eclectic volume of essays examining different readings of fantasy in three main periods of history: the early and medieval periods, the early modern period, and the twentieth century. Individual essays examine a variety of modes of fantasy, from chivalric romance to travelogues, cowboys to ghosts. There is a good mix of alternative understandings of the term and derivations (popular and otherwise) of *fantasy*, here.

Swinfen, Ann, *In Defence of Fantasy: A Study of the Genre in English and American Culture.* London: Routledge and Kegan Paul, 1984.

Swinfen derives her understanding of fantasy from conceptions of the marvellous. One of the more original aspects of Swinfen's study is her treatment of 'Talking Beasts,' which she examines in some detail, comparing animal fable with naturalist tales of animal life. The work of Ursula LeGuin also features strongly in this book.

Todorov, Tzvetan, *The Fantastic: A Structural Approach to a Literary Genre,* trans. Richard Howard. Ithaca: Cornell University Press, 1975.

This is the landmark study in the field. See Chapter 7 for more details.

Tolkien, J. R. R., 'On Fairy-Stories,' in *Tree and Leaf.* London: HarperCollins, 2001, pp. 1–81.

A key essay and a 'must-read' for any scholar in the field. See Chapter 7 for more details.

Zipes, Jack, *Fairy Tales and the Art of Subversion: The Classical Genre for Children and the Process of Civilization.* New York: Routledge, 1983.

A socio-historical account of the development of the fairy tale and its political importance to the child reader. See Chapter 7 for more details.

Index